CULTURES OF OPPOSITION

SUNY Series in American Labor History
Robert Asher and Amy Kesselman, editors

CULTURES OF OPPOSITION

Jewish Immigrant Workers, New York City, 1881–1905

Hadassa Kosak

State University of New York Press

Cover photo: **Moe Levy's Workshop (clothing), Walker and Baxter Streets, 1911,** Museum of the City of New York, Byron Collection, 93.1.1.18159

Published by
State University of New York Press, Albany

Printed in the United States of America

For information, address State University of New York Press
State University Plaza, Albany, New York 12246

Production by Dana Foote
Marketing by Dana E. Yanulavich

Library of Congress Cataloging-in-Publication Data

Kosak, Hadassa, 1938–
    Cultures of opposition : Jewish immigrant workers, New York City, 1881–1905 / Hadassa Kosak.
        p. cm. — (SUNY series in American labor history)
    Includes bibliographical references (p.) and index.
    ISBN 0–7914–4583–6 (alk. paper) — ISBN 0–7914–4584–4 (pbk. : alk. paper)
        1. Jews—Employment—New York (State)—New York—History. 2. Alien labor—New York (State)—New York—History. 3. Jews—New York (State)—New York—Social life and customs. 4. Jews—New York (State)—New York—Politics and government. I. Series.
    HD8081.J4 K67 2000
    974.7′1004924—dc21   00-026553

10 9 8 7 6 5 4 3 2 1

CONTENTS

ILLUSTRATIONS

Acknowledgments

I wish to acknowledge my great debt to the enthusiastic support of the late Herbert Gutman, who first inspired me to take a fresh look at the world of Jewish immigrants. At the many stages of my work, I derived considerable benefit from the advice of Eric Foner and Irwin Yellowitz. The writings of Margaret Somers in the field of sociological history and her suggestions for further reading in that field opened new avenues for a historian venturing into the fields of sociology and anthropology. Throughout this project, my colleague Ellen Schrecker offered me her clear-sighted substantive and editorial comments. My friends Ellen and Neal Wood provided valuable and detailed comments on the whole text. Uri Ram, a sociologist and a historian, was always generous with his time, as was Daniel Soyer, whose writings and advice I have always valued. My friend and fellow historian Annie Chamberlin was indefatigable in helping me research unusual illustrative material and shared with me the excitement of those discoveries.

The staff of the Jewish Division of the New York Public Library, the American Jewish Historical Society, and Marek Web and Fruma Mohrer of YIVO Institute for Jewish Research all assisted me in my searches for material and resources. Their helpfulness went well beyond the call of duty. In the last stages, I was enormously encouraged by the enthusiasm and suggestions of Paul Buhle, the comments of Dorothée Schneider, as well as the comments of the anonymous readers for State University of New York Press and its editors. Amy Kesselman in particular, the co-editor of the American Labor Series, was most helpful and patient in her suggestions and in piloting the book through publication. Yeshiva University, where I have taught for many years, has always shown support for this project. In particular, I wish to mention Karen Bacon, Dean of Stern College for Women, Carole Silver, Judith Neaman, Doris Goldstein, Shlomo Eidelberg and Ephraim Kanarfogel. The Stern College Ivan L. Tillem Fund provided generous financial assistance for securing the rights for the use of the visual material in this book. I also wish to thank Nava Schreiber for her friendship and her generous assistance in locating images.

Finally, my thanks go to my immediate family. To my sister Marion Kozak, also a historian, for many discussions on the detail and general outline, and for trips to libraries and archives; to Eli Epstein for unstinting moral support; to my late brother-in-law Ralph Miliband, and to my nephews David and Edward Miliband, my gratitude for their comments on parts of the text. I wish to acknowledge my gratitude to the late Lydia Auerbach for her help in translating some of the Yiddish source material. I treasure also the gift of friendship of Beadie and Harry Magdoff, whose conversations and reminiscences about their own families in the 1920s and 1930s provided me with a rich tapestry of Jewish political history which will remain with me forever. Thanks also to Ira Katznelson for alighting on a title in a moment of serendipity in the summer of 1998, and to David Szonyi, Noa Kleinman, and Judy Wilcox for much appreciated editorial and technical advice. Needless to say, the responsibility for the contents of this book is mine alone.

Introduction

> They do not understand the duties and rights of American citizens. They do not have inbred or acquired respect for law or order as the basis of the life of the society into which they have come. They have known authority mainly as wielded despotically, and as something to be submitted to under compulsion. . . . Resistance to authority does not seem to them necessarily wrong, only risky, and if it ceases to be risky the restraint it can have on their passion is very small.
>
> —Editorial, *New York Times*, 24 May 1902

Thus the *New York Times* warned its readers about the first Jewish immigrants, who had arrived in the United States in the years 1881 to 1905 from Eastern Europe, mostly from czarist Russia. A few days before this editorial was published, widespread disorder had erupted on the Lower East Side when angry Jewish housewives, protesting the high price of kosher meat, had attacked butchers, thrown meat at the police, and imposed a boycott on meat consumption. In its outraged editorial, the *Times* was reacting not so much to the behavior of these women but to a "dangerous class" of people who, in taking the law into their own hands, presented a threat to American society if not subdued effectively and decisively.

This study examines the Jewish immigrant political culture and the circumstances in which the community gained a new identity. It seeks to explore the dynamics of a new, oppositional culture and its manifestations, which informed the actions and the practices of a Jewish working population remarkable for a confrontational culture. These were new immigrants who, despite their recent arrival in the United States, were determined to participate as self-conscious actors in social and political struggles. They demanded, at all times, full economic and political rights for themselves and their community.

These early immigrants had come mostly from rural areas or small towns, where they worked as artisans or tradesmen serving the needs of the

1

local population. Their social, economic, and cultural milieu changed dramatically upon their arrival in the heart of the world's most advanced urban economy. They differed from the post-1905 generation of immigrants who, because they experienced the beginnings of industrialization and political change in Russia, would undergo a growing secularization, enabling them to participate increasingly in political life, particularly in working-class organizations, in the Russian Empire. Historians have noted that this experience enabled the later group to make a concrete contribution to the foundation and organization of more stable trade unions on American soil.[1] In contrast, the earlier immigrants of the 1881 to 1905 period had been largely cut off from mainstream Russian society. They were strangers to factory production, the wage economy of advanced capitalism, and the organization of the tailoring trades, which became their major source of employment.

The American industrial setting of 1881 to 1905, into which they were thrust, was characterized by mass production, irregular work, sweatshops, speed-ups, and declining wages. In the garment industry, the immigrants also confronted German Jewish employers, most of whom had settled in the United States during the period from 1820 to 1870. These owners of industrial capital also assumed the roles of educators, guardians, and philanthropists and aspired to transmit the American values of individualism, industrial discipline, and work ethic to the Jewish immigrant masses, goals which met with resistance and considerable hostility. Many of the newcomers may have aspired to material success, but they did not unequivocally embrace entrepreneurial individualism as the preferred route to social mobility and material advancement. They also embraced the culture of protest, which became their hallmark.

Only through an analysis that integrates the newcomers' working lives with their cultural practices can their distinctive experience be fully understood. This book reviews the whole variety of immigrant economic and political experience in the context of a changing culture and reassesses the widely held belief that members of the first generation of Jewish immigrants from eastern Europe were passive historical agents overwhelmed by industrial capitalism. On the contrary, the community's political culture was pervasive, distinctive, and influential. That culture's longevity had an impact as late as the 1930s and, as the following chapters will show, influenced the subsequent formation of Jewish working-class identity. The general contours of the story of Jewish labor, particularly in the needle trades, are well known. The work of Melech Epstein, Moses Rischin, and Irving Howe, among others, viewed the activism of the first generation of immigrant workers as anticipating the successful Jewish unionism of the International Ladies' Garment Workers' Union (ILGWU) and the Amalgamated Clothing Workers of America (ACW) in the 1900s.[2] Howe, in particular, offered a rich, detailed, scholarly testimonial to the Jewish immigrant community and its culture, ranging from trade unions to theater and the arts. He is especia interested in the politicized expressions of that culture, including its articulation of socialist ideology. However, Howe also believed that, in the context of social and cultural developments, the early immigrants failed to leave a mark: "nature had given . . . no voice . . . history no claims," to that first generation of newcomers.[3] He saw them as a "stunned" generation, overwhelmed by the problems of migration, too politically immature to be significant in the making of an American working class.[4]

The fascination of historians with the politicized expressions and eventual success of working-class protest explains their focus on the post-1905 immigrants, who brought with them a greater organizational and ideological maturity acquired through participation in the revolutionary Russian struggles. Their experience is credited with the success of effective trade union organization through which Jewish workers won their rightfully respected place in the annals of American labor. However, the emphasis on employment, workplace struggles, and subsequent union successes cannot fully explain the early history of Jewish immigrant militancy, because it overlooks the rich variety of social practices, beliefs, and traditions that helped the first wave of Jewish immigrants to forge a new political language and to establish their identity as active social citizens. It is remarkable that many of the social struggles concerned community issues outside the economic sphere of worker and employer relations. Other contested areas included the nature of class relations as manifested in the dispensation of charity by the German Jews, concerns about profiteering by shopkeepers and landlords, and the broad issue of the relationship of the individual to society. The involvement of unwaged workers, notably women, as well as members of other trades, shopkeepers, and others not visibly connected to the workplace disputes, is a remarkable feature of the community struggles of the period.

Most immigrant women were young and unmarried, and their role in workplace activism has been well documented.[5] The role of married women in community life and labor, although central to the political culture of the Jewish community, has received less attention. Yet married women were visible social actors as consumers, wives, housewives, neighbors, tenants, and social organizers, though usually not as factory workers. They participated in and led struggles within a sharply bound geographic and social space.[6] In similar ways, other members of the community not directly linked to a workplace demonstrated their solidarity with the working community.

The political participation of these groups is an essential part of the history of the immigrant experience and contributes to a fuller understanding of the community's culture and political language. It helps explain the divide between the Jewish immigrant labor movement and the established mainstream American labor politics based on craft unionism. While contemporary advocates of craft-based unionism believed that trade union structures were an effective model of industrial action, Jewish immigrants, employed for the most part in unskilled jobs in the garment industry, developed organizational strategies based on communal support. The seemingly "anarchic" tendencies of Jewish immigrant workers pervaded both community unrest and labor conflicts and were consequently viewed as wasteful and "un-American."[7] However, contrary to the criticism of contemporaries, the enduring, sometimes anarchic, social unrest in the Jewish neighborhoods reflected the community's need to forge a new political language in which to think about, struggle for, and evaluate political goals.[8] In short, this was the process through which a new political culture was being articulated.

Within the Jewish community, the process of inventing the new language was based on a dynamic reinterpretation of different cultural components. As a result of the encounter with American society, its agencies, and the resources of the democratic and republican system, the immigrants redefined the values of their homeland culture, founded on common geographic roots and a shared sense of ethnic identity. Although the immigrants had had little experience of organizing politically within the larger society in their native lands, they had been sophisticated participants in *shtetl* politics and the rich and varied world of Jewish associations *(hevrot)*, in religious dissent, and in the power struggles within the Jewish community in czarist Russia. In the American context, they gained the additional tools of democratic citizenship and political action. The new experience of the wage economy, the market system, and the socioeconomic dynamics of the urban setting as exemplified in tenement housing and street life provided the immigrants with a fresh context for the political adaptation of traditional symbols, ethical codes, and language. The new political culture was forged in shopfloor struggles, consumer boycotts, rent strikes, street demonstrations, and parades. These previously unfamiliar aspects of political life provided the immigrants with a new language whose vocabulary drew its inspiration from work experience and community politics. For example, the insult "scab" acquired several meanings; it was used both in the workplace and against social transgressors in the communal sphere.

The emergent new practices had nothing to do with Luddite methods against industrial modernizers, nor were they the first stirrings of later trade union successes. Rather, they articulated a culture that served as a benchmark to evaluate, explain, guide, and express public dissent from the assumptions of mainstream American capitalism. The men and women who represented this new culture challenged the fundamental premises of social relations and the allocation of power, as well as traditional categories of class and gender, and other issues of political importance. Ultimately, the immigrants' new vocabulary and practices transformed the social ethos of the old world community from one which had been severely constrained by the political restrictions of the Russian Empire and by a communal power structure marked by rigid traditionalism into something very different. It became a new community where "people walk on their heads," according to one contemporary observer who bemoaned the lack of old-world deference and hierarchy.[9]

POLITICAL CULTURE AND COMMUNITY: THE HISTORICAL PERSPECTIVE

The lens through which this book investigates the history of the immigrant community is that of "political culture," a concept that encapsulates the cultural and social characteristics of a group and the way these traits are demonstrated through political action. The study shows how this political culture was developed and disseminated, through collective action on the Lower East Side, by means of new vocabulary, symbols, rituals, religion, and, above all, moral codes of behavior. Examining immigrant institutions, organizations, values, and practices through the prism of political culture will, therefore, focus on the politically confrontational practices initiated by these immigrants who became new Americans.

The contribution of culture to labor history has long been recognized. E. P. Thompson pioneered this approach to historical analysis to explain the formation of working-class culture in nineteenth-century Britain.[10] Thompson's concept of political culture embraces a variety of religious, social, and economic practices. By subjecting to historical analysis the reappropriation by the nascent working class of "customs in common" springing from culture and tradition, he helped incorporate the concept of the "political" into the analysis of popular cultures. Since the publication of his groundbreaking study, *The Making of the English Working Class,* in 1964, historians have been free to search for political expressions in the everyday social context through language, symbolic behavior, and religion. Under Thompson's influence, the durability of the cultural legacy became an accepted category in labor and immigrant studies. Most historians have come to endorse the view that laboring people were not helpless victims lacking resources and destined to fall prey to the overpowering impact of industrial society. This includes workers in societies like the United States, where a pronounced majority were immigrants. Historical writing has also come to reflect the impact of Herbert Gutman's contribution in his seminal article "Work, Culture, and Society in Industrializing America, 1815–1919," published in 1973.[11] Addressing the uniqueness of American working-class formation, Gutman emphasized the persistence of the imported cultural characteristics among newcomers to the American industrial system. Preindustrial traditions and institutions were, according to Gutman, the determining factors in shaping and sustaining the resistance to industrialization of the many diverse groups entering the alien factory world between the years 1815 and 1919. Consequently, the defining feature of the American working class was the successive historical entry points of different "cultural" groups who, in turn, periodically redefined the American working class.[12]

In Gutman's analysis, immigrant culture emerged as an autonomous category of values and practices that was imported by the immigrants from their preindustrial experience and that survived and even flourished, to a varying degree, among immigrant groups according to class, occupation, location of city and industry, and size of the community.[13] "Work, Culture, and Society" has less to say about the potentially dynamic and transformative qualities of immigrant culture in relation to the demands of the industrial system and institutions of the host community.[14] Following Gutman, historians of immigration stressed the endurance of imported culture throughout the process of adaptation to the American milieu and its role in the subsequent emergence of ethnicity. Influenced by Thompson and Gutman, historians of immigration have focused on ethnic continuity and the powerful resilience of "inherited" values. For example, Virginia Yans McLaughlin's account of the Italian immigrant experience emphasized the family's role in reinforcing its traditional primacy as a symbol of the Italian community.[15] Thus, immigrants from the southern region of Italy preserved family cohesion by seeking out jobs that guaranteed the maintenance of close ties to immediate and nonimmediate relatives. But in time, historians, including Gutman himself in his later work, recognized the limits of this approach and raised objections when it was used to represent culture in a static "traditionalist" dimension. Class conflict, according to Gutman, did not remain immured in stubborn precapitalist work habits. Rather, as suggested by some contemporary historians, after the first generation, such conflict took new forms and acquired a new cultural and political character.[16]

CULTURAL STRATEGIES AND POLITICAL CULTURE: THE SOCIOLOGICAL PERSPECTIVE

In addition to some dimensions of the historical-cultural approach discussed above, this study applies concepts developed in the fields of sociology and anthropology to address the nature of transformation in Jewish political culture and its practices. Sociologists have elaborated on the role of culture in social action and political mobilization. Following anthropologist Clifford Geertz, they argue that social action and political movements are powered by specific cultural symbols and public meanings that, in turn, inspire certain patterns of action.[17] This view emphasizes the importance of publicly negotiated meanings in contrast to individually internalized values.

Culture thus signifies shared meanings inherent in public behavior, in institutions, and in language.

In this context, culture's significance, and specifically, "culture as a strategy for action," according to sociologist Ann Swidler, lies not in defining the "ends of action" as dictated by internalized values and ideals, but in providing publicly available "cultural components that are used to construct strategies of action."[18] Cultural heritage, therefore, is not an end in itself but a "tool kit" for action, offering a selection of strategies. This construct can illuminate the political culture of the Jewish immigrant community, whose actions were not predetermined by any particular aspect of a uniquely "essentialist" Jewish tradition, religion, or value system.[19] These cultural weapons represented resources that were brought into play selectively as circumstances dictated. The immigrants thus used the socially shaped, culturally recognized, and familiar ways of evaluating reality and forming social bonds as their key resources for constructing action.[20] Immigrant strikers and protesters on the Lower East Side demonstrated a capacity for mobilization, using a variety of cultural tools. Notions of justice and fairness informed their actions. Of no less importance was their ability to assert their power in the workplace and in public spaces, such as the streets, parks, and synagogues, through a repertoire of publicly understood language and symbolism. In their struggles, immigrant men and women mobilized traditional institutions, such as local mutual-support and benefit organizations, as well as newly formed and fluid neighborhood networks. Swidler's analysis of cultural heritage as a "tool kit" for action is particularly apposite in the early period of Jewish mass migration. She notes that, in general, in "unsettled" periods when new forms of action are being developed, culture "makes possible new strategies of action."[21] The early period of Jewish migration and settlement was precisely such a time, when traditional hierarchies based on wealth, religious learning, and social pedigree had collapsed and new claims for citizenship rights were being staked out.

This was also a time of intense contestation between the immigrants and the settled cultural conditions of industrialized America. Although the immigrants resisted the American philosophy of rugged individualism by asserting their own widely accepted ethos of mutuality in human relations, they also rejected the way work had been practiced in their homeland. By means of boycotts, strikes, and ostracism campaigns, they opposed those who violated their ideas of fairness and justice. In the new setting, the language of political culture was not merely an expression of material interests. The Wards Island revolt in 1882, described in chapter 2, exemplified the assertion of civil rights against the indignities meted out by Americanized German Jews to the low-status immigrants. The history of this incident illustrates how political culture manifests itself in struggles that have no material objective. The incident demonstrates that political culture is imbued with its own logic and that cultural durability is independent of economic factors.

Although the underlying assumptions of this work are that political culture informs all social behavior and that cultural codes are more enduring than any set of material circumstances, it is these codes which are pivotal in their relationship to the exercise of political culture. Useful to this approach is the framework offered by sociologist Margaret Somers, who sees political culture "as a configuration of representations and practices that exists as a contentious structural social phenomenon in its own right. . . . By existing as something apart from either the economy or the state, a political culture, when *acted upon,* will shape the outcome, the meaning, and the very course of political action and social processes" (emphasis in original).[22] Accordingly, political culture is not only the result of social and material factors, and it is more than an instrument in sociopolitical conflicts. Somers, however, warns of the dangers of "false dichotomy," as practiced by cultural historians who have abandoned material determinism and embraced the concept of autonomy of culture, through investigating such concepts as political language and public ritual, as detached from the material world.[23] Somers maintains that although political culture has its own logic and durability, it is not insulated from social and economic reality since it interacts with issues of power relations.[24] In the new setting of the Lower East Side, issues of economic character became intertwined with an array of cultural practices. Jewish immigrants forged a language of political culture to describe workshop practices that was used in social relations and other aspects of communal life. Conversely, cultural or religious practices and symbols were applied to commercial and industrial conflicts.

Contemporary sociologists and historians have highlighted the dynamic power of culture and its contribution to the reading of history. Lynn Hunt, in her pathbreaking study of the French Revolution, which explores the "text" of the Revolution—its calendar, icons, and parades—argues that its language created new forms of revolutionary content.[25] She suggests that revolutionary political texts not only signify the building of a political community but also provide the foundation "to establish new fields of social, political, and cultural struggle."[26] The harnessing of symbols, strategies, beliefs, and customs for political initiatives produced an oppositional language that defined new social and political aspirations.

In the case of the Jewish community, the political struggles were symbolized by a new language that expressed and also nurtured political goals by opening new terrains for contestation. The newly minted vocabulary inspired and elaborated a binary moral code of rights and wrongs, which counterposed fairness against exploitation, community welfare against individual gain, public good against private greed. This code of symbolic logic was shaped in concrete, political struggles against profiteering and exploitation, as in the meat boycott and rent strikes. By setting public standards of fairness, the community of Jewish immigrant workers succeeded in mobilizing the support of outsiders, such as contractors and even landlords and shopkeepers. By invoking these moral tools to challenge power relations, the community acquired and sustained a unique political voice and a capacity to define new goals.[27]

Ethnic identity and culture contributed to communal strategies in staking out the political claims and counterclaims of the group. The Jewish immigrant community demonstrated the power of their political culture through public articulation of language, ritual, and religion at a moment when social relations and power structures were being questioned. At that historical conjuncture on American soil, culture and ethnicity were transformed from an insular tradition into an armory for purposes of political contestation and as a tool for appropriating political power. A historically significant moment arose with the act of migration itself, when the cultural and social constraints of traditional patterns were weakened or suspended.

THE ETHNIC IDENTITY PERSPECTIVE

Historians of ethnicity in recent years have challenged the idea of ethnic values and culture as static and timeless. Using the concept of ethnic "invention," elaborated by Eric Hobsbawm and Benedict Anderson in their studies of nationalism, they have demonstrated its dynamic potential in new and perceptive ways.[28] Applied to the Jewish community on the Lower East Side, this perspective shows how exiles from a small-town community reorganized themselves in the metropolis to set up new networks and to press for new goals. In order to elucidate this process, this study incorporates the approach suggested by Werner Sollors, one focusing on "invention" and "construction" of ethnicity, that is, on its changing character, its adaptation and selectivity.[29] Or, as Kathleen Neils Conzen and the co-authors of the influential article "The Invention of Ethnicity: A Perspective from the U.S.A." interpret it, ethnicity is "a process of construction or invention which incorporates, adapts, and amplifies preexisting communal solidarities, cultural attributes, and historical memories," thus emphasizing culture as an evolving, rather than a fixed entity.[30] According to this view, adaptation and selectivity characterize the formation of immigrant culture, a process that unfolds in the public sphere through such civic institutions as unions, schools, and associations. Above all, the conceptualization of a dynamically constructed ethnic culture suggests the primacy of the collective sphere over the individual as the locus where cultural meanings are contested and reconstructed over time.

This view of ethnic culture focuses on the vital engagement by members of the community as active participants in shaping community life and identity.[31] By recognizing the dynamic character of group identity, this perspective challenges the hitherto accepted belief among historians of immigration, as well as ethnic leaders, that ethnicity serves simply as a means of cultural and group preservation.[32] On the contrary, ethnicity is driven by multiple factors. The relationship of the ethnic group to the dominant culture is as much the subject of negotiation as is its internal power structure. These negotiations may have a conflictual, competitive, or cooperative character.[33] The history of the period from 1881 to 1905 suggests that contestation and conflict were prominent features of life on the Lower East Side. Both men and women participated in the process of redefining themselves as members of an ethnic group. They did so through forging a political culture rooted in the immigrant experience, earlier political traditions, and the material conditions in which they lived.

A new construction of Jewish ethnicity appeared as the first Jewish immigrant group from Eastern Europe redefined itself in response to a new economic system and by encounters with the German Jewish community and other ethnic cultures. The ethnic community provided its members with a wide variety of political tactics for redefining the realm of social relations. The new American context and its impact on the community's definition of its associational life are of particular relevance for the Jewish ethnic group. For many Jews, the act of migration represented emancipation. Relegated to the margins of economy and society in czarist Russia, Jews sought both individual and group remedies to their problems either by participating in the revolutionary movements of their day or by emigrating. These secular solutions to Jewish marginality undermined and ultimately transformed community bonds and the traditional power structure.

Released from the confines of tradition, Jewish immigrants entered a pluralistic American society, conducive to a diversity of civil associations. Free to seek new and competing visions for their reconstructed identity, Jews could now redefine their cultural language. But they did so within a context of collective memory, historical experience, and communal ties and symbolism.[34] Ethnicity did not disappear, despite the decline of the traditional; it thrived in a context of new possibilities and through competing definitions of its identity.[35] As with other immigrant groups, Jewish ethnic redefinition was riven with tension. However, in contrast to such groups as the Germans, the Poles, and the Italians, whose identification with a nation and state became a source of pride, the Jews were unique in their lack of a common political organization of nationhood. While Zionism was beginning to capture the imagination of some Jews, its appeal in America during this period was limited.[36] They also lacked any synthesis between national religion and national consciousness. While national holidays or church-centered celebration found general acceptance among Poles, Italians, or French Canadians, similar symbols were accepted only by some groups within the Jewish community.[37] Nor was religious observance a unifying bond among Jews. Traditions, such as Sabbath worship, were highly valued but flexibly practiced. Religious organization and control lacked the kind of hierarchical unity which existed within the Catholic Church. Jewish religious observances, as well as the rabbinate's authority, remained highly contested. The institution of Reform Judaism, on the one hand, and the setting up of alternative places of worship in backrooms *(shtieblach)* on the Lower East Side, on the other, did not require the same kind of sanction as that prescribed by the Catholic Church. In the absence of agencies capable of enforcing ethnic or cultural consensus, Jews battled against each other in all aspects of communal life; most prominently over issues of social, economic, and cultural significance. The main intracommunal struggle was waged between those who advocated compromise with the dominant political culture and those who fought to assert a competing set of values.

German Jews, easily identified by their higher economic status, language, social origins, and greater assimilation within U.S. economy and society, represented the former group. They were willing to extend a protective mantle over the newcomers from Eastern Europe by providing a charitable safety net and, in some cases, by helping them to immigrate. German Jews dominated the oligarchic Jewish welfare organizations, which were intended to mitigate the worst instances of suffering among the very poorest immigrants, but they showed little interest in promoting ethnic bonding. Instead, they preached a new culture of American values such as individualism, self-reliance, and upward social mobility. On the Lower East Side, they also became identified with exploitation in the workplace. Whatever differences existed within the Jewish community among groups who came from different East European countries or regions, they were united when it came to labor struggles or confrontations with well-known manufacturers who were mainly German. They were a target for the forces of opposition, particularly the Socialist press.

The struggle between the new East European immigrants and German Jews was mirrored by conflict within the recently arrived immigrant community. The newcomers harbored a similar, though somewhat more ambivalent, hostility for contractors and subcontractors—themselves often immigrants—who served as intermediaries between the workers and the large manufacturers. The social and political drama of the shopfloor struggles, rent strikes, consumer boycotts, and street protests on the Lower East Side was the means used by immigrants to contest the legitimacy of the market and to demand alternative arrangements. The opponents in these encounters were landlords, commercial interests, and strikebreakers, as well as state institutions, such as the American justice and educational system.

The immigrant community acquired a distinctive ethnic voice that differentiated it from the dominant national voice of American society. The Jewish immigrants gained recognition by building a cultural apparatus, which included a variety of working people's organizations and political groupings. Their main weapon of self-defense was labor militancy, but as Daniel Soyer has so authoritatively shown, the formation of such new communal institutions as *landsmanshaftn* played a key role as well. These were organic and independent, mutual-aid, hometown organizations, which originated in the old country but which acquired a new purpose by responding effectively to some of the immigrants' needs.[38] The newcomers' organizing strategies contributed to and fashioned their political culture and formulated their political demands. In the case of the Jewish immigrant community, these "local" and concrete meanings constituted a political idiom that translated, at particular historical moments, into aspirations for increased democratic rights.[39] The ability to effect such a transformation depended on their capacity for participatory democracy, whether in the form of associations and organizations or in street and crowd activism. The newcomers—being employed in an almost exclusively immigrant industry, the needle trades, and living in an ethnic neighborhood where sweatshops, schools, and synagogues existed in close proximity—were able to crystallize their particular concepts of justice and rights. All of this activity articulated a need to capture a political space and to express claims to citizenship rights within the community and larger society.

This book describes the democratic impulse at work in constructing the community's identity. It was not an orderly process, in which the host country's institutions gradually bestowed rights, but an unruly, if highly participatory, struggle that unfolded in the Jewish neighborhood. Popular activism and collective actions did not recognize the accepted divisions of public and private. No home was sacrosanct in the social upheavals, as crowds appropriated the streets as well as homes. Both public and private spheres were transformed into arenas for competing social classes and ideologies.

SYNTHESIS AND NARRATIVE:
JEWISH IMMIGRANTS, 1881 TO 1905

The history of social unrest initiated by the immigrants will be explained by identifying institutions, organizations, values, and practices through the prism of political culture. Specifically, this book describes the character of labor activism and how it reached new heights in the garment industries of New York in the 1880s and 1890s.

Chapter 1 examines the Jewish homeland culture in the Russian Pale of Settlement, which provided the foundation for subsequent developments on American soil. It describes the material organization of the shtetl economy, the allocation of power between the czarist state and the Jewish community, and relevant aspects of ethnic practices, experiences, traditions, and collective memory. The last quarter of the nineteenth century was a defining period in the history of Russian Jewry. It was characterized by official anti-Jewish policy and spontaneous popular outbursts of anti-Semitism, as well as by deeper fissures in both Russian and Jewish society. The sudden migratory tide among vast numbers of Jews was the result not only of persecution but also of conflicts within the Jewish community on issues of religion, culture, and political control.[40] The wave of out-migration can be traced to the political and economic transformations taking place in czarist Russia as well as to new discontents and expectations inspired by the growing secularization within the Jewish community itself. These were some of the trends which contributed to the formation of a culture of opposition in a period of turbulence and transition before the emigrants arrived in the United States.

Chapter 2 describes the process of emigration and settlement in New York that engendered a new dynamic. It brought the immigrants into contact and, later, into confrontation with, representatives of assimilated American and West European Jewry, who had assumed a philanthropic role toward the immigrants. From the very beginning, the relationship between these two groups was fraught with conflict over the definition of rights and the nature of social support services. It became clear from the start that the immigrants rejected the notion of charity if it was conditional on accepting client status and loss of rights. Through the process of immigration they developed new networks of mutual aid as alternatives to those provided by American philanthropic agencies.

Chapter 3 analyzes the economic setting in which the immigrants found themselves and which became fertile ground for the expression of their political and social demands. Emerging from an artisanal economy in their home country, the immigrants entered a system of wage work in the needle industries that was characterized by mass production in factories, sweatshops, and homes. New York's garment industry was growing fast, but the system of subcontracting, as well as growing consumer demand for affordable goods, led to declining pay and increased exploitation. This economic setting once again brought Jewish immigrants into conflict with German-American Jews and, eventually, with immigrant employers. This resulted in confrontation over economic issues and power struggles at the workplace level as well as within the political and social sphere described in chapter 2.

Chapter 4 describes how the concentration of the Jewish population in the "ghetto" on the Lower East Side was instrumental in forming a distinctive Jewish working-class culture, which linked the workplace to all aspects of social organization. The indivisibility of workplace and public and private spaces facilitated the development of a Jewish political culture and a commitment to collective action.

Chapter 5 surveys the manifold manifestations of collective actions and crowd activity which were spurred by economic grievances. Immigrant workers protested the conditions of their employment, including wages, hours, hiring and firing procedures, and the contracting system. These issues served as the catalyst to mobilize support beyond factory confines and merged with community activism. Strikes were neighborhood-based activities that not only aimed at redressing economic justice but also were popular expressions of citizens' rights.

Battles in the realm of industrial relations on the Lower East Side informed a new political language, which was forged in public power struggles over concrete social and economic issues. At the core of the new vocabulary, as chapter 6 shows, was a binary code which counterposed values of fairness and equity to those of exploitation and injustice. This shared language, with distinct roots in material struggles, became a familiar metaphor in contesting the dominant system of justice and rights.

The concluding section summarizes the impact of the political culture forged during the first waves of migration and shows how it imprinted its long-term ideological stamp on the Jewish American community even after the decline of the Jewish working-class community.

CHAPTER ONE

Jewish Immigrants to the United States, 1881 to 1905: The Decline of the Old Communities

> It is right to draft the hard-working masses;
> Shoemakers or tailors—they're only asses!
> But the children of the idle rich
> Must carry on without a hitch.
>
> —Folksong

From 1881 to 1905, approximately three quarters of a million Jews emigrated from the Russian Empire to the United States.[1] They were part of large waves of immigrants responding to powerful economic and demographic developments in eastern and southern regions of Europe.[2] Jews emigrated in proportionately greater number than any other European group except the Irish. In absolute numbers, they ranked second after the Italians among the newcomers. During the peak years of their immigration, they constituted 10.5 percent of all new Americans.[3]

Why did Jews leave the old country at that point? What kind of society and culture did they come from? Who were the most likely to leave their homes and their communities? Responses to these questions indicate the social and cultural determinants that guided the newcomers in America. Spurred by economic necessity resulting from changes in world economic systems and the oppressive policies of Czar Alexander III, Jewish emigration also followed a long-term deterioration in social status and a curtailment of autonomy of their communities during the second half of the nineteenth century. A series of reforms initiated by the czarist government had a pro-

---

Folksong dating to the years of the oppressive conscription laws of 1827, quoted in Isaac Levitats, *The Jewish Community in Russia, 1772–1844* (New York: Columbia University Press, 1943), p. 65.

found impact upon its Jewish subjects, particularly after the abolition of the autonomous Jewish community *(kahal)* in 1844. No longer bound and regulated by governmental authority, the community and its leadership also lacked the power and the authority that the state had previously conferred on it. These developments, reinforced by secular trends sweeping the Pale in the last half of the nineteenth century, undermined old hierarchies of authority and directed many Jews' political energies "outward" toward the wider society—and the new world.

Traditional historical narratives have emphasized increasing economic hardship and the discrimination practiced against Russian Jews as primary causes for their late-nineteenth-century migration. Accounts of the period do indeed confirm that those most exposed to the growing perils of impoverishment and proletarization were more likely to emigrate. However, material objectives alone cannot account for the group's evolving identity and subsequent history in America. Rather, in order to understand the formation of this group's identity, we must view its total social experience as defined by its interaction with existing institutions, economic life, cultural practices, and strategies of political action. In the words of sociologist Margaret Somers, we must understand "the structural and cultural relationships in which they are embedded."[4]

THE EMIGRANTS

An examination of the Jewish emigrants' occupational structure indicates a marked preponderance of skilled workers and artisans, accounting for 64 percent of all Jewish immigrants between the years 1899 and 1914, while skilled workers represented only 37.7 percent of all gainfully employed Jews in Russia in 1897.[5] Predominant among them were tailors and seamstresses, who together comprised 44 percent of all skilled newcomers.[6] The next largest group, representing 21 percent of all Jewish immigrants during the 1899 to 1914 period, consisted of laborers and servants, classified by U.S. immigration as unskilled workers. They represented 18.5 percent of all gainfully employed Jews in Russia in 1897. In contrast to these two groups, the commercial and professional occupations, whose combined representation among all Jews in Russia amounted to 30 percent, accounted for only 6.8 percent of Jewish immigrants.[7] The pronounced numerical presence of nonrural laboring occupations distinguished the Jewish immigrants from other national and ethnic groups. In contrast to the Jewish experience, "laborer," "farm laborer," and "servant" were much more frequently listed occupations among Italian, German, Polish, Slovak, and Greek immigrants in the years from 1899 to 1910.[8] Also distinctive was the relatively high influx of Jewish immigrant women. Jews ranked second to the Irish with a rate of fifty-four males to forty-six females, an almost equal distribution, in contrast to Italian, Croatians, Russians, and Greeks, among others.[9]

The high proportion of skilled workers among the immigrant men and women merits further analysis. What were the reasons for this pronounced tendency of craftsmen-artisans, especially of those engaged in the manufacture of clothing, to emigrate? The socioeconomic and cultural situation of the groups provides some explanation. Skilled Jewish workers emigrated in large numbers because of declining opportunities to earn a livelihood in Russia. The swelling class of artisans and their impoverishment were in part the result of the dramatic growth in Jewish population in Russia, from 1.6 million in 1825 to 3.98 million in 1880 and 5.175 million in 1900. Simultaneously, there was a noticeable reversal of the Jewish occupational structure, characterized by a marked increase in the numbers of those engaged in handicrafts and a decline of those engaged in trade. The data available for 1818 indicates that, in sixteen Russian provinces, those engaged in trade accounted for 86 percent of all Jewish occupations, while only 12 percent of Jews were artisans. By 1897, however, the category of trade occupations decreased considerably, so that they represented only 32 percent of all Jewish occupations, while the proportion of artisanal work increased to 37.7 percent.[10] Even more telling are data available for the period between 1887 and 1898 which indicate that, in absolute and relative terms, Jewish artisans increased considerably in fifteen out of twenty provinces of the Russian Pale, while the other five provinces witnessed only a slight decline.[11] Within the swelling ranks of artisans, tailoring and related occupations were more numerous than other skills; they came to represent 38.7 percent of all Jewish artisans. In some provinces, especially in the south, their ratio was even higher. In the city of Ekaterinoslav for example, clothing workers comprised 46.4 percent of all artisans.[12]

A similar occupational distribution existed among women in the Pale. Of Jewish women aged fourteen to fifty-nine, an estimated 27 to 28 percent were working. Women's employment in paid work reflected economic necessity. The traditionally high esteem that Jewish tradition assigned to lifelong religious learning for men meant that women played a central role as providers. Women, like men, were engaged in petty commerce or crafts such as shoemaking, weaving, lacemaking, and baking. Among the many occupations in which Jewish women were engaged, the sewing trades represented the largest group. Of all registered female artisans, 70 percent worked in some aspect of this craft.[13] It was unusual for women to be employed as tanners, butchers, barbers, or engraving photographers but not unknown for men to be employed in women's occupations such as knitting, which was poorly paid, with earnings of as little as fifteen kopecks per day, practiced in villages for city markets.[14] A minority of women ran small dressmaking establishments with one or two employees or apprentices, earning

a bare subsistence minimum for themselves and their families.[15] The preponderance of handicrafts, particularly sewing, among Russian Jews
reflected a disadvantageously high ratio to local population, leading to cutthroat competition and pauperization.[16]

The declining living standards among Jewish artisans were also partly
caused by legal restrictions on domicile imposed on Jews and by the low standard of living among the Russian population in general. Apart from professionals and merchants, the majority of Jews were forbidden to live outside
the restricted areas of the Pale. Within the Pale they were excluded from the
countryside and confined to the provincial towns and incorporated villages.[17] Geographic restriction accompanied economic prohibitions; Jews
were barred from owning land or real estate outside urban areas and also
from liquor production. The latter restriction had a particularly severe impact on the Jewish economy.[18]

The Jewish community suffered from poverty as did the rest of the local Russian population. Even the emancipation of the serfs in 1861 did not
generate a viable economic base which could revive local demand. The position of peasants was further aggravated by the worldwide fall in grain prices
during the 1870s, which adversely affected the Pale's economy. A Russian
government committee reported in the 1880s that 90 percent of Jews living
in the Pale constituted "a proletariat living from hand to mouth in poverty
and under the most trying and unhygienic conditions."[19] The growing numbers of itinerant beggars and recipients of charity further reflected the vast
scale of pauperization. In 1898, for example, the number of families requesting Passover assistance reached 132,855, representing nearly 19 percent of all Jewish families in Russia and as many as one in four in some regions.[20] Among the poor, artisans were the most numerous, followed closely
by manual laborers and beggars.[21] The largest single group of artisans, including tailors, seamstresses, and other occupations related to clothing, suffered most in the declining Jewish economy. Their growing numbers "could
supply clothing for half the population of the Russian Empire," but their
ability to provide for their families at the turn of the century declined pre-
cipitously.[22] Thus, for instance, though the national average annual income
of all tailors in 1897 was 250 to 400 rubles, "the average income is only a
dream for most artisans-tailors, a dream which will never be fulfilled." Most
tailors, as well as shoemakers, had to subsist on 80 to 120 rubles a year.[23]

The declining economy had far-reaching effects on the Jews' occupational structure. Those engaged in skilled artisanal occupations increased
at the expense of occupations related to commerce. Sources confirm that
the economic decline undermined the living standards of religious profes-
sions such as *melamdim* (teachers), rabbis, talmudic scholars, and ritual
slaughterers. Many were forced to seek alternative ways of earning a living,
and the acquisition of skills became a necessity dictated by their economic

circumstances.[24] From the economic point of view, an artisan's life appeared relatively attractive, primarily because little capital was required—a factor applying to all artisan work in the shtetl economy—and secondly because of the short apprenticeship. Jewish artisans, both men and women, worked mostly from home. Such occupations as tailoring or shoemaking were done mostly by hand and usually to order for local customers who supplied the necessary materials.

Manufacturing on a large scale was "relatively rare."[25] Thus, the use of sewing machines did not spread among the Jewish tailors, and as late as the 1890s, the typical small-town tailor worked "with his own two hands; each had his workshop, or a workroom, or at least a work table."[26] For some, the acquisition of a sewing machine seemed prohibitively expensive.[27] According to one account, some workers stubbornly refused to believe in the sewing machine's ability, which "will not and cannot tell between good and evil" and was incapable, therefore, of performing quality work. Declaring that no seam "sewn by machine could be stronger than a seam sewn by human hand," the same old-fashioned tailor refused to buy a machine, despite the growing competition from the more mechanized tailoring shops.[28] Jewish artisans compensated for the absence of capital equipment by the intensive use of labor and particularly of cheap apprentices, but rarely waged workers. For instance, in Vilna and Kovno, two of Lithuania's provinces, fewer than half of the master-artisans in 1898 employed one worker, and more than half engaged the services of an apprentice, defined as a child aged ten to fifteen.[29]

It was estimated that at the end of the nineteenth century, there were about 100,000 apprentices within the Pale, of whom about a fifth were girls.[30] In seven of the twenty provinces of the Pale (not counting Poland), tailoring bosses employed Jewish boys and girls as apprentices rather than qualified adults. In the remaining provinces, the average shop employed one to three wage earners. Larger shops were generally confined to the Pale's bigger cities.[31] In reality, though largely independent, Jewish artisan-craftsmen were unable to employ workers or to compete with the consumer goods industry that served the general market. Those aspiring to achieve the status of master-artisan had to undergo a period of apprenticeship of three to four years. They spent their first year helping the masters' wives in household work and childcare. After three years, they earned low wages of 40 to 75 rubles annually. In reality, many apprentices left their masters before completing their training, to begin working as independent craftsmen, while others skipped their apprenticeship altogether.[32] As a result, "one could encounter a self-taught artisan whose products will not be satisfactory outside the poor districts of the shtetl; in large cities these craftsmen could not survive."[33]

Impoverished Russian peasants, the main customers for Jewish artisans' products, were consumers of cheap, all-purpose goods, a situation

1478. — L. & P., Praha. — Ręcznie kolorowane.

Figure 1.1 Jewish cobblers and apprentices, postcard, Eastern Europe, ca. 1900. The Jewish National and University Library, Jerusalem. Courtesy of Beth Hatefutsoth, Tel Aviv.

which discouraged any form of specialization. Thus, for example, the limited and simple needs of the local population dictated the presence of one all-purpose tailor, rather than a number of craftsmen specializing in different garments. According to the recollections of M. Alper, an immigrant who came to the United States aged forty in 1902 and whose father was a tailor, rough local peasants required the services of tailors capable of making a wide variety of garments: "a fur coat or an overcoat, or a pair of linen trousers or a linen dress for women."[34] Tailors providing more specialized services were generally confined to the larger towns. For example, in the town of Spola (Kiev district), with a population of twelve thousand, half of whom were Jewish, two categories of tailors existed: those who catered to the richer clients and those who made clothes for the poor. The former specialized in making superior quality coats in fur, sheepskin, or superior cloth, designated for the Sabbath. The latter made "trousers of cheap black shining material, short jackets of wool and cotton."[35] Sarah Reznikoff was a Jill of all trades in czarist Russia, capable of running up almost anything from men's underwear to ladies' dresses, but she took the initiative to improve her skills: "I sent for Glazhdinsky's *System of Cutting for Dressmakers and Tailors.* . . . I was soon able to make dresses that fit."[36]

During the last decades of the nineteenth century, even independent or semi-independent gainfully employed Jewish artisans faced poverty and proletarianization. The wretchedness of their life was matched by their equally inferior social standing in the Jewish community, caused by both limited religious learning and low income. Jewish men's devotion to scholarly activity, which traditionally afforded them high social esteem, presupposed an existence free of economic worries, a luxury open to few; the majority were forced to seek more practical pursuits. Many fought "tooth and nail" against the possibility of social degradation and clung to old values of "clean work," fearing a loss of status. Abraham Solomon Melamed, who was born in 1862, remembered his grandmother's grief after she was widowed and forced to give her five-year-old son (Melamed's father) away, as an apprentice to a tailor. All her life she mourned over the great tragedy imposed on her by poverty which forced her to

> give away her son to learn a trade. She was the daughter of Rabbi Solomon and the daughter-in-law of Rabbi Abraham Schechter, and among her relatives on her father's side there was not one artisan. And now her only son, one of thirteen sons she bore to her husband, of whom twelve had died before reaching the age of studies, her one child had to become an artisan.[37]

Similarly, a widowed mother, one of M. Alper's ancestors, who couldn't afford a decent dowry to marry off her two daughters, refused to consider artisans as future sons-in-law. It wasn't to her liking because in those days [1860s] an artisan was considered crude and boorish. And she insisted on the respectable lineage of her late husband as well as her own lineage, since she herself came from religious parents and was a learned woman well-versed in Yiddish and could translate the whole Bible [into Yiddish].[38]

Others clung tenaciously to their precarious economic status by refusing to admit their poverty; doing a lot of "cheek pinching in order to get the color," in order to pass as respectable, well-off Jews, even though "poverty whistled in all corners," remembered A. Berlow, whose father sold leather to Russian peasants and shoemakers.[39]

Tailors were considered disreputable in some sections of the Jewish community. An anonymous immigrant, who came to the United States so he would not have to "live on air any longer," could not contemplate learning a trade in Russia because

> it would have shamed my family. My father-in-law used to say that if one finds a needle in the stomach of a chicken, the chicken is *treyf* [nonkosher]. What can one say then about a tailor who holds in his mouth so many needles? And that was also the rule for other trades.[40]

Tailors were also accused of cheating their customers by retaining pieces of cloth provided by clients. One observer portrayed the tailors of the town of Spola as unreliable, especially in the days before the High Holidays. They apparently liked vodka and, like some of their English counterparts,

> all took off some of the cloth given to them by their customers, claiming that it was "left over." Although some used to deny it vehemently in the name of all that was holy, some . . . would say in jest: "Get one yard more, because whether you provide it or not, I will have to take the equivalent of my vest." People used to say that this custom of remnants was the means for some tailors to become rich and respectable.[41]

In response to similar accusations, Abraham Solomon Melamed remembered a humble tailor who, on his death bed, asked the head of the town's burial society to

> have his coffin made of the board of his work-table which he had used for thirty years. These boards will be the testimony on Judgment Day that "I have never stolen any of the cloth provided to me and that I did my work with honesty." [His wish was fulfilled]. . . . They carried his table which they broke into boards to the cemetery. The boards served as sides of the coffin and the legs of the table as tombstones.[42]

The artisans' declining material circumstances in the late nineteenth century played a pivotal role in influencing social and cultural relationships and in forging the identities of distinct social groups. New social categories emerged under the impact of economic hardship, which were equally shaped and defined by their social and cultural position in contemporary Jewish society.

JEWISH CITIZENSHIP IN ACTION

Social divisions were part of the traditional Jewish community despite its sense of unity when facing danger from the outside world. By the mid-nineteenth century, however, solidarity had been severely tested by what one historian calls the "conscription debacle."[43] The ensuing social antagonisms and mass discontent generated a process that would erode the social and cultural leadership's power.[44]

Until about 1850, Jewish communities in Russia and Poland were self-governing political entities, a status which allowed the leaders considerable executive power in internal communal affairs. The kahal was "the guarantor of civil order of the Jewish society and the effective fiscal administrator on the state's behalf," noted one historian.[45] Throughout the history of the independent Jewish communities, artisans were excluded from public offices, which, along with the right to vote, were granted in exchange for financial contributions.[46] Between 1827 and 1844, the kahal's power to exert social control was further augmented by its responsibility for supplying recruits to the Russian army.[47] Central government required a certain quota of conscripts from every community. The draft law's administration and execution were handed to community leaders who, in turn, apportioned the number of recruits to be supplied by individual families. Given the exemption of rabbinical students and tradespeople's sons from military service, a disproportionate burden of the draft fell on the poor. During the early years of the draft laws, the length of army service was twenty-five years, and boys as young as eight were recruited. Traditionally, the recruitment laws have been viewed as expressions of state-motivated anti-Semitism, which aimed effectively to remove young recruits from their religious and cultural continuity. Ultimately, however, decisions about who was recruited were the responsibility of the kahal rather than of czarist institutions in choosing to draft youngsters under the marrying age of eighteen.[48]

The unfairness of the draft process remained etched in popular memory. Abraham Solomon Melamed remembered, "It came the turn of my father's family to send a son to serve in the army. And because my father was the only artisan [a tailor] among them, the whole family decided to send him to the army as a scapegoat. And because he was an orphan nobody objected."[49] To meet the demands of the Russian government, Jewish communal authorities had the right to draft idlers or vagrants who paid taxes irregularly or were guilty of other offenses.[50] Thus, short of self-inflicted mutilation, there was no escape for the poor, artisans, laborers, and other socially marginal Jews. Moreover, those who attempted to circumvent the law or to escape were thwarted by the communal authorities, who often resorted to the services of kidnappers or informers. Although the new recruitment law of 1874 decreased the community burden of supplying an annual quota of recruits, it did not erase the memory of the injustice and the feeling of resentment expressed in popular lore.[51]

Those opposed to the kahal's claim to power and control defied the community council's absolute power by a variety of means. The most extreme was that of informing on enemies to outside authorities or resorting to Gentile courts, a known recourse for settling grievances, as in the case of Hasidim informing against the Vilna kahal in 1799. In another case, Jewish artisans demanded representation on the town's council independently of the recognized Jewish authorities.[52]

Discontent was expressed more commonly through the longstanding practice of participatory associations such as the autonomous voluntary associations known as *hevrot*, guilds, and breakaway synagogues. In these traditional formations, subordinate groups fought for inclusion and exercised their rights as full citizens of the Jewish community. An integral part of Jewish communities, the hevrot fulfilled the functions of social welfare agencies, offered mutual aid, and dealt with the religious needs of the Jewish population. The most important was the *hevra kadisha* (burial society), which was in charge of burials and the cemeteries. Other religious societies devoted their activities to recitation of psalms for sick or deceased members, visited the sick and provided religious instruction. There were societies that assisted the poor, including the provision of food, clothing, shelter, and dowries to destitute brides.[53]

The proliferation of autonomous associations and congregations was integral to the culture of religious dissent in an unequal setting where ordinary people had no recognized voice. Secession from established synagogues constituted a means of cultural and social self-expression at all levels of social conflict. The kahal had historically exercised control over artisans through its power to grant or revoke artisanal guild charters and to supervise their affairs.[54] Moreover, the kahal was eager to centralize all places of worship for tax-collecting purposes.[55] Jewish guilds sought a greater share in religious ceremonies and rituals and, ultimately, religious autonomy by holding services in their own places of worship. Guild-based synagogues also established their own hevrot for the fulfillment of religious and social duties. Membership dues financed the acquisition of the basic Torah scroll, ceremonial objects, and the hiring of preachers. Usually, when a guild's constitution was drafted, all its members signed it, irrespective of their status.[56] However, despite the commonality of universally accepted ceremonial symbols, these synagogues differed from established ones. For example, some of their members were illiterate, and, as in the case of the Bialystok tailors' guild, there were far fewer Talmudic tracts in the guild's library, an absence which symbolized the more humble origins of its members and the rejection of domination by a learned elite.[57] Sometimes journeymen vented their grievances against artisans by seceding from artisanal synagogues to establish their own places of worship, as well as forming their own guilds and hevrot.[58] Journeymen tailors of women's garments in the town of Moghilev, for example, split from the parent guild in 1850 and formed their own organization, which remained active into the 1900s. Following the split, the journeymen established not only their own synagogue but also their own free loan (interest-free) association, and cared for their sick. The breakaway from the parent organization offered them freedom to develop their own traditions and culture. In subsequent years, for example, the seceding journeymen took great pride in an annual celebration commemorating the release of their leaders who had been imprisoned at the instigation of the master-tailors.[59]

Establishing breakaway synagogues was a traditional expression of religious and social discontent. At one level, it claimed commonly accepted and familiar religious rights of honorific and ceremonial participation previously enjoyed by better-off Jews. When seceding groups used such established symbols as Torah scrolls and other expressions of liturgy and ritual, they indicated their acceptance of established religious models. On occasion, religious rituals and customs were a terrain for openly expressing social and cultural antagonisms. They provided opportunities for open clashes between artisans and well-to-do communal officials, as in the case of the town of Keidany, where a worker entered a synagogue on Rosh Ha'shana (New Year's Day) wearing a silk skullcap, a privilege reserved for the wealthy and the powerful. That evening, he was summoned before the communal elders of the community, who imposed a fine and ordered him to surrender his silk cap. In response, local artisans defied the edict by coming to the synagogue wearing silk caps, velvet gabardines, and fur caps. Thereupon, community officials denounced the undisciplined artisans to the local Polish nobleman, who imposed a sentence of flogging. Ultimately, a settlement was reached between the two warring factions that allowed artisans to wear silk and velvet. The agreement also coopted an artisans' representative onto the kahal's board and provided the opportunity to choose their own representative rabbi in all legal disputes.[60]

The proliferation of voluntary associations of journeymen and artisans shows the cracks appearing in the oft-assumed loyalty and cohesion of the community.[61] Secession from established synagogues and the founding of new hevrot effectively acted as a counterweight to the rule of an oligarchy and helped to provide democratic outlets in Jewish political life. The silk skullcap incident provides a poignant illustration of both class conflict and an expression of political culture. The incident symbolized oppositional practice that went beyond the immediate sources of tension, such as army recruitment. The background of the declining rural economy served to bring into sharper relief the unequal distribution of cultural and religious space, and this became the arena of social conflict. The skull cap incident provides a microcosmic example of how contestation over cultural symbols, apparently insignificant customs within the Jewish community, sometimes became lightning conductors in struggles for greater democratic rights. On this occasion, the leadership of the Jewish community colluded with the state in order to preserve ethnic hierarchy. The journeymen of Keidany claimed the formal religious dress code as a universal right, held in common, in contrast to the elite's exclusive claim to a symbol of its power.

The hevrot, guilds, and synagogues were institutions of participatory democracy. They were a mobilizing force organized around common concerns and claims for a more equitable share of religious honors. Ultimately, these claims contested the accepted practices and defied the Jewish elite's cultural and social status.

Many years after the incidents mentioned above, Abraham Ain conveyed a similar structure of social relations at the turn of the century in Swislocz, a shtetl with a population of about 3,000, of whom 2,000 were Jews. He described the Community Council as a self-perpetuating elite which ran community affairs, made decisions about religious and charitable matters, administered the bathhouse and poorhouse, and collected the tax on kosher meat—the *korobke*. The council members were the "choosers and the chosen," or the Jewish equivalent of an oligarchy.[62] These memories of grievances constituted a force that resonated powerfully in a new and dynamic world view.

The culture that inspired the expression of such tensions transformed itself on American soil to confront new issues in innovative ways. The platform for the enactment of social practices was no longer confined to the shtetl or local synagogues, but encompassed neighborhoods and streets.

THE DECLINE OF TRADITIONAL COMMUNITIES

With the abolition of the autonomous Jewish communities in 1844 and the changes in the laws regulating taxation and draft that followed in 1863 and 1874, the power of the official leadership significantly decreased.[63] The tax reform of 1863 abolished mutual responsibility for tax payments, which were thereafter paid directly to the Russian authorities on income and property. The military reform of 1874 decreed that all twenty-one-year-old men had to come before a draft board where recruits were picked by lot for a four-year service. Officially, the reforms, particularly the new draft law, liberated ordinary people from their leaders' unlimited power. However, although the reforms effectively deprived community representatives of the means of disciplining unruly members, in reality the community retained much of its power. In some cases the kahal continued to exist secretly, or even with the knowledge of the Russian authorities, and to regulate internal life, supervise residency laws, and grant exemption from army service by special authorization to those who wanted to study in secular schools. At times it became a kind of clearing house for recruitment, as when the community raised money to pay those who volunteered for the army while exempting others from service. In reality, the administration of the draft remained discriminatory, providing loopholes for the wealthy and the well connected.[64]

In the long run, these events, coupled with economic and cultural changes in the Pale, unleashed powerful forces that resulted in the secularization and modernization of Jewish life. Contemporary commentators noted, for example, the new spirit of rebellion around the institution of the "crown rabbi." These rabbis, whose official appointment dated back to the regulations imposed by Alexander I in the early nineteenth century, were vested with increased powers after the abolition of the kahal. The qualifications for the job included a secular education and the ability to speak and write a language other than Hebrew or Yiddish. This lent the institution the support of secular Jewish circles in Russia. Moreover, unlike traditional rabbis who were elected by Talmudic scholars and community notables, the authorized rabbis were, at least in theory, democratically elected. Not surprisingly, the balloting, especially in the larger communities, mirrored the social and political tensions in the Jewish community. In many cases, these rabbis were symbolically embraced by the "riff-raff," according to one contemporary observer's complaint.[65] Popular support for the crown rabbis reflected the common people's mistrust of the traditional leadership, which was known for its discriminatory practices and its use of the korobke, a meat tax that financed traditional rabbis' salaries.[66] At times, the clashes between the traditional rabbis and the crown opponents mirrored the conflict between the poor and the traditional hierarchy. For example, in Ekaterinoslav, in 1888, supporters of Rabbi Nahum Zeev Shahor, who were described as "the lowest social element," allegedly terrorized his antagonists.[67] Conversely, those candidates who derived their support from "shoemakers and tailors" or from the Russian authorities, did not gain any support from the communal elites.[68] Some contemporary observers bemoaned the passing of an era and longed for the years when "the people saw and feared the awesome whip" of the official kahal. "Today's lowly people signed a covenant to oppose all that leadership holds holy," complained one writer in 1888, lamenting communal elections as a "victory of the sheep over their worthy leaders."[69]

Intra-Jewish social and political divisions intensified and the new individualism was particularly manifest in the changing character of charity distribution. The traditional charitable services provided by the kahal and the hevrot in the past declined during the decades of general impoverishment.[70] Although benevolent voluntary associations continued to exist, they were often dependent on the financial assistance of individuals who were not synagogue members. Departing from tradition, new rules concerning charity distribution stated that the needy could no longer ask for alms unless they could prove need.[71] The new philanthropists found it necessary to discourage a culture of dependency. To reeducate and discipline the poor, they embarked on new efforts to centralize all charitable funds, especially in the larger communities, thereby hoping to put an end to the proliferation of beggars. Thus, for example, the poor of Bialystok received booklets in which each weekly stipend was duly marked, while the out-of-town poor were allowed to appeal directly to the prosperous Jews of the town on three designated days and were entitled to food from local charities. They also got a three-stop railway ticket, possibly to encourage them to leave town.[72]

Contemporary sources reacted with alarm to the new spirit of "each one for himself and each little *minyan* [quorum of ten men for worship] for itself," which replaced what some concerned contemporaries perceived as old communal cohesiveness and solidarity.[73] Lamenting the demise of the old unity, and alarmed by the frequent collusion of communal leaders with the Russian government, one critic noted a damning incident from the town of Berditchev. According to a newspaper report, the town's Jewish leaders requested that a local official coerce an elderly Jew to pay a poll tax for himself and for his long-deceased son. The town clerk ordered the elderly Jew to do so, but his inability to pay landed him in jail. Although two well-to-do community members eventually paid the debt, the author of the article marvelled "how a respectful and large community as this would miscarry justice."[74] The article concluded with the remark, "The emigration to America from our town has not abated, and three to four families leave every day. Most of them are artisans, along with few adventurers and young men who have to flee the military draft board this year."[75]

THE IMPETUS TO EMIGRATE

Economic dislocation and pauperization underscored the growing divide between rich and poor and the latter's increasing dependence on the former. Artisans and their families suffered the hardships of poverty as well as low esteem. Their marginality was reflected not only in the distribution of charity, but also in the way they were treated socially, in schools and in the synagogues. The recollections of B. M. Laikin, born in 1896, testify to the power of privilege. "I always felt that my two teacher-rabbis never hit me because my father was a respectable, well-to-do Jew and not just an artisan, as were the fathers of the other children." The only artisan who attained respectability, according to this account, was a shoemaker who employed other workers and had some education. But even he was excluded from the "respectable" group that met at the rabbi's house on the Sabbath.[76] In view of the low esteem in which artisans were held, the prospect of joining their ranks signified a social degradation "worse and more sinful than converting to Christianity," according to S. J. Levy, who came to the United States in 1902 at age nineteen and subsequently became a dentist. According to him, "the whole town lived on charity."[77] With poverty growing throughout the Pale during the 1880s and 1890s, many teachers, rabbinical students, and slaughterers, as well as petty merchants, faced the prospect of joining the ranks of the poorest proletariat. A weakened allegiance to the community led many individuals to a critical view of Jewish leadership. Ben Reisman, who came to the United States in 1896 from the Ukraine, brought "no sweet memories of youth" from his hometown, only his mother's cynical view of the town's Jewish notables, who

> study Talmud day and night . . . [and] provide for the cost of the synagogue and the religious school, but charge high interest rates when the poor come to borrow a few pennies. They squeeze out his soul, but to others they appear as great scholars and so they fulfill the command of "righteous life."[78]

Growing secularization within the Jewish community further sowed the seeds of economic and social discontent. The cultural transformation began under the rule of Czar Alexander II, who granted privileges of domicile and occupation to students and to professionals, thus increasing the number of Jews entering government-sponsored Jewish schools as well as Russian schools and universities.[79] Russification and the new secular ethos released hitherto unknown aspirations among Jews and promoted new challenges to the established order. The foremost expression of the secular mentality was a new emphasis on the future, as opposed to the traditional "timelessness" of Jewish historical experience. While religious beliefs held out the promise of future redemption, social changes undermined the traditional Jewish quietism and the belief in a divinely ordained history.[80]

The challenge to the old order was universal. Growing numbers of Jews experienced exposure to Russian culture and Russian society through the Russian "crown school" or university, while many others, who grew up in traditionally Jewish homes, also gravitated, mostly in secret because of parental opposition, toward Russian culture.[81] The resulting russification and secularization of the Pale assumed a variety of political expressions. While some considered cultural assimilation as the solution to the Jewish problem and rejected the notion of Jews as a people apart, others aspired to reconcile the Jewish tradition with modern secular culture. Still others, who aspired to liberation from the confines of Jewish tradition, linked their struggle to the revolutionary movements for emancipation from the oppressive czarist regime. The dominant political trends of the day, especially populism, called for politically engaged Jews and Russians to agitate among workers and the newly emancipated peasantry to support a revolution against the regime. "Going to the people" was the principle underlying a populist credo. The Jewish revolutionary intelligentsia took up the mission to educate the people and help them shake off the yoke of oppression. They hoped that revolutionary agitation would bring nearer a free society based on a philosophy of solidarity and emancipation. Many Jewish intellectuals believed that secularization and radicalization of the masses would ultimately solve the so-called Jewish question, in other words, stop anti-Semitic persecution.

However, the promise of emancipation through participation in the revolutionary movements was shattered by the pogroms of 1881. The effect of the pogroms was deeply and widely felt. Irrespective of the degree of assimilation within the Russian revolutionary movements, "virtually every major figure in the Russian Jewish intelligentsia was drawn to some sense of solidarity with the Jewish people," observed one historian.[82] Some became Palestinophiles; others, forced to seek new answers to Jewish survival and freedom from oppression after the trauma of the pogroms, sought refuge in America. Here, russified revolutionaries Abraham Cahan, Morris Winchevsky, Philip Krantz, Morris Hilkowitz (later Hillquit), Louis Miller, and Emma Goldman would become prominent in new political struggles, which linked most of them inexorably to the Yiddish-speaking masses.[83]

While some Jews were exposed to secular learning and to Russia's radical political movements, others on the socioeconomic margins remained untouched by contemporary politics, although secularism affected their world view. This was particularly the case in the days before the founding of the Bund in 1897, a movement mostly confined to industrial workers in large cities. Many others were also influenced by the prevailing secular currents. As immigrant accounts testify, a new orientation toward future possibilities and the new belief in the ability to shape one's life characterized their perceptions of social and economic reality. Unlike the older generation of parents who experienced economic decline but determinedly clung to their familiar way of life, the shtetl youth rebelled. "To go on and suffer so much will never satisfy us, the young," declared A. Berlow, who decided at thirteen to stop his studies because "Talmud will not provide a livelihood," and at age fifteen made his way to the United States.[84] Similarly, Joseph Esrick, who emigrated to the United States in 1888 at the age of fourteen, while still a student in a religious school, began to think about possible options open to him. He rejected the career of a rabbi or a *shohet* (ritual slaughterer), who could not earn enough to pay for water "to prepare kasha."[85] Although he expressed a preference for the tailoring and shoemaking trade, he did not take up these plans until emigrating because his parents considered themselves "respectable people."[86] Another immigrant, who moved to Ekaterinoslav and then emigrated to America in 1902, rejected his parents' plan for a good match with a sizeable dowry, which would finance a peddling stand: "Though I was young . . . I understood that this is no practical solution for me."[87]

Young people's rejection of traditional livelihoods, coupled with practical considerations for their own future as well as that of their children, lay behind many decisions to emigrate. They did for Philip Bernhardt, who came at age eighteen. His father, who was a religious teacher, had said that he "didn't see great hopes for his children in the old country" and decided to emigrate.[88] Another immigrant was torn between the desire to return to his native Russia where he had left his wife and children and concern for their future there. He observed:

> In Russia, there was no possibility for Jewish children to achieve a goal, not in commerce and not in learning a profession . . . people had to leave home and look for luck abroad. But my children were still small, one was five and the other was three. Do I have to worry already about their future?[89]

This was also a generation which was prepared to defy the dictates of religious authorities. In fact, their very decisions to emigrate constituted a defiant act in view of the rabbinical authorities' widespread image of America as a "treyf land." The image was intensified through Russian Jews' contacts with emigrants who became a living confirmation that Jews forsook their religion in the new land and that their children "don't know the difference between the middle of the week and the Sabbath."[90]

In the changing climate within the Pale, news about America found a receptive audience. At times, such stories assumed a mythical character analogous to the apocryphal tradition reserved customarily for the Holy Land. Folk imagery in Hasidic tales focused on the symbol of the coming of the Messiah, who would lead the exiled to the Holy Land through subterranean tunnels. Sam Langer, who emigrated in 1902 as child, remembered how he loved to hear the story that America "is located under our feet and we are walking on the heads of the Americans and if one were to dig a tunnel into the ground one could reach America."[91] Personal accounts and apocryphal stories described America as a magical country, a land that epitomized freedom and opportunity. America was seen not only as the land where "everybody is free to move around and do what he pleases" or as the land of plenty where "one can pick up money lying around in the streets," but also as a place providing a potential for personal renewal.[92] "I heard that it was a new land and I was young—twenty-two years of age—I wanted to see the world, to see what the world looks like and to see whether I could take part in the direction life takes," recalled Bernard Fenster, who had been a tailor's apprentice before coming to the United States in 1891.[93] America also carried the promise of freedom from religious oppression for nonconformists who had found it impossible to escape the watchful and intolerant community of the old world. S. Ginsburg, once a Talmud student in Ukraine who was supported by his wife in petty commerce, compared his struggle for religious freedom in the old country to that of Baruch Spinoza, the seventeenth-century Jewish philosopher who had been excommunicated in Amsterdam. He dreamed of a "free land" where he would be able to follow his convictions.[94] Another immigrant searching for a "free republic" traveled to Austria and Germany and finally set his heart on Switzerland, which he thought was a land of freedom, but because of that country's stringent immigration laws, he eventually decided to emigrate to America.[95]

America, a land free of limiting social conventions, was associated in the minds of future emigrants with a promise of new beginnings. As one immigrant recollected, when he was thirty, the head of a family, and forced to look for new sources of livelihood, he found himself "in a frame of mind which led me to think that I had to do something drastic. I felt I had to smelt over my old personality into something new, to knead out a new being out of the old components. To learn a trade and to become an apprentice and so to become a new 'being' that could not happen, not in my old home."[96] Similarly, Ephraim M. Wagner, who had been a teacher in Russia, decided to emigrate in 1888 because "I often used to consider the matter of changing my occupation, and the happy idea of emigrating to America occurred to me."[97] Above all, America came to symbolize a land not only unfettered by the confines of political and religious intolerance, but free of the traditional social stigmas perpetuated within the Jewish community. The same immigrant who sought to become a new being set out for a country "where it is no shame to work; on the contrary, it is even an honor, and this country is America. So, I am going to America."[98]

The process of secularization had far-reaching effects on the traditionally circumscribed lives of women. As the providers in families where men devoted their lives to learning, East European Jewish women were more in touch with the secular world. The exalted ideal of Torah study for Jewish men also meant that Jewish learning for women was neglected. Free of cultural or educational expectations, girls in Russia were more likely to avail themselves of public secular education, unlike their brothers who were still confined to traditional *cheder* schooling. Girls represented only 5 percent of those attending cheder, but 40 percent of those filling the few primary school places available.[99] According to historian Paula Hyman, exposure to the secular world meant that a new generation of women were able to detach themselves more easily from the traditional way of life and readily embrace the radical movements of the day.[100]

Women were also more likely to acquire a knowledge of Russian and Ukrainian, enabling them to act as intermediaries in business affairs on behalf of their families.[101] Sarah Rothman described her mother as "modern" because of her ability to read Russian and her secular independence. She was the only watchmaker in her town in the 1900s, meeting all kinds of people through her shop, some of them socialists. She eventually became a Zionist and refused her father's suggestion of marrying a religious man.[102] Emigration was an attractive option for such women, who not only defied tradition by seeking secular education but also sought better prospects overseas. Those who emigrated were largely young unmarried women, but there were also some who followed their husbands. Other women, like men, wanted to leave behind the poverty and social degradation they had experienced in the Pale. By emigrating, they rejected the traditional roles assigned to them. Rose Pesotta, the future labor activist and anarchist, decided to go to America, "where a decent middle-class girl can work without disgrace."[103] As A. Berlow recalled, his sister decided to leave home because she knew that the lack of an adequate dowry meant she had "no future."[104] Fannie Shapiro, a young woman who left in 1906, begged her father to allow her to go to America and even threatened suicide: "I want to go to America, I want to learn. I want to see life." Her father agreed and paid $30 for her ticket.[105] Ella Wolf (Misolovsky), who arrived in 1891 from Vilna, savored her freedom:

> Of course, the conveniences were downstairs, the water was in the hall, but I was young and I was free here . . . the freedom that I had here in comparison with the school in Vilna was so great that America was my life. The only place we didn't have freedom was the home because my father was so deeply religious.[106]

The image and promise of America, as well as the new country's economic prospects, influenced the decision to emigrate. Different aspects of the American experience were related in contemporary Hebrew and Yiddish newspapers. Most recommended emigration but disagreed on the desirability of various destinations. For example, the *Yudishes Folksblatt*, which was influenced by the budding Zionist ideology of the 1880s, favored Jewish exodus and settlement in the historical homeland, while *Ha-melitz*, one of the two major Hebrew newspapers of the period, tended to favor the United States as the future homeland. It portrayed America as the land of toleration and of plenty where, under the Homestead Act, Jews received free land. In contrast, Palestine was presented as an undeveloped and uncivilized country where new settlers did not have much opportunity to find an adequate reward for their toil.[107] Newspaper accounts of the pros and cons of emigration were less important than personal impressions communicated by friends' and relatives' letters.[108] Reports from those already in America were an invaluable source of information. As one contemporary said, "no one can tell the relative difference of conditions between this country and the old as well as those who have tried them both."[109] The dissemination of these letters to shtetl inhabitants was of major importance. References to and from other emigrants provide proof that the information was fully shared. Firsthand experience, related by a friend or a relative well-acquainted with the needs and the expectations of the future immigrant, carried much more weight than images propagated by governmental or communal agencies. For example, one man, who feared America's corrupting influence upon his religious son, refused to allow him to go there. His fears were alleviated only after a visiting emigrant, who brought regards from his sister in America, assured him that in America "one can be as religious as in Baltermanz (the name of his village)."[110]

In the letters Jews in the Pale received from friends and relatives in America, the correspondents' use of images and idioms familiar to their readers served as a convenient shorthand by which to convey impressions and make comparisons.[111] One immigrant informed the recipient of his letter that "I live here a much better life than many Polish noblemen." Another, a cloakmaker, though unemployed at the time, expressed regret at not having emigrated earlier and enthusiastically compared the plentiful diet in America to the basic fare and the hunger he experienced in his old home. In a much less enticing letter, one new American informed his reader that "we are suffering here more than soldiers in the Czar's army. We work hard from morning till late at night to earn a few dollars to guarantee our livelihood." In general, the new experience of work in America determined the tone of other letters. "Here in America it's not so good . . . here as you know, if one doesn't work, one doesn't have anything. And now, my husband doesn't work, but hopefully he will start working again soon," one daughter informed her parents.[112] It was generally agreed that one had to work hard in America. Irregular employment, long slack seasons, and the desperate need to accumulate the means to survive in difficult times were problems expressed in many letters.[113] Yet, despite the hardships and disillusionment often implied in the letters, in only one of the sixty letters did the writer inform his wife of his intention to return home. He wanted to do so as soon as he married off his son and explained, "It is difficult for an old man in America."[114] The remaining letters, though often expressing disappointment, tacitly or openly subscribed to the belief that America guaranteed a livelihood to all willing to work hard, and that "whoever did not succeed in making a living here, will never make it."[115]

The correspondence is also replete with expressions of concern about families and relatives in the old country, toward whom many immigrants assumed tangible obligations. "I will support you both as long as there is life in my body," vowed one immigrant in a letter to his parents. Another assured his sister and brother-in-law that, had it not been for his "limited wages" because of scarce job opportunities, he would have sent them the money they needed to purchase a lease. Similarly, another immigrant defended himself against his widowed mother's accusation of having a "cruel heart," explaining that the "few dollars I had were spent on doctors" for his sick child, who subsequently died.[116] The practical assessment of chances for success in the new country, based on information communicated in letters, played a significant role in many people's decisions on whether or when to emigrate to the United States. This is borne out by the drop in the number of immigrants during the depression of 1893.[117] However, the expressions of familial solidarity and obligation, and the ardent wish to reunite families, were more decisive than the actual information and experience related in the letters. The mere presence of relatives in America became a powerful magnet that succeeded in drawing an ever-growing number of Jewish immigrants.

The impact of modernization and secularization on the traditional economic and social relations in the Jewish communities in Russia was dramatic. Released from religious and social constraints, the immigrants set out to seek a new emancipatory path in a society free of communal, social, and political bias. The repressive state of czarist Russia gave way to new political and economic opportunities for exercising citizens' rights, free markets, and waged labor. Patterns of participatory activities emerged in this new setting, and claims to universal rights supplanted the discretionary authority assumed by the traditional elites within the Jewish community. Particularly revealing is the story of a group of immigrants in transit in the town of Brody, on the Austrian side of the Russian border, who compared their exodus from Russia and their hopes for America to the goals of the French Revolution. Before setting out on their voyage from Brody to America, they printed the history of their departure in a gold-lettered scroll, bound it together with tri-colored silk threads, the colors of the French Revolution, and handed it to the officials of the Alliance Israelite Universelle.[118]

This and similar accounts forecast the future transformation of the political culture of immigrants. The economic, social, and cultural changes within the Jewish community, as well as in Russian society, crystallized the fissures within the Jewish community in the Russian Pale. The social fragmentation so noticeable throughout the nineteenth century bears out the claim that solidarity was not a fixed cultural or an essential characteristic of Jewish ethnicity. In the fluid and changing economic and social conditions, contours of new group solidarities emerged. A new articulation of shared experiences of men and women who had suffered increased poverty shaped a common understanding and evaluation of their conditions. The changes and the experiences that impelled them to emigrate would become their universal discourse and would supply a vocabulary that would enable them to interpret the new social, economic, and political relations in America in novel ways. Although alienated from the traditional social institutions of their old communities, they now possessed indispensable tools that would aid their survival in the encounters with new social and economic challenges. With this armory, the first generation of Jewish immigrants struggled to understand the meaning of America and to fulfill its promise of equality, freedom, and civic rights.

CHAPTER TWO

Conflicted Cultures:
West and East European Jews

[A]n angel of forgetfulness sits at the door leading to America, slapping the newcomer on his face. He in turn, forgets his sins, his humble origins, his lack of education and becomes immediately a holy, saintly, wise man, a know-all.

—*Ha-Ivry*, 10 July 1892

The decision to emigrate from the shtetl was inspired by social and demographic factors. While family ties and community networks were crucial in the mass exodus from Russia, the urge to emigrate was imbued with quasi-mystic symbolism, through the evocation of Biblical narratives of flight from oppression and the coming of the Messiah. The significance of these symbols situates the decision to emigrate in a broader cultural perspective and beyond purely economic, individual, or family motivation. The promise of salvation inspired the hope of deliverance from the old world. The Messianic image, so much a part of Jewish traditional culture, was a readily comprehensible emblem of redress for those who had suffered cataclysmic changes in Russian society, including repeated pogroms and oppression. In the initial stage of the mass exodus, the "Messiah" was embodied by the Alliance Israelite Universelle and other organizations representing Jewry in the modern, industrialized West. Soon, however, the emerging hopes of the immigrants defied the political quietude linked to Messianic notions. In the years under discussion, new social forms and practices were forged from the immigrants' shared experiences and expectations. New webs of relationships based on solidarity provided instruments for articulating immigrants' needs and demands.

The decision to emigrate was predicated on having family and contacts in the United States, including neighbors and friends from the same

---

"Concerning the leaders of the community," *Ha-Ivry*, 10 July 1892, p. 1.

province or village. Like all immigrants to America, Jewish newcomers relied on letters for information about work, housing, and passage. Their networks, which were largely informal, provided them with a protective cushion against the impact of the great unknown American experience.[1] These links, originating in Russia, survived in America because newcomers were channeled into specific neighborhoods and types of work. Poles found jobs in the steel mills of Pittsburgh; Italian women in Buffalo canneries; Jews and Italians in the clothing industry of New York. Although individual skills, family pressures, and the labor market had an influence on patterns of immigration and settlement, ethnic and kinship ties provided moorings central to the process. The history of the Jewish community on the Lower East Side is one of a transplanted community adapting to new circumstances but fully conscious of the importance of its forms of sociability. In the newly created ethnic neighborhoods, the shtetl communities reestablished versions of the rich and varied old world web of independent associations and networks.

The Jewish model of the complex links that tied individuals and families to networks was the *landslayt* (the plural form of landsman, a person from the same hometown). The landslayt comprised a system of independent, neighborhood-based associations, some of which eventually became formally organized as unions, fraternal societies, and synagogues. These tended to be organic, mutual-help groups based on social trust, which provided a basis for claiming the rights of citizenship in the new country. The landslayt was based on the unifying principle of mutuality among social equals, providing social and practical support for daily survival and helping to foster a new ethnic identity. The immigrants used these networks for help in many aspects of the settlement process. Informal gatherings based on commonality of origin soon assumed a more formal character, which developed into *landsmanshaftn*, hometown mutual aid associations, which were authentic, homemade civic institutions that became essential resources for the immigrants' survival. They served as strategic vehicles of collective action and as forums for political struggle, where socioeconomic conflicts were played out. The landslayt and its formalized version, the landsmanshaftn, were more meaningful to immigrants than the alien, ready-made American organizations. They did not trust the top-down approach to welfare and assistance that had largely been devised by Americanized German Jews.

The predominantly German-led Jewish charities' stated mission was to assist those who clamored to emigrate to the United States, but their other agenda in the first years of mass immigration was to curtail the large numbers of would-be emigrants and to regulate their settlement by dispersing the new arrivals among far-flung American Jewish communities. The charitable role of well-established American Jews embodied prevailing cultural and social attitudes toward the poor, particularly in the determination to assimilate all newcomers into American values and social norms. The ethos of these welfare institutions, established by the better-off Jews, was based on a philosophy of self-improvement and moral uplift that contrasted sharply with the newcomers' expectations. In the resulting clashes, the immigrants largely rejected this alien ethic. Having their own democratic institutions, they rebelled against the patronage of outsiders. Familial and communal ties, sustained throughout the migratory experience, supported a specific repertoire of practices. The egalitarian and democratic character of the immigrants' own associations, such as the landsmanshaftn, was their alternative to the paternalistic, westernized model of assistance. These hometown associations contributed to the emerging identity of immigrant Jews and ultimately to a democratic and egalitarian tradition.[2] "Clientelist" welfare structures and practices, based on an unequal donor-client relationship administered by a foreign Jewish elite, were alien to the political culture of East European Jews. Characteristically, they did not take into account the fact that their clients had their own organic system of support and political culture that could not be brushed aside in favor of an externally constructed model. In fact, both the donors and the recipients rejected social welfare as construed by the opposing side. While the East European Jews were committed to a nonbureaucratic, need-targeted approach, official welfare, administered by agencies outside the community, was concerned with merit. Westernized and at least partly assimilated Jews were represented by the Board of Delegates in the United States, the Mansion House Committee in Britain, and the Alliance Israelite Universelle in France. These institutions hoped that the migratory process could somehow be contained to an orderly and gradual trickle. The project to curtail the first scramble out of Russia into Brody, a town on the Austrian side of the border, however, failed to stem the tide. The classic divide between German and East European Jews was acted out at Brody and reflected a clash between a vibrant civic tradition and the aspirations of those who wanted to exorcise "underdevelopment." The conflict between the two cultures eventually conditioned and politicized the life of newcomers in the United States. It also presaged future clashes between Jewish labor and capital in New York City, where German Jews controlled large American clothing interests while newly arrived immigrants from Russia became the labor force. The Brody experiment illustrated the great divide between the organic community organizations, such as the landslayt, and the official charitable structures. The landslayt endured long after the Brody experiment had failed.

A PROLOGUE: THE BRODY EPISODE

The immigration of 1881 was galvanized by a pogrom in Elizavetgrad following the assassination of Alexander II.[3] What followed was a mass exodus, parallel to the historic migrations by followers of Messianic movements and inspired by blind faith in the ability of Western Jews to deliver their oppressed brethren from slavery.[4] The impetus was a letter, supposedly written in August 1881 and ascribed to Sir Moses Montefiore, whose concern for the political and economic welfare of Jews throughout the world was well known. There is no proof that the letter was ever published, but what was disseminated rapidly throughout the Pale was the claim that the Alliance Israelite Universelle, an organization composed of upper-class French Jews, was urging Russian Jews to migrate to America. It was rumored that the Alliance would not only provide the emigrants and their families with the money for the trip to America but also, once there, "give everybody a plot of good and fat land, a house equipped with the necessary things . . . and everyone will live happily."[5] Despite vigorous denials by the Alliance of its willingness to provide such aid, thousands of Jews sold all their belongings and flocked to Brody, expecting that their French benefactors would take them to America. The Alliance dampened this enthusiasm with warnings to community leaders and rabbis in the Pale to discourage the flight. Instead, news that Alliance officials were in Brody spread quickly, and thousands of immigrants poured in. Their stubborn faith in an American refuge astonished official representatives. "I could never persuade them that they are committing a grave mistake," complained one, "they insist on going to America no matter what. They do not ask anything of the committee in New York, they only ask for funds for the trip."[6]

It soon became clear that neither the Alliance nor other organizations representing West European Jewry intended to subsidize a mass emigration, and that neither economic need nor sincere willingness to work hard in the adopted country would suffice to obtain financial assistance.[7] Those who were denied passage to America or to West European countries eventually were sent back to Russia. Officials in Brody unsuccessfully tried to persuade the refugees that they had better chances of establishing themselves in Russia than in America. However, the applicants were not to be persuaded, as evidenced by repeated tearful scenes involving those unwilling to board the train back to Russia.[8] The stiff selection criteria illustrated the anxieties of assimilated West European and American Jews about the consequences of admitting an "alien community." Their main concerns were to control the number and the type of immigrant allowed to enter the United States. This policy became the keystone of their differences with the French Alliance and the British Mansion House Committee, which were eager to help Russian Jews escape the pogroms and oppression—but to be rid of them by sending them en masse to America.

American Jews feared the stereotypical East European Jew as much as did their counterparts in Paris, London, and Berlin. They worried that their poverty and ghetto mentality would reflect badly on the more established

American Jewish community. They regarded the East European immigrants as clannish, incorrigibly dirty in their everyday habits, overly inclined towards peddling, at best a source of social embarrassment, at worst a cause of anti-Semitism. Thus, in addition to claiming financial inability to absorb the cost of emigration, German Jews maintained that they could not "afford to run any risk of incurring the ill feeling of their fellow citizens."[9] As comparatively newly accepted members of the American community, they believed that it was their foremost civic obligation to prevent "the infliction of permanent paupers upon the already over-burdened city."[10] American Jews exerted strong pressure on the Jewish representatives in Brody to undertake a strict and systematic screening of applicants for immigration to determine the fittest. Large families had less chance than others of success. The Alliance warned the prospective immigrants "not to count on us to accept married men and fathers of families." One applicant pleaded with the committee: "If Lord gave me children, shall I now drown them?"[11] "Absolute paupers must on no account be chosen for emigration," decreed HEAS (Hebrew Emigrant Aid Society) of New York, and only "those having a trade or willing to settle on the lands of the Society, or to work as laborers on railways and otherwise should be selected for emigration."[12]

One possible solution was settling the immigrants on farms, based on the model provided by the Mennonites' successful settlement in the United States. Unmarried and unattached mechanics, farmers, or laborers were preferable to married men whose wives had remained in Russia and so were likely to become homesick and "cause us trouble."[13] Moreover, all prospective immigrants were to be instructed that "they must work hard for daily wages at anything that comes their way, and that a rigid adherence to the rites of Judaism will in many cases be entirely impossible." The New York relief organizations also insisted on restricting the number of immigrants, recommending an annual quota of three to five thousand who could be successfully integrated without becoming a burden on the labor market and the charities' finances. Finally, they advised the committee in Brody, and all other European charitable societies involved, to discourage future immigrants and to resist "our humane impulses and check the tide of emigration [even] at the cost of much human misery." Thus the American committees, such as the Board of Delegates, as well as other Jewish officials in Brody, assumed the role of immigration controllers, determining the preferred demographic patterns of settlement even before the immigrants reached U.S. shores.

Nevertheless, it soon became apparent that the European committees in Brody, London, and Paris, as well as the more remote American HEAS, had failed in their task of rooting out so-called undesirables. The leaders of the New York refugee committee complained: "Fully one third [of the newcomers] . . . possess none of the requisite qualifications, and . . . their

unfitness must have been apparent to your agents if they exercised any discrimination whatever."[14] Attacks and recriminations between Europe and
New York increased as the waves of immigrants, many of whom had been assisted by charities at points of embarkation—mainly London, Antwerp, and
Hamburg—continued to arrive.[15] The New York refugee organizations accused the Mansion House Committee of flooding New York with Jewish
refugees at the rate of thirty-five hundred a month.[16] These immigrants had
reached England through their own efforts and were given £8 by local Jewish charities to continue on to America. Moreover, the New York committee
blamed London for indiscriminately sending all refugees, including some
alleged "schnorrers" (beggars) disguised as Russian refugees.[17] In addition
to claiming that the United States was becoming a dumping ground for all
the unassimilable Jews of Europe and Russia, American Jews also complained that the expenses incurred were exhausting their financial resources, which were "moderate" in comparison to the supposed fortunes of
their European counterparts: "[H]ad American Jews in [their] possession a
fiftieth part of the riches of the European Jews, the American Jews wouldn't
be asking for help."[18] However, the leaders of Western and Central European Jewry turned a deaf ear both to the Americans' demand to stem the
number of immigrants and their pleas for financial aid. The squabbles between European Jewish charities and their American counterparts
abounded, each accusing the other of shirking their responsibilities.[19] This
conflict was but one example of the "pot calling the kettle black" since, during the years 1881 and 1882, neither American nor European Jews were willing to welcome waves of Russian refugees into their midst. The specter of
anti-Semitism, provoked by the presence of a large army of foreign unem-
ployable and unassimilable paupers, haunted both communities.[20]

Between 1881 and 1882, about six to seven thousand emigres fleeing
Russia received a subsidized passage to the United States, while another ten
to twelve thousand who had arrived in Brody by June 1882 were forced to
turn back.[21] By August 1882, the number of refugees in Brody reached fourteen thousand. A special conference in Vienna of all organizations involved
in the Brody rescue project resolved that refugees should not be directed to
a Western destination unless it could be proved that their lives were in danger.[22] Participants proposed sending the refugees to Spain, Albania, and
Santo Domingo.[23] Eventually, approximately eight thousand were returned
to Russia, while the rest were sent to Egypt, Turkey, and Western Europe.
The Brody project came to an end in December 1882, when all the organizations involved decided to withdraw their support from the task of assisting
the passage of Russian refugees to America. Simultaneously, the Austrian
government changed its liberal policies toward the refugees and closed its
Russian frontier. The Brody experiment, as well as other programs intended
to channel emigration, accentuated the importance of family and commu-

nity resources for successful migration. Significant numbers went to the United States without any official aid.[24] A steamship agent's observations explain how the immigrants of 1881 could afford to come: "The transportation expenses were paid by their brothers, sisters, sons, etc. Those who were already in America and had earned money there had sent me money for bringing over their parents."[25] Familial obligations, as indicated in immigrants' letters, to bring wives, brothers, sisters, parents, and in-laws, corroborate this observation. The majority of Russian immigrants reached America through family and community contacts. However, the conflict of cultures, exemplified in the Brody incidents, was also replicated on American soil.

SETTLEMENT

Links between the immigrants and their kin survived the families' geographic separation. The emigres continued to seek information and exchange impressions with family in the old country. They were eager to provide and to receive news about not only blood relatives but also a wider circle including parents, siblings, in-laws, friends, and acquaintances at home as well as in neighboring towns. We are fortunate to have this information in the letters preserved for posterity by the czarist censor and retrieved half a century later.[26] The Kula collection, which includes letters composed by Jewish immigrants to the United States in 1889 and 1890, reveals a detailed familiarity with the lives of as many as ten, even a dozen, relatives and friends, all of whom are mentioned by name by the American correspondents. Concern for those who stayed behind was genuine. Goldie Wolf wrote in 1890, "My head begins to ache when I remember the troubles at home." Miriam Goldberg, writing to her sister Yetta Rebecca in 1891, declared, "I cried because we are so far away" and expressed her worry about her niece's illness, assuring her sister that she was praying day and night for her health. Others reproached their families for failure to answer their letters and for betraying their obligation to provide those in the United States with news from home. Longing for kin is a motif in numerous letters. "How lucky is the child who comes to America with parents," exclaimed Goldie Wolf, and an anonymous woman writer from Chicago promised to send $10 for a photograph of her mother.[27]

Financial help sent to Europe further tightened the bonds of kinship. In 1890, J. Harris of Orchard Street in New York apologized to his mother for failing to send her more than five rubles. "I would do everything for you," he assured her, explaining that medical expenses for his sick son were the reason for his failure to fulfill his filial obligations. The same year, an anonymous correspondent from Newark, who had already brought over his sister and planned to finance the passage of his brother, promised his parents, "As long as there is strength in me, I will support you." Similarly, in a letter to a brother-in-law and a sister, David Arenzon pleaded for indulgence. He was living on income from a part-time job and could not offer his family the help they expected, but promised to send money as soon as he could. The obligation to help was so strong that he found it necessary to provide proof from a friend, who corroborated the fact that he would have sent money had he been able.[28] Financial responsibilities toward those left behind included the unwritten promise that immigrants would make arrangements for family re-unification. Rarely did a whole family emigrate together, as was observed by a steamship agent in 1881, who stated, "Women and their children are not accompanied by their husbands. The husbands of those women have gone by themselves because of not having the necessary money for taking their families, but once they earned money they brought over their families."[29] Those who stayed in Europe depended on relatives to provide them with tickets to reach America. Until that time, some wives and children remained under the watchful eye of parents or other family members in their home-towns. Mordechai Bloom thanked his in-laws for taking care of his wife un-til he sent for her, while Isaac Hartbrojt promised to send tickets to the rel-atives who looked after his wife.[30] Women-centered households, left behind in Russia, had to fend for themselves as best they could. When winter came, Rose Cohen's mother bought feathers to pick and her "grandmother knit-ted stockings for the women of the village."[31] Eventually, Rose Cohen fol-lowed her father as a twelve year old, traveling with her aunt.

These reciprocal arrangements and mutual obligations broadened the familial links and created intricate networks that bonded immigrants with extended families and other networks left in Europe. Immigrants helped siblings and parents as well as wives and children with the migration process. Joseph Dyenson, an immigrant who arrived as a young man of nineteen in 1892, brought over his sister two years later, and together they shared the expense of financing the passage of two younger brothers. Ten years later, they all contributed to the expense of paying for the tickets of their father and his family.[32] Rachel Lea and Abraham Gottlieb of Delancey Street, on being asked by a brother to pay for the traveling expenses of the latter's son, told him, "You should not think that the streets in America are paved with gold." Nevertheless, they pooled the necessary money for the promised ticket.[33]

Although it was the men who normally came as a socioeconomic van-guard, there is also evidence that women, some very young, migrated in their own right and not as family members. Jewish families did not oppose the emigration of daughters, in the expectation that after settling, they would assist in bringing over the others.[34] For example, Emma Goldman's half-sister Lena, who emigrated in 1881, settled in Rochester. Her presence there was a decisive factor in the emigration in 1885 of Helene, another of Emma's half-sisters, and of Emma herself, who was determined to escape an arranged marriage. Moreover, Emma's parents, Abraham and Taube, and her brothers soon followed the daughters to America, accompanied also by Freda, Abraham Goldman's elderly mother.[35]

Having relatives abroad was an asset not only for immediate family but also for other members of the community, including total strangers. Steamship tickets that arrived for named relatives who, for a variety of reasons, gave up their right to them were passed on to others with a promise to repay the debt in America.[36] Some individuals, like S. Ginsburg, who came in 1892 aged twenty and who did not have relatives or the benefit of a ticket, borrowed fare money from strangers, promising to repay his debt after arriving in America.[37] There were exceptions to the pattern of individuals leaving alone. For example, men who emigrated through Brody often were accompanied by wives and children. Others, who wanted to settle on farms in America, emigrated in groups, such as a group of seventy from Elizavetgrad who came to Brody with their families, requesting passage money to go to Texas, where they intended to earn their living by farming. Only a small number of young men was selected from the larger group and offered free passage to America, but they refused, explaining that they had decided to go together "in order to work and help each other." For these Am Olam (Eternal People) groups, who adopted a communitarian culture of collective settlement, group emigration was an alternative to emigrating with a family. Another group of emigrants, the *fusgeyer* (walkers), gained fame when, in 1899, its members decided to walk all the way from Rumania, their homeland, to Hamburg.[38] Similarly, other smaller groups of immigrants, from different communities in the Pale, banded together for the duration of the journey.[39]

For most emigrants, who didn't have the appropriate exit permits, the arduous journey to America began with an illegal crossing into Germany. Obtaining exit permits was a lengthy and expensive procedure, necessitating trips to the provincial capital for the legal stamps required for the numerous certificates and frequent bribes that were costlier than the fees paid to professional smugglers operating along Russian borders. Despite these dangers and hardships, the emigrants were determined to leave a country where they had no civil rights. Setting foot on German soil was an exhilarating experience: "We all cried 'hurrah.' . . . This is a free land; here we are not downtrodden." The enthusiasm, however, soon gave way to disappointment after the rough treatment they received from suspicious German authorities, unscrupulous shipping agents, and lodginghouse owners.[40] The hardships and ordeals the emigrants endured at Hamburg and Bremen were only the beginning; a trying boat journey lay ahead. Scanty supplies of kosher food, shortages of drinking water, and the hostility and contempt of the crew and wealthier passengers were the lot of the steerage immigrant.[41] For some, however, the most arduous and trying crossing could not dim the prospect of America, which still seemed like the promised land. "Nothing was missing from my happiness. I had my whole future before me," was one immigrant's recollection of his trip.[42] Moreover, the first glimpse of New York confirmed their hope. The sky, which "seemed bluer and the sun much brighter than in the old country," corresponded to one hopeful immigrant's image of the Garden of Eden.[43]

For others, the "seven stages of hell" through the long and grueling procedure of immigration and the interrogation by Jewish charities in Castle Garden or Ellis Island soon marred America's image as the Garden of Eden. On being released, the immigrant was met by money changers, hotel and boardinghouse owners, and sometimes labor agents, all competing for potential clients and victims.[44] To the immigrants, the appearance of these agents did not bode well.

> We were all shocked looking at our little Jews who were standing around Castle Garden, their appearance as black as Egyptian darkness, all dressed in torn rags. I asked them: "Brethren, what is this? Can it be that there are poor people in the Golden Land?" "Wait, wait," they said, "you will soon see."[45]

The newcomers were overwhelmed by the crowds and the sheer size of the city. New York appeared "like a huge anthill with millions of ants; each ant wants to snatch a granule of grain for itself," to one newcomer, who wondered how he, "one little ant without money, without language, without trade, will be able to fight all other ants and get for myself a granule of grain?"[46] The presence of relatives, landslayt, and other immigrants to New York, willing to share their accumulated experience with the newcomers, was both indispensable and, usually, available. These people helped newcomers adjust to their new surroundings and assisted them with the search for shelter, training, and jobs. A cousin who cared for an unknown newcomer was praised for being "kinder than a real brother." Another immigrant informed his relatives in 1890 that an uncle welcomed him "as warmly as parents would" and paid his rent as a boarder, while another uncle taught him machine operating. Yet immigrants' expectation of familial assistance were not always forthcoming, as reported by Edith and Sarah Pilep, who complained to their mother in 1890 of the "haughtiness" of a sister, or Chana Klein, whose letter told of "mistreatment" by her sister.[47]

Through the agency of landslayt, the more settled immigrants helped those who did not have relatives. One newcomer, who had experienced exile to Ekaterinoslav in 1899, prior to his arriving in the United States, concluded, "The green years [first years] in America were like paradise in comparison to the first years in Ekaterinoslav. In Ekaterinoslav there were no landslayt to extend you a helping hand." Another wrote, "Brothers meeting in their native town are not as happy as strangers from the same town meeting in exile."[48] Immigrants who crowded into New York City, and, particularly, the Lower East Side, created a communal space from the start. Sometimes community networks provided by the landslayt were more important than family and relatives in supplying a supportive social, economic, and cultural milieu. Abraham Balson, a newly arrived immigrant whose relatives took him to Massachusetts, decided to go to New York, where, among his fellow newcomers, he finally "felt at home." Similarly, immigrants often refused employment opportunities outside New York because of the absence of landslayt and friends.[49]

By contrast, immigrants who had no links with their landslayt, relatives, or friends, had to resort to charities for food, shelter, and jobs. According to the reminiscences of Joseph Dyenson, Hachnasat Orchim, an immigrant hostel on 210 Madison Avenue founded in 1889, was not a welcoming shelter for the poor and needy. An official greeted the newly arrived immigrant and his wife in 1892 suspiciously:

> [F]irst [he] did not believe that we were married . . . and [asked] why we looked so young. We were lucky because we had our *ketuba* (marriage certificate) with us and my Russian passport. After he saw that we were married, he began to yell that there were enough schnorrers already without us and that he cannot do anything to help us. When I explained to him that I am not a schnorrer and that I have enough money to last for a few months and that I only wanted advice from him, only then he calmed down.[50]

Abraham Cahan, the celebrated editor of the *Forward,* who immigrated in 1882 at the age of twenty-two, described his first adversarial encounter with the German-Jewish welfare agencies at Castle Garden:

> When I arrived there, I was interviewed by an American Jew who talked with me in German. . . . Unable to communicate effectively, we were uneasy with each other. I left with a strong impression that he was a heartless bourgeois. And he probably suspected that I was a wild Russian. This is what they called us immigrants at that time, sometimes even to our faces.[51]

Here were examples of officialdom working through its means-testing drill. The refugees at Brody had experienced similar officious and intrusive manners and attitudes. The humiliation inflicted by the shelter's management stood in stark contrast to the welcome and assistance Joseph Dyenson had experienced when reunited with his uncle: "Within one hour I saw about ten landslayt, among them my second uncle and my rabbi, who taught me Talmud. They immediately rented rooms for me at the back of a store belonging to a landsman. We bought some old furniture and I became my own master."[52] Like Dyenson, Samuel Cohen, who came to New York in 1880 at age sixteen from Balbirishok in Lithuania, fondly recollected his first visit to a synagogue on the Lower East Side of New York:

> After it was over, I was not quite sure that I was transplanted. In that synagogue alone, I met enough relatives to form another Shupowitcher clan. Some I remembered; others, long away, I had only heard about. Groups had gathered all around, talking and looking at me and nodding. Some had drawn something from their pockets and handed it to one man who gave it to Fetter Itselle. I did not look, but I felt that all the hubbub concerned me. Finally, Fetter Itselle called me aside. Handing me some American money, the value of which I did not know, he said, "This is for you."[53]

In 1884, Cohen temporarily moved to Worcester, Massachusetts, where, according to him, 98 percent of the Jewish people were from his home town.[54]

In addition to meeting the newcomers' urgent material needs, relatives and landslayt provided them with a sense of continuity, a link to the "old country" community. Joseph Dyenson recalled the meetings of his landslayt, which used to take place in a watchmaker's shop on Norfolk Street that belonged to a landsman. The shop became the post box for letters as well as a meeting place where "we would drink a glass of tea and receive news and regards from home." Similarly, the home of a relative of another immigrant became a clearing house for news and information and also a shelter open to newly arrived individuals in search of work, who frequently drifted in and out of the city.[55] These informal interactions would eventually serve as nuclei for the institution of landsmanshaftn. So important were these contacts that some new arrivals were willing to pay a fee for locating relatives and friends.[56]

Yet, despite the landslayt community's intricate webs of assistance and mutualism, there was a significant gap between the oldtimers, with their accumulated experience of American ways, and the "green" newcomers. One immigrant, who arrived in New Haven in 1904, noted that the easy friendliness of the landslayt was not reflected in their attitude toward the "greener." He remembered his Americanized friends who "in my presence all spoke English, which I didn't understand, and soon began to criticize my Yiddish, which I mixed with Russian words. I felt their contempt for me."[57] Such scorn, whether real or imaginary, drove some newcomers to cities where they could meet with people like themselves. No place provided a better setting then New York City, where the large immigrant community tempered dependence on an unfriendly landslayt or relatives by offering a greater variety of social contacts.

OFFICIAL PHILANTHROPY AND COMMUNAL NETWORKS

The history of the relationship between officialdom, represented in this instance by the American Jewish charitable organizations like HEAS, and the client community of newcomers resembles many other historical instances of patronage and client status. However, the resistance and even rebellion of people who were the targets of such philanthropy against its mechanisms of control provides a unique illustration of the emerging independent culture and identity of the early Jewish immigrants. They were people who, despite living in poverty, refused to accept encroachments on what they viewed as their civil rights. Their definition of these rights was forged through common experience and embedded in the emerging ethnic community born out of the process of immigration. While immigrants saw themselves as equal members of that community, they also were inextricably tied to a broader historical perception, a moral dimension that guided their social actions and gave them a particular ethnic identity. Their experience of high-handed treatment by charitable and welfare organizations echoed a historical memory of oppression. This in turn provided them with a guide for interpreting contemporary experience and with tools for action. Memories of "enslavement" and "tyranny" were immediately comprehensible and powerful symbols that the newcomers expressed in their conflicts with the hierarchical charities. In contrast to later immigrants, who had the benefit of experience accumulated by those already here, the first wave of arrivals had few informal or mutual aid networks. The harsh conditions they faced and their struggles for daily survival often were so overwhelming that they were forced to resort to the charity of the German Jewish agencies, who provided the only visible source of support. The case of Aleksander Harkavy illustrates this dilemma. As a member of the Am Olam group, an early example of the "back to the land" movement and subsequently the author of the first English-Yiddish dictionary, Harkavy and his group felt defenseless and helpless, "like babies dependent on their mother's milk," so dependent were they on aid from charitable organizations for food, shelter, and jobs. Later on, from 1904 to 1909, Harkavy himself became an advocate on behalf of immigrants arriving at Ellis Island, helping them to deal with American immigration officials.[58]

The Am Olam group, which took up the romantic ideal of farming in America, was quite unprepared to meet the hardships of the new world. Their experience, however, was shared by many other new arrivals, especially in the 1880s. HEAS, which was largely administered by German Jewish charitable organizations of New York, ran shelters for immigrants and their families in three main locations: Castle Garden, Wards Island, and Greenpoint. With the rise in the numbers of newcomers to thirty-five hundred a month in 1882, these charities also rented boardinghouses in New York.[59] According to HEAS reports, the average stay for an immigrant family was four to six weeks, at an average expense of 23 cents a day for each immigrant in shelters and 60 to 75 cents in boardinghouses. The shelters, especially the one at Castle Garden, also served as clearing houses where many nonresident immigrants congregated in search of employment and where prospective employers came seeking cheap or scab labor. In addition to housing, shelters provided kosher meals to hungry immigrants upon production of a required certificate.[60] However, contemporary accounts testify to the meals' poor quality and small quantity, a typical feature of charitable alms. Consequently, according to Aleksander Harkavy, many hungry immigrants "used to fake the pieces of paper in order to fill their empty bellies."[61] Julius Gershin, a Bundist who came to the United States in 1903 as a trained tailor, had to rely on charitable soup kitchens until the arrival of his wife. He remembered the patronizing attitude he encountered in the soup kitchen sponsored by Jacob Schiff on East Broadway, where "for 3 cents they gave you a piece of meat, a little soup, bread, and a glass of tea where . . . Jacob Schiff would come and say, in German, 'eat, my children, eat.'"[62]

Despite strenuous efforts to discourage migration, the activities of German Jewish welfare groups failed to stem the tide of immigration or to regulate it. Nor could they stop the influx of immigrants into the New York labor market, either by keeping newcomers in designated centers or by sending them to other American cities.[63] The origins of the project which aimed to disperse immigrants far away from New York City, may be traced to fears of anti-Semitism as well as disdain for East European Jewish culture and a belief that cities bred vice. German Jews regarded East European immigrants as the most disadvantaged group to arrive in America in terms of labor skills. In addition to being unskilled and having large numbers of dependents, the immigrants allegedly came from a socioeconomically disadvantaged country of origin. They had no experience of "mercantile activity and therefore, unlike the previous immigrants of Continental Europe, the Jews were to suffer the hardships of simple and arduous jobs, very much like the poor Italian 'Lazzaroni,'" a designation which symbolized the depth of poverty.[64] German-American Jews were not alone in holding these opinions about immigrants from Eastern Europe, but in translating them into social welfare methods, they were acting from a powerful financial base. Their autocratic approach to social welfare clashed with immigrants' notions of fairness and the use of power. The Wards Island incident of 1882, described below, as well as other clashes between newcomers and the dispensers of welfare, reflected the emergence of Jewish immigrants as historical agents who asserted their power to define New York Jewry's ethnic identity and the right of well-settled, respectable Jewry to speak for all Jews.

Wards Island was a typical immigrant quarantine for poor, ailing, and aged immigrants, but the incident of 1882 illustrates the adversarial relationship between official welfare agencies and the impoverished but uncowed immigrant population. It represents the indignities suffered by those who were forced by circumstances to become the beneficiaries of German Jewish goodwill. A contemporary sympathetic observer remarked that they suffered a fate "worse than the fate of the black slaves. They are literally captives of the charities . . . which use them to get more money out of the European Jews for support of Russian refugees."[65]

The Wards Island incident, or uprising, was the culmination of long-standing grievances. The Russian immigrants, who were held at Wards Island virtually as prisoners and forbidden to leave the island without permission, complained of poor nourishment and of being penalized, according to one report, for their refusal to work on Saturdays. Furthermore, the tyrannical superintendent of the facilities, Blank, known for his penchant for humiliating the residents of the shelter, insisted on being addressed as "sir" instead of the customary first-name familiarity. Corporal punishment was administered on the merest pretext of a breach of discipline. Isaac Goldstein, one of the "inmates," had his hands tied together behind his back as punishment for his habit of holding his arms behind his back, a seemingly disrespectful posture that had infuriated Blank. Blank had also demanded that his own name be included in Hebrew prayers of thanks that in Russia, at the insistence of the government, included the czar's name. Not surprisingly, the inmates of the camp resented this high-handed treatment, which was expressed to the congregation in a sermon on Saturday, when an allusion was made to the "local tyranny." Significantly, the implied parallel between czarist oppression and the superintendent's autocratic enforcement of rules, together with other accumulated grievances, drove the immigrants to open rebellion on the same day during dinner.

The rebellion ignited when one inmate questioned the meager portion of food he had received and expressed a preference for serving himself rather than receiving his share from one of the officials. This was refused, and he was asked to leave the island. His supporters persuaded him to stay, while the whole group proceeded to take revenge upon the hated superintendent. A full-scale riot broke out when police from Manhattan arrived, ending only after Blank was forced to flee the island by swimming to the opposite shore and the mutinous residents were promised a grievance committee. The next day, the strikers demanded "bread and humane treatment" and release from "this prison." However, the grievance committee decided that the main cause for agitation was the immigrants' inactivity and compelled them to work in a factory owned by a Jewish philanthropist at half the standard wage. This plan also backfired when dissatisfied workers rebelled against this injustice. However, despite what had happened, the immigrants still had expectations of an alternative and fairer system. They retained an

Figure 2.1 "Looking Backward. They would close to the new-comer the bridge that carried them and their fathers over." A cartoon from *Puck*, 11 January 1893, of five wealthy "old immigrants" trying to stop new immigrants from coming to the United States. © Collection of The New-York Historical Society.

awareness of why they had made the long journey from oppression to freedom, and they demanded an "American wage" for "American work," ultimately forcing their employer to raise their pay.[66]

The Wards Island incident expressed the pent-up frustrations among immigrants who came to America to enjoy their rights as free citizens to humane and dignified treatment as well as to improve their living standards. Instead, they suffered virtual imprisonment and loss of liberty at the hands of people who were supposed to help them in their settlement process. Wards Island's bad reputation was confirmed by American immigration officials. Edward Corsi, a one-time U.S. Commissioner of Immigration and Naturalization for the New York District, described how "riots frequently occurred" and that many immigrants escaped, preferring to be arrested and confined in New York jails.[67] The treatment received on Wards Island persuaded one immigrant that America was not "half the country he once thought it was" and added that he would be glad to be back in Russia. Others expressed despair, wishing "that the Lord take our children to Him. We then would be able to drown ourselves in this river flowing in front of our eyes so to put an end to our terrible slavery."[68] For the immigrants, the tactic of collective action against the charities' paternalistic attempts to assert their authority symbolized similar instances of resistance against oppression, especially as expressed later in the workplace and in the community. The incident among the first wave of immigrants on Wards Island illustrates a rebellion by a subordinate group that had just arrived in the United States but that shared a claim to definite political and social rights. The immigrants' experience of "enslavement" in Russia and their emancipatory expectations determined the character of their protest, and their conceptions of justice and rights clashed with the control practices of those in charge of Wards Island.

The incident exasperated the philanthropists by confirming their worst fears of the unmanageability, lack of discipline, and unassimilability of the East European Jews. In keeping with their objectives of discouraging the newcomers' supposedly parasitic instincts and further waves of immigrants, the philanthropic institutions soon decided to abandon the project of shelter facilities. In June 1882, the Russian Aid Society of New York, which was managed by German Jews, informed the Castle Garden Commission "that they are no longer responsible for Russian-Jewish emigrants arriving there. They now wash their hands of all connections with them. This results from the indefensible conduct of these emigrants, who think they will be supported indefinitely without work."[69]

Another project undertaken by the German Jewish charities was to disperse newcomers, by finding them employment in different cities, as soon as they arrived in the United States. This policy came up against unexpected obstacles and appeared to justify the fears expressed by the Brody committee. German-American Jews presumed that settled Jewish communities would concur with their reforming zeal and help check the growing concentration of unskilled paupers in New York. Accordingly, they began to send newcomers to other cities, claiming that they were fulfilling the need for mechanics, farmers, and laborers expressed by other Jewish communities. One immigrant's letter, published in the *Yudishes Folksblatt,* noted that barely two days after his arrival in New York, he and thirty others were shipped to Pittsburgh, where they were promised what appeared to be average wages of $1.50 a day. Another group of immigrants arrived in Cincinnati and favorably impressed the local people because they were "well dressed and combed in a European fashion."[70] Although nothing is known of what became of these groups, others clearly were unhappy away from New York and were soon returned, while other "deported" migrants even begged to return to Russia.

Accounts show that New York organizations sent immigrants to cities and regions without either being asked to do so or consulting the newcomers. Protests from different communities were quick to follow. St. Louis remonstrated against being treated by the New York Jewish welfare societies as a "distributing depot for Russian immigrants who are sent to Southern and Western states" and about being used by other neighboring cities as a destination for paupers.[71] The city's charity leaders issued a strong warning that "any person sent here who may become a subject for our charities *will be immediately retransported to the place whence the same have been sent.*"[72] New Orleans, implying that there had been previous shipments of immigrants, complained about a group of over one hundred immigrants, of whom only five or six were "practical or laboring men." A similar letter from Texas read, "Texas is no country for paupers . . . or peddlers and petty merchants. There are more than enough in the state . . . and . . . we can no longer afford to act as wet-nurses for the helpless people that have been sent us." Detroit protested the presence of thirty new paupers who had been requisitioned by a lumber merchant from Grayling, Michigan. After having worked in the woods for four days, they were paid three dollars each and told to cope on their own. They walked twenty-four miles to Grayling, which was quick to send them off to Detroit. However, that city's Jewish leaders were looking for skilled mechanics and complained about the quality of immigrants New York had sent, men who were "so little able to help themselves."[73] Similar complaints were received by the New York refugee committee. A HEAS account shows that local Jewish host committees in the different cities complained about having "their patience sorely tried" when immigrants refused to work and became a burden to the local charities.[74] The majority of Jewish communities that received immigrants were keen to send them back, even to finance their return to New York.

It is not known how many immigrants were dispatched from New York to other cities by the welfare charities. According to an 1882 report, the second and the last year of the project, HEAS sent a total of 3,693 Jewish immigrants to other cities. Of these, 2,145 were men, 508 women, and 1,040 children. The result of this largely unsuccessful attempt to provide the immigrants with jobs and to steer them away from New York was the creation of an army of hundreds of pauperized drifters who wandered among various American cities, further aggravating the traditionally negative view of Eastern European Jews as parasites, "schnorrers," swindlers, and idlers.[75]

Other methods of securing employment for immigrants were shown to be unfair. In the first years of mass immigration, the newcomers were confined to shelter facilities and consequently became easy prey to questionable hiring practices by employers, who were given a free hand by both the American immigration authorities and the staff of Jewish charities. The availability of a large labor pool in immigrant hostels and shelters led to hiring of newcomers as strikebreakers. For instance, one group was sent off the boat to do scab work during a freighthandlers strike, which ended in violent clashes between strikers and immigrants.[76] This and similar incidents provoked the bitter remark of the Freighthandlers' Union vice president in summing up the causes of the defeats of strikes in the 1880s: "It's that ____ ____ Castle Garden that's killing us."[77] In another initiative to find employment for new Jewish immigrants, HEAS, which also served as a labor exchange for newcomers, was said to have exploited the eagerness of Am Olam's young idealists by finding them work on farms in Massachusetts, Connecticut, and New York. They were forced to work hard, "harder than in Egypt," ploughing, milking cows, and washing pigs, replacing the Negroes "who with great effort had won their freedom from slavery."[78] Although many of these jobs were accepted enthusiastically by would-be Jewish farmers, the work meant severing their ties with other Jewish immigrants and being condemned to a life of cultural isolation, without having the means to communicate with their American employers on the farms.

An account by Aleksander Harkavy illustrates how important it was for an immigrant to be part of a group. He found his first job as a farmhand in Pawling (Dutchess County), New York, but decided to leave after one month, even though he was to be paid only half his monthly wages if he did not stay for the whole season. While walking back to New York City (in order to save his train fare), he came upon a crew of ditchdiggers in White Plains. Although offered a job digging, he refused and hurried back to his friends in New York. There they reproached him for forsaking paid employment in view of the desperate job situation in the city. The whole group then decided to walk back to White Plains to find employment with the same group of ditch diggers. However, the jobs were no longer available there, and they walked back to New York.[79] Possibly, there were jobs for immigrants outside New York that could be obtained with the help of the philanthropic organizations and through the services of unscrupulous labor contractors. Such schemes exposed newcomers to isolation and exploitation.

One immigrant related his experience in a letter to the *Yudishes Folks-blatt*. He had been placed in his first job by an unnamed labor exchange, which promised a group of newly arrived immigrants jobs in Baltimore paying $13 a month and free lodging. In Baltimore, he was taken to a boat and, to his surprise, found himself employed in an oyster fishing operation. He worked in insufferable conditions from early morning until night, "the sweat running like rivers, feet and legs buckling under. . . . We slept in cages where we couldn't even sit up and at night I used to crawl out on all fours to catch a breath of some fresh air."[80] After two weeks, he was told that from the $13 promised, $6.60 would be deducted for the train fare and $5.60 for the clothes provided, which meant the company owed him a balance of 80 cents. The immigrant and a friend decided to escape in a small boat. When they finally landed in an unfamiliar place, they ran into a wood where "broken twigs and branches fell on our heads and it seemed to us that the whole wood pursues us and hits us with sticks. We flew like birds until sundown." Their escape was foiled, but a second attempt brought them freedom. After this bitter experience, the immigrant warned his fellow Russian Jews "not to trust strange people to find a job for him. No immigrant should sign papers which he doesn't understand." He concluded with the advice that representatives of the government at Castle Garden were more trustworthy than private labor contractors.[81]

The initial hardships the newcomers encountered, especially those forced to accept charity, inspired a wave of pessimistic reports and warnings. Under pressure from organized charities, many young, able-bodied men had to accept whatever jobs they were offered, read one report. If they refused, they were denounced as lazy and probably denied all forms of help. As a result, the account continued, the number of those clamoring to go back to Russia was growing daily. "We left our homes because we were promised paradise on earth," read one complaint "and now we are guilty if we ask for bread, not free bread, God forbid, but bread in exchange for work, or ask to be sent back where we came from."[82]

SELF-HELP NETWORKS AND THE MAKING OF SOCIAL SOLIDARITY

Jewish aid societies, which were established with the specific purpose of helping the poor, were not carrying out their purpose, a newcomer wrote to people back home. Although the charities in Castle Garden customarily asked the new arrivals where they intended to go and whether they had any money, those were dangerous questions, warned the writer. If immigrants replied that they had no financial means to reach their destination and asked to be provided with the necessary funds, the charities would be inclined to return them to Russia. These fears were not unfounded; between 1882 and 1889, for example, the United Hebrew Charities recommended that a total of 7,850 Jewish immigrants be sent back to Russia. Over 4,000 were returned on cattle ships; they paid their way by feeding and cleaning cattle on board, thus not only saving the United Hebrew Charities the expense of their passage but also bringing in a profit of five dollars for each returning immigrant.[83]

What were the immigrants' options apart from the assistance of outsiders? Above all, the newcomers needed to find employment. Upon arrival, a person was informed by awaiting relatives that "in this country everybody works. Nobody will give you anything for nothing. There is no eating by day here," referring to the ancient Jewish custom of feeding poor religious students who had no other source of income.[84] For the masses of skilled and unskilled immigrants, however, employment opportunities were limited. They had neither the necessary contacts to find apprenticeships nor the ethnic ties of veteran workers that provided access to skilled jobs. Only with the growth of community and networks would the immigrants gain access to unskilled and skilled jobs. Skills were less important than contacts in the community. After a disappointing stint at peddling, Samuel Cohen finally found a job in a cigarette factory through a cousin, who also trained him in the skill of rolling cigarettes.[85] He soon learned that the Irish foreman did not treat all workers equally. For example, he allowed old-time Irish employees to continue working during slack time and granted them small benefits, while assigning harder jobs to newcomers. Another foreman in the same factory used to place Jewish newcomers near the steam pipe, which caused the tobacco leaves to dry out and break, making the job much more difficult and lowering productivity and take-home pay. Several months later, after accepting a bribe, the foreman agreed to move Cohen to a better place.[86]

Aleksander Harkavy's fortunes illustrate the importance of having work-related contacts. Through an acquaintance who had been in New York for some years, Harkavy found his first job in metalwork, which paid two dollars a week, although he lacked the skills or experience for this work. He was soon promoted to a more specialized job working ten hours a day at a filing machine, for which he received a considerably higher weekly wage of six dollars. Harkavy lost his job three months later because of a recession but, also through an old acquaintance, found a new job in a soap factory. He had to leave this position because he suffered from the harmful effects of the plant's chemicals. In both jobs, being introduced to the position through an insider was more important than work experience. However, regardless of contacts, there were few job opportunities for the unskilled, and sometimes immigrants were treated better in jobs outside their immediate community. Like others, Harkavy was frequently exploited. He described his experience of working in a matzoh factory:[87] Having found out about the job through an ad in a newspaper, he quickly concluded that employers preferred immigrants because it was easy "for the bakers to cheat them and to suck their blood like leeches."[88] On his first day, he was told that he would be informed about his wages after the first week's work. This was standard practice in the hiring of "greeners." After working nineteen to twenty hours a day and living on matzos, Harkavy waited impatiently for his reward at the end of the week, hoping to receive at least five dollars, but his pay amounted to only $2.50. He then left the "accursed job," only to learn that washing dishes in a restaurant owned by an immigrant paid one dollar for two weeks' work.[89] This and many similar cases of exploitation prompted the *Yudishes Folksblatt* to state that New York Jews "are worse than strangers . . . they take advantage of the fact that we are like mute animals."[90]

For many immigrants, sometimes the only possible viable occupation was to become a peddler, especially in periods of unemployment. Younger people, unlike the older and probably more orthodox generation, viewed peddling as abhorrent and took it up only as a last resort. Although the immigrants rejected peddling, landslayt and relatives recommended it as the fastest introduction to American life and as a useful schooling for newcomers.[91] Old-timers with extensive networks favored peddling as profitable, since they could subcontract newcomers, their landslayt, and relatives to dispose of their wares. However, many found peddling degrading. M. Turitz, an immigrant who came to America in 1889, agreed with the poet Elyakum Zunser, who maintained, "What is peddling if not begging."[92] Ironically, assimilated American Jews regarded immigrants as having inbred peddler instincts, although nothing could have been further from the truth. Immigrants forced to take up peddling found it deeply humiliating, particularly on the Lower East Side, where profit margins were extremely narrow and peddlers had to travel beyond the familiar districts in order to make a profit.[93] Nathan Reznikoff described how he paid $3.75 for a basket full of stockings and only managed to bring back $3.50: "I took my stand on the corner of Stanton and Ridge Street and became a peddler. I felt like a beggar. This was not an honest way to make a living." Some were eager to become wage earners as soon as was possible. One man decided to leave his profitable peddling business in Perth Amboy and become a worker, despite his father's warnings.[94]

The Baron de Hirsch Fund survey of 1890 found that, while 76.5 percent of the Jewish population on the Lower East Side were employed as wage earners, only 16.8 percent were engaged in peddling.[95] It should be noted that, unlike door-to-door peddling, pushcart peddling gained "occupational legitimacy," becoming a hallmark of the streets of the Lower East Side.[96] The reputation of newcomers as instinctive peddlers was formed, no doubt, because of the many market stalls on the streets of the Lower East Side and the dense crowds they attracted, which became a distinctive mark of Jewish immigrant culture. These outdoor merchants answered the needs of the poor immigrants of the growing metropolis, offering wares and foods at affordable prices. Of the estimated five thousand Manhattan pushcart peddlers in 1906, approximately 61 percent were Jewish.[97] Many were women. The Mayor's Pushcart Commission of 1906 found that many men had "other occupations regularly and let their wives and children attend to the pushcarts."[98]

For those who chose waged work, the transition to employment in the clothing trades was the result of extensive and intricate webs of association. From the moment of their arrival, newcomers were often warned that "whoever comes to New York must forget all he knew in Europe, because all his knowledge or wisdom will not bring him one cent in return. Unless he becomes a different person he will never find his way here."[99] Some newcomers came to America hoping to learn new and more secure skills and trades.[100] However, others, despite having skills in other trades, had no other option but to enter the clothing industry because they could not obtain employment in their own trade. A newly arrived carpenter could not find employment in his craft because neither his relatives nor his landslayt knew much about the skills or job opportunities in his trade. Instead, they talked him into peddling newspapers on East Broadway. Soon after he began his new job, he was approached by yet another well-meaning person who advised him, "Young man, you'd better start with a *machinke* [sewing machine]; you will be better off."[101]

Networks based on community, family, ethnicity, and religion channeled most Jewish immigrants into the clothing industry. The attraction of the industry and the process whereby so many went into the same trade were an enigma to the contemporary American public. An inspector of factories in New York State marveled at

> who it is, or what powerful influence is brought to bear upon them that thus diverts these people into an occupation which is no longer renumerative or attractive, and confines them in dense masses in foul quarters, where they must labor extraordinarily long hours for a mere subsistence.[101]

In his attempt to shed some light on the problem, he voiced a suspicion that there existed

> some sort of arrangement, the precise nature of which it is difficult to determine, by which the Polish and Russian Jewish immigrants are controlled so that they may be easily congregated and utilized in the clothing industry.[102]

The attempts of outsiders to impose control over newcomers clearly failed. The coercive methods, practiced in the Wards Island shelter and reminiscent of czarist absolutism, met with resistance. The immigrants also rejected the paternalistic power that was disguised as economic assistance. They did so by acting collectively through a language of familiar symbols of enslavement and oppression.

In the first years of mass immigration, new forms of democratic, participatory practices began to emerge in the Jewish community. Inspired by a rejection of the hierarchical, "patron-client" system of welfare, they provided an alternative, solidaristic model of mutuality based on reciprocity. Although loosely defined and informal, the landslayt relationships carried with them rights and obligations that helped to foster the democratic character of its formalized successor, the landsmanshaft, in contrast to charitable agencies in which ordinary people had no voice.

The immigrants flocked, against better advice, to New York, and to the horrors of slum dwelling, and entered a trade that suffered from an exploitative subcontracting system. The logic of these alternatives remained a puzzle to contemporaries, but to the newcomers they represented routes that were clearly charted within their cultural and social universe of associational networks.

In the garment manufacturing industry's sweatshops and factories, newcomers came face to face with employment practices that reflected the hierarchical values being imposed by welfare agencies. The large clothing manufacturers, who were mainly German Jews, asserted their authority in the workplace just as they dominated welfare organizations. Their attempts to establish control over newcomers outside the factory gates met with resistance. Inside the factory and the sweatshop, immigrant workers rejected employers' culture—whether articulated by German manufacturers or East European contractors—as they had rejected it in the contested sphere of the welfare process. They were motivated by the practice of equitable mutual aid, a value system that looked toward emancipation from social and political oppression, and acquisition of full citizenship rights. Coming to America spelled the beginning of a new, more democratic process, and the newcomers were determined to make full use of its potential.

CHAPTER THREE

Jewish Immigrants and the New York Clothing Industry

The angel of work in this country is one whose name is Hurry Up. And even though our brethren the green workers are complaining silently about their bosses saying that they work as hard as in the days of the golden calf [days of slavery], their complaint does not receive any attention because who can arbitrate between them and the mighty bosses and also the stomach demands its share and that is why the green workers work as hard as they can for a very small remuneration.

—"Letters from America," 1893

This chapter will explore the contribution of economic factors to Jewish immigrant history, including the links between economic life and social politics. Margaret Somers has called this concept, which situates historical actors in their full social environment, the "relational setting." This concept permits the historical exploration of relationships, practices, perceptions, and identities, as well as the full range of political and social forces which "configure together to shape history and social action."[1] The relational setting includes all the social components that affect historical actors over time, without ascribing direct or exclusive causal relationship to any one factor or the contribution it makes to historical events. The concept frees the historian to search for a fuller narrative, which encapsulates and informs historical life and shapes the course of social action. It also allows the fluidity of overlapping issues over time to be considered, rather than presenting one factor, or even a series of factors, as having the most decisive impact on historical events.

The concept of relational setting recognizes that material factors, such as work experience, are inextricable from an array of other relation-

---

"Letters from America," *Ha-Ivry*, 6 August 1893, p. 5.

ships. It is particularly relevant in the exploration of Jewish immigrant social actions. For example, the Wards Island incident discussed in chapter 2
illustrates how the struggle for civil rights could not be explained by economic factors alone. The immigrants felt impelled to contest the arbitrary
despotism of a jumped-up local autocrat on the Wards Island immigration
colony. Despite the intolerable material conditions there, it was the assault
on personal dignity that ultimately provided the breaking point. The identity of Jewish immigrants can be constructed from several perspectives: as
members of an ethnic group, as wage workers, and as members of emerging and frequently overlapping social groups within the community. As
chapter 5 will show, the protest and strife that characterized economic relationships stemmed from the interdependence between the social world
and the world of work. The question of how the experience of work relates
to a community's social life and activity has long preoccupied historians.
The premise that workplace experience and economic grievances generate
class consciousness and collective action has always been implicit in working-class histories. However, in E. P. Thompson's analysis of the formation
of the English working class, culture became the critical mediating element
between workers' experience and behavior. According to his study, the
English working class evolved through popular resistance and opposition
and were inspired by older societal customs that challenged the new demands imposed by industrial capitalism. Since Thompson's study, historians have continued to analyze the role of cultural struggles expressed in
popular political discourse and instances of workers' resistance to the industrial system. Labor historians have paid particular attention to new industrial forms of production in the process of the formation of the working class. Specifically, they have noted the role of surviving traditional craft
identity and artisanal solidarity in politicizing artisans-turned-workers.[2]
One such example is the instance of the shoemakers in Lynn, Massachusetts. Although by 1860, advanced factory production had driven out the
craftworkers, their independent artisan culture survived nevertheless. In
their opposition to the encroachments of capitalism and in their labor
struggles they continued to invoke symbols and rhetoric rooted in republican craft traditions.[3]

However, the historical experience and the oppositional culture of ar-
tisan-turned-worker cannot be applied to immigrant Jewish workers in
conflict with factory and sweatshop production in the United States. Most
East European Jewish immigrants were unskilled workers who shared the
experience of the world of waged work mainly through the diversified and
fast-growing needle trade, which became identified almost entirely as a Jewish occupation. Although the newcomers perceived work in the needle
trades as being akin to enslavement, the workshop emerged as a social as

well as an economic institution. Production units were frequently based on family or landslayt ties, with the subcontractor—in contrast to the main contractor or manufacturer—being a familiar person whose economic status was not markedly different from that of his workers. There was also a significant degree of mobility between workers and small contractors. Their political culture inspired them to use tactics of confrontation different from the craftspeople or older German and Irish master-tailors.

The clothing industry at this time was undergoing rapid changes as a result of powerful market forces characterized by mass production, a growing division of labor, speedups, and declining wages. Different types of entrepreneurs, contractors, and subcontractors were in control of factories, workshops, sweatshops, and the putting-out system. Subcontractors, the smallest employers, whose profits were sometimes minuscule, represented a new stratum and were derisively called cockroaches or undesirable parasites on the trade. Garment making became fractionalized in terms of method, management, and workforce. Whereas up to the time of the Civil War workers had confronted an identifiable employer "class," Jewish unskilled newcomers were pitched against fellow Jews, some of whom were living on the margins of poverty and sometimes even supported the workers in their struggles. This feature of the garment industry therefore determined a new type of contestation, one marked by complexity of social relationships.

For Jewish workers, in contrast to their German and Irish counterparts, a sense of craftsmanship was not part of their identity. As noted in chapter 1, although most artisans in the Pale had been Jewish, the group's economic importance had been in decline throughout the nineteenth century. The economic stagnation of the population in Russian towns and countryside had caused the impoverishment of Jewish craftsmen. Furthermore, during the last decades of the century, the Pale's industrial development was slow in creating new opportunities for its Jewish inhabitants. Thus, although a Jewish proletariat existed in czarist Russia by the 1880s, Jewish representation in the industrial workforce amounted to only 10 percent of the total in 1898.[4] No longer identifiable as craftsmen, and not yet wage workers, the newcomers did not fit into an accepted labor typology. Most workers had no previous industrial experience, while many future laborers in the needle trades were so-called Columbus tailors—that is, newcomers who had only recently "discovered" the industry.[5] The tradition of a particular skill unifying a disparate group cannot explain their political culture. Unlike Thompson's handloom weavers, they were not craftsmen defending their way of life against modern capitalism; nor did they, like Lynn's republican shoemakers, have a collective memory of the dignity of their craft. Rather, united by common ethnicity, they generated a new political language reflecting concerns and demands for economic and social rights.[6]

GARMENTMAKING: FROM CRAFT TO INDUSTRY

The expansion of the ready-made clothing industry began during the second half of the nineteenth century with the widespread adoption of the sewing machine, first introduced in 1847. New cutting techniques and machines were perfected in 1874, followed by steam, gas, and eventually electrically powered tools. These technological advances ushered in a new era of mass production and of subdivided tasks, which facilitated the absorption of unskilled immigrants, and led to falling wages and increased hours. These changes undermined the traditional skills of artisan-tailors, who struggled unsuccessfully to protect wages and hours.[7] The industry's transformation ultimately resulted in a new type of labor organization that superseded the traditional craft unions. Yet, during the last two decades of the nineteenth century, two labor forces vied for control in the garment industry. One was an older class of skilled workers who invoked the language of American republicanism by emphasizing rights to regulated work hours, a decent wage, and time for leisure. The other voice, that of unskilled Jewish immigrants, demanded fairness and justice based on a different perception of community rights and a newly acquired language of democracy, reinforced by the process of emigration. The schism between immigrant and settled labor was well illustrated by the view of an Ohio farmer: "In Europe labor is accustomed to oppression. . . ." In America, however, "our people have been carefully educated to consider themselves the best on earth and they will not patiently submit to privation."[8]

The industry's rapid growth after 1870 was largely due to the development of the ready-made sector, especially in the fast-expanding category of women's garments.[9] Though practically nonexistent before the mid-1880s, mass production of women's cloaks and, later, shirtwaists, suits, skirts, kimonos, and dresses was a new and growing feature after 1890. At the peak of this development, during the years from 1899 to 1909, the number of establishments manufacturing women's garments nationwide grew by 86 percent, wage earners employed in the industry by 111 percent, and the value of their production by 159 percent.[10] New York's share in the expanding women's ready-to-wear industry was preeminent. In 1909, the city produced 69.3 percent of the national total, its share amounting to $266,477,000, followed by Philadelphia as a distant second, producing only 7.8 percent of the national output at a value of $30,130,000.[11] Within the ready-to-wear women's garment industry, cloak manufacture expanded more rapidly than any other branch. For example, Meyer Jonasson, a leading New York cloakmaker, increased his business fifteen-fold between the years 1874 and 1885, with sales growing from $110,000 to $1,700,000.[12] Shirtwaist production also rose rapidly. Although still a fledgling industry in 1895, it employed 17,922 workers by 1900; by 1907, the number of workers had nearly doubled to 34,234, half of them women.[13]

New York's expanding clothing industry affected the mode of production and had an adverse impact on the status of the city's old-time, skilled tailors. According to Conrad Carl, a veteran New York tailor and a witness in the 1883 Senate hearings on "Relations between Capital and Labor," the industry's organization had undergone fundamental changes. Tailoring work had been traditionally divided according to garment: coats, vests, and pants.[14] Although clothing manufacture, especially the manufacture of better-quality clothes, relied on the services of competent master-tailors the system was already dependent on "outside," often sweated labor. For example, the production of suits, the largest source of employment for artisan-tailors, was monopolized by a number of firms that specialized in both wholesale and custom-made clothing. As a rule, leading clothing firms maintained a large labor force of "outside" tailors while employing only a small workforce on their premises.[15] "Outside" tailors worked at home or in small subcontractors' workshops on all stages of the production of precut garments, which they received from the manufacturers, utilizing family labor for nonskilled finishing jobs. In Conrad Carl's words: "A tailor is nothing without a wife and very often a child."[16] According to Charles Miller, another witness at the Senate hearings and an old-time tailor-cutter, the elite master-tailors produced a suit of clothes "clean out," or from start to finish.[17] By the 1860s and 1870s, however, a formal and detailed division of labor was adopted for all processes of production including basting, trimming, felling, finishing, and buttonholemaking, thus diminishing the range of skills of the traditional tailor, who previously had been in overall charge. What resulted was the team system of production, which came to predominate in coat and cloak manufacture. First introduced in 1877, it resulted, according to John Commons, not only from the immigrants' willingness to use sewing machines but also from their acceptance of a division of labor that American tailors shunned.[18] The team consisted of an operator, baster, and presser, with additional nonskilled labor employed in finishing, buttonholemaking, tacking, and felling. A shop's size and the number of teams it employed were determined largely by the speed of pressers. As a rule, two were needed to iron coats produced by three teams, which meant that a coat shop employed an average of ten to twenty people.[19]

Tailors universally hated the team system based on piece work, which also was known as the "task system." Although workers were paid weekly, wages really were determined by the amount of work done on a daily basis, fixed at a level that was hard to fulfill. As time went by, tasks increased, from eight to ten coats being produced daily in the 1880s, fifteen to twenty in 1896, and twenty-two by the 1900s.[20] The team/task system resulted in speedups.

Conrad Carl saw the operator as setting the pace of work: "If a piece comes from the machine to the presser it has to be done just as quick as the other ones. One has to work as quick as the other. They all are good workers and have to work together; one wheel goes into the other wheel and they have all to run together."[21] Despite working twelve to sixteen hours a day, a team rarely could complete more than four to five tasks.[22] By 1892, it was calculated that in order to earn $3 a day or $18 weekly, a machine operator had to work sixteen hours a day to finish sixteen to eighteen coats.[23] In contrast, the "Boston system," also known as the "scientific" system of production, which entailed a more specialized and minute subdivision of labor, predominated in large shops and factories employing one hundred to two hundred workers. This system, which enabled the employer to hire low-skilled labor, was practiced in the manufacture of shirts and vests. Bernard Weinstein, the secretary of the United Hebrew Trades, an early umbrella labor organization, reported that vest manufacturers replaced old-time Jewish workers from Manhattan and Brownsville with cheap labor by opening large new shops in Brooklyn, where they quickly trained new workers.[24] Shirtwaist manufacturing, the fastest growing branch of the women's garment industry, was organized in larger premises and followed the same principle.[25]

The expanding clothing industry's most prominent feature was the growth of the contracting system. An important principle in the organization of production, already operating in the 1830s, it involved the manufacturer providing precut materials for a process which was contracted out to a middleman. He, in turn, either employed others or subcontracted or "put out" the work to tailors or seamstresses, who completed the garments in their homes. The system was advantageous for manufacturers because it enabled them to save on rent, fuel oil, machines, and administrative costs. The contractor's profits came from the difference between the pay he received from the manufacturer and the wages he paid to workers or the subcontractors. Clearly, it was in his interest to keep down labor costs. Contracting and subcontracting naturally evolved from the putting-out system, which predated the Jewish immigrants' entry into the industry. Later, the availability of relatively inexpensive sewing machines enabled contracting and subcontracting to flourish. During the 1850s, large wholesale firms that had employed outside, independent artisan-tailors working on precut garments adopted the highly exploitative contracting system. The tailor-contractors "are hungrier than the others," testified Conrad Carl. They would bribe the foreman of large manufacturing houses to get bigger consignments and hire "poor men and women" to do the work.[26] Contracting was solidly entrenched by the 1880s, due to the influx of thousands of unskilled, mainly Jewish immigrants. Contracting and subcontracting became ever more specialized, assigning such unskilled operations as finishing, buttonsewing, and felling.[27] The immigrants became laborers in a simplified and expanded production process. In 1892, for example, of 350 major wholesale clothing manufacturers in New York, only five had their work done on the premises. Of the sixty-thousand clothing workers in the city, two-thirds worked in tenements and thus were probably employed by contractors and subcontractors. By 1907, the situation had not changed markedly, and of the 850 major wholesalers surveyed, only one did all its manufacturing on the premises.[28]

The industry's new features reflected social power relations. The industry's top echelons represented German Jewish entrepreneurs, who assigned the work to contractors and subcontractors, who then undertook the responsibility to find workers at short notice from within the community of which they were a part. They knew where to find men and women with sewing machines at short notice. For the entrepreneurs, the contractors and subcontractors were a valuable resource that offered them freedom from administrative worries.[29] The manufacturer removed himself from the process of production, thus making the contractor responsible for all aspects of labor management. In the words of one manufacturer, "I have addresses of these people [the contractors] who have our work and that is about all."[30] Contracting existed at all levels of production and for all garments, although shop sizes differed. While some shops working on coats and pants employed as many as two hundred to three hundred workers, others, on vests for example, employed only ten, while still smaller units produced garments using the labor of a single family and their lodgers.[31]

Industrial developments were mirrored in the changing labor force. Since the 1820s, tailoring had been a typical immigrant trade, and it remained so in the era of mass production, with foreign-born workers representing 73.1 percent of the total workforce.[32] The labor force's ethnic composition, however, slowly began to change. Thus, while the garment industry continued to serve as a traditional immigrant trade and was described by John Commons as "the school of his Americanization," German and Irish workers were supplanted by Jews.[33] In 1890, according to the findings of the Baron de Hirsch census, out of a sample of 26,058 interviews with Jewish workers, 14,770 were engaged in clothing production, representing about 25 percent of all hands employed in the manufacture of ready-made clothes in New York.[34] According to the New York factory inspector, by 1897 there were approximately 49,875 Jewish clothing workers, constituting 75 percent of the total of 66,500 workers employed in garmentmaking on the Lower East Side.[35] Jewish workers had come to dominate the garment industry in New York, which was increasingly carried out on the Lower East Side. Changing modes of production and the increase in the proportion of male operatives had adversely affected women's role in the industry's labor force,

despite their continuing involvement in seasonal home production, particularly in the large garment centers on the east coast.[36] Once essential to
garment production, women were being displaced by male workers and relegated to inferior, poorly paid tasks. Jewish employers in men's clothing
preferred to employ men rather than women, especially in machine operating and basting.[37] The exception to this rule were the larger German Jewish manufacturers, such as Meyer Jonasson and Albert Friedlander and Co.,
who at one period willingly employed women because they could pay them
lower rates and also because women would be less likely to join unions.[38]
Thus, while in 1888 women employed in cloaks represented 45.5 percent of
the total workforce, in 1891 they comprised 39.1 percent; by 1896, this
dropped to 29 percent and in 1900, to 23.6 percent. The number of women
workers in absolute numbers, however, kept pace with the growing labor
force of the entire garment industry.[39] In 1890, for example, the number of
women employed in garmentmaking was 11,798, which more than doubled
to 25,318 by 1900. Jewish women, young and unmarried, were present in
significantly greater numbers in large shops and factories, which may explain the mass strikes by women in 1909 and, thereafter, the organizational
successes of the ILGWU.[40] The large shops, such as the Triangle Waist Factory, provided a public space for women's political action, as well as routes
into the labor and political movements.

The garment industry provided a cohesive economic arena for the Jewish immigrant community. It largely employed poor people, who struggled
together against the oppressive conditions defined by their industry and
against their social and cultural disadvantages. Their ambiguous class situation lay in the many subdivisions of the economic, but not the cultural,
sphere. Their social actions were inspired by alliances across the easily
bridgeable divides between economic subgroups. For example, even subcontractors, who often were a despised group regarded as exploitative
agents of the contractor, occasionally made common cause with workers, as
the following chapters will show. Their social position was characterized by
only marginally less grinding poverty than that of the operatives and a
higher degree of independence but not of status. Operatives might advance
to the position of subcontractor and even small-scale manufacturer but be
driven back into the drudgery of machine operating because of some acci-
dent of fortune. On the other hand, subcontractors and contractors could
never cross the divide that separated them from the German Jewish entrepreneurs. "None of the petty bosses became wealthy, but only the manufacturers," observed I. A. Benequit, an anarchist and sometime shirtmaker,
peddler, and contractor.[41] All workers and subcontractors spoke Yiddish
and lived, for the most part, in the same part of New York. Whatever their
socioeconomic status, it could not compare with that of the German Jews,
with their dominance of charity foundations and other civil institutions.

Routes of Entry into the Garment Industry

Jews were able to enter garmentmaking in great numbers, and eventually become the industry's dominant group, because its skills were easy to acquire. According to an inspector of factories in New York State, those who "became familiar with the language and customs of the country, do not scruple to take advantage of the ignorance and poverty of their newly arrived brethren," thus creating a "conveyor-belt" effect in introducing the newcomers to the industry.[42] The inspectors accurately grasped the ethnic and religious dimension of the exploitative process. German Jews, including clothing manufacturers, became self-appointed guardians, Americanizers, and philanthropists for the newly arrived. They exercised control through a vast network of middlemen-contractors, in whose shops the newcomers found work and acquired skills. The immigrant laborers were not indentured into the garment industry by evil bosses but were recruited into the shop via grassroots links. The guidance of more experienced immigrants proved invaluable in gaining access to training, skills, and jobs. While old world community networks were important, no less instrumental were new contacts that extended beyond family and land-slayt networks. In many instances, the route to a job was circuitous. For example, Joseph Guterman was introduced to the shirtwaist trade by his landlord's uncle. A weaver unable to find work was introduced to his first job, where he learned the skills of a skirtmaker, by a neighbor who shared the same Lower East Side courtyard. The go-between was a ritual slaughterer's daughter, who had heard that "a greener had come and had nothing to do."[43]

The introduction to the garment-manufacturing shop brought immigrants face to face with the unfamiliar industrial world, probably for the first time. The grim exterior of the building, the site of her first employment, reminded Ella Wolf, who began work when she was eleven, of a prison in her native Vilna; Isidore Schoenholtz, who later became secretary of the Dressmakers' Union and vice president of the ILGWU, first found employment in shirtwaist production housed in a building reminiscent of an army barracks.[44] The latter image reflected the interior's starkness and discipline. No talking or singing was allowed at the Triangle Waist Company, remembered Pauline Newman. Workers vividly recalled the dingy quarters of small subcontractors and particularly the numerous wooden stairs they had to climb daily, carrying bundles of clothes or their sewing machines weighing twelve to twenty-five pounds. Inside, the noise produced by sixty to eighty machines was as deafening as Niagara Falls, remembered Isidore Schoenholtz.[45] Another newcomer to a garment shop recalled a typical scene reminiscent of of Blake's "Dark Satanic Mills":

> [D]irty workers sitting undressed, almost naked. They work furiously with their foot under the machine. The eyes glued to the needle of the machine.

And they snatch with the hand different pieces of cloth and push it under the needle. And the flies and the noise. Difficult to imagine. I saw dark in front of my eyes. And I think—this is what I will become—a machine. But there was no time to think. My landsman brought me over to an operator and said to him: "This is the greener, do you want to seat him down?". . . The operator asked: "Can he thread a machine?" "No," said I. "Well," he said while starting to sew at the same time because time is money, "He has to pay ten dollars and work one month free and then we shall see."[46]

After meeting a contractor or foreman who would train newcomers, the learner would pay a prearranged fee, which ranged from $5 for pressing and $10 for learning the skills of a knee-pants operator or collarmaker, to $30 for learning the skills of a necktie cutter and $50 for a skilled cutter. The apprenticeship period varied from two weeks for the simpler sewing tasks to six weeks for the more specialized skills. Because of the high fees and long apprenticeship demanded for garment cutting, simple pressing and sewing-machine operations were more popular among newcomers. Immigrants obtained apprenticeship fees from various sources, often borrowing the necessary amount from relatives who had come earlier and accumulated some savings. Others started work in different jobs, such as peddling, and only later chose to learn a skill.[47]

German Jewish charities also offered routes of entry into the industry. The United Hebrew Charities (UHC), known also as "Eighth Street," because of its address, was an organization funded and run by the "uptown" German Jews, who were well connected with the leading manufacturers in the industry. The UHC claimed that it sent "green" job seekers to be trained at its expense. The prevailing view, however, was that it really had the bosses' interests at heart. Workers complained that employers with ties to the UHC trained workers only after a full eleven-hour workday. The owner of Lichtman's shirt factory of Union Hill, New Jersey, who had close ties to UHC, came under attack for his "unfair" practices. According to the *Arbeiter Zeitung*, Lichtman divided the work process in his factory so that each trainee learned only a fraction of the production process.[48] One young woman complained that the charities refused to pay her rent and board for one month while a relative taught her a trade and instead offered to teach her button sewing in Lichtman's factory. Teaching button sewing, "a job that any woman can do anyway," was a way of exploiting cheap labor, as was the training of able-bodied men who were compelled by the charities to spend four weeks learning shirt packing, not a marketable skill or one which required apprenticeship. Trainees who complained about Lichtman were attacked by his men and denied help by the charities. Similarly, in Wallach's factory in Hightstown, New Jersey, immigrants who complained about low wages were threatened by UHC with arrest if they quit. It was common

Figure 3.1 Workers in a sweatshop, ca. 1905. Brown Brothers.

knowledge, according to one source, that the UHC usually paid the immigrants lower rates, thus depressing general wage levels. The UHC also allegedly sent trainees to act as scabs.[49]

Charities and garment manufacturers colluded in exploiting newcomers also in the case of the Woodbine colony in New Jersey. Established in 1891 as a sizable, five thousand-acre agricultural colony, it was financed by the Baron de Hirsch Fund with the goal of assisting Jews to become farmers and achieve economic self-sufficiency. Before long, however, the Fund's trustees, mostly German Jews with strong ties to the garment industry, changed their policy. They regarded charity giving as inhibiting self-reliance, but they were determined to keep the two thousand colonists away from New York City. They therefore persuaded Meyer Jonasson, one of the leading manufacturers, to open branches in Woodbine, thereby providing a geographically isolated and therefore docile labor force tied to one location and one employer. Thus, the lofty ideal of becoming self-sufficient farmers living outside the traditional Jewish ghetto was compromised by turning Woodbine into another garment-industry venture, with some small-scale farming attached.[50] Woodbine and similar experiments exposed the ambiguous nature of philanthropic projects, which purported to help workers while at the same time exploiting their labor.

As a rule, newcomers were victims of exploitation right from the start. Easily identifiable because they looked like foreigners and sometimes because of the lingering smell of disinfectant, the greenhorns were an easy target for abuse by employers and even fellow immigrants. "Yesterday's greenhorns made fun of us," recalled one immigrant. However, the same man, after being taken to a public bath and a barber, acquiring button-up shoes and learning to say "all right," mocked a train full of other greenhorns. Above all, newcomers knew nothing about wage rates or hours of work. "You are a greener, you are an apprentice and that's it," summarized one newcomer in the clothing industry.[51] The length of apprenticeship, though discussed and agreed at the outset, often was extended under the pretext that the worker had not mastered the requisite skills. Sam Langer was told, after the initial four weeks of learning the machine operator's trade, that he had not yet acquired the art of sewing and was asked to pay an additional $5. Two weeks later, the boss still refused to pay him wages, claiming that he was still an apprentice.[52] Another immigrant, introduced by a landsman to a shop where he was supposed to learn a machine operator's skills, was employed for four weeks carrying bundles. After finishing his term, he had to be reapprenticed, this time as a dress operator, in exchange for an additional five dollars.[53] Even this so-called apprenticeship system was not available to women, who were intimidated by male superintendents, as in the case of Lena Weinberger, who was given her first instructions by a seventeen-year-old man who shouted at her in English. After the intervention of her brother, a friendly woman was substituted. Other women depended on a friend or working partner to teach them the ropes. Some used an astute, if risky, method of short-term jobs to pick up skills and experience.[54]

Upon completion of their training, some immigrants stayed on as wage earners. Their unfamiliarity with the industry laid them open to exploitation in terms of employment, wages, hours, and tools. Sam Langer remembered the boss saying that his wages would be determined later, according to "how much I was worth." Louis Glass, who apprenticed as a cutter in 1891, was told after six weeks that the boss would determine his pay.[55] Abraham Solomon Melamed, another newly graduated cutter, was informed that he would receive only $5 per week. When he complained, the boss informed him that no newcomer would be paid as much as a veteran worker, even though the newcomer might be better qualified. When Melamed inquired when he would "green out" and be properly paid, he was told, "Fruit that ripens falls off the tree by itself." Taking this as a hint, he decided to look for work elsewhere. Lack of confidence put newcomers at the mercy of employers. Even after inflating the extent of his work experience in his second attempt to find employment, Melamed did not dare insist on a standard wage and allowed the boss to decide. Melamed soon realized that his diffidence about wages gave him away: The boss "suspected my green color because an old timer would have demanded a certain pay."[56] After two weeks, however, Melamed moved on to another job which paid $20 weekly, and soon after he found yet another, paying $24. Sam Langer, who came in 1902, had an even more humiliating start. When he went looking for a low-skilled presser's job, he was not offered a specific weekly wage but was given only $1. His boss said that even that was too much, but "he sees that I am trying, and he hopes that I will become faster."

Work hours were a mystery to newcomers; as Sam Langer observed, "one worked without a clock."[57] Rose Cohen was told by her boss "no office hours in my shop" when she arrived to work at seven in the morning. New workers soon realized that unless they kept up with the pace the boss dictated, they would lose their jobs. "That bench must bring me profit, and you sit on my bench and I don't have any profit from you," Bernard Fenster was told on being fired. Long hours prevailed, especially for newcomers, and overtime was not paid. Abe Herschowitz, who worked sixty-two hours a week at a low-skilled job as a helper to a pocketmaker, could not afford a watch. Rather than arrive late he used to come as early as six o'clock to the shop and found many people already working. Pauline Newman also remembered that the boss fixed the length of the workday. All piece workers had to do overtime at his discretion. Protesting risked losing one's job.[58] Speedup and growing subdivision of work threatened working women as much as men, although, as Susan Glenn perceptively points out, labor history is often written as if the loss of craft identity were limited to male artisans. For women, as much as for men, who had been trained or accustomed to produce an entire garment, under the modern industrial tailoring system, skill counted for less than speed, which made adjustment difficult. The new system required a transition from dressmaker to operator.[59] Furthermore, work in garment shops meant working under the control and supervision of, and alongside, men. Rose Cohen wanted to sit at a separate table to escape crude jokes and stories. Cohen remembered the stinging insult and embarrassment she felt at the vulgarity of her male coworkers: "We [women] sat with our heads hanging."[60]

Religious workers were particularly exploited, as most shops did not give time off for the Sabbath. Observant Jews often had to undergo repeated apprenticeships and earned less. One religious immigrant, after repeated periods of training and several years of experience, only earned $4 a week, or half the average wage.[61] Bernard Fenster, who immigrated in 1891, began working in Friedlander's cloak factory at $5 weekly, making up Saturdays by working on Sundays in the boss's home. Although Fenster originally clung zealously to his religious beliefs, he soon learned that he could not earn a living and yielded to the "temptation of evil" by working on the Sabbath. Ephraim Wagner found out that he could not support his family on his meager wages and also began to work on Saturdays, justifying his decision with a quote from Talmudic law: "A life in jeopardy overrules the Sabbath." Giving up religious observance created unbridgeable rifts in families, especially between the newcomers and the old-timers, the former identifiable by their uncompromising religious convictions. One immigrant, who arrived in 1894 and began to work on Saturdays, was threatened with divorce by his wife, who came over a few years later, if he did not stop. She declared she would not bear "a criminal's child." These and similar cases helped create the image of America as a godless land where all Jews sooner or later tasted the fruit of "the American tree of knowledge" and forsook their religion.[62]

Work dominated immigrants' lives, casting a shadow on long-established religious practices and leisure habits. Communal solidarity was achieved in the exploitative atmosphere of a single industry to which newcomers flocked, where one individual's experience was mirrored a hundredfold. The growing role of the ethnic community in channeling newcomers into garmentmaking further enhanced links among nonskilled needle workers. These factors contributed to the dissolution of old occupational identities and enabled the newcomers to embrace the goals of a community of nonskilled immigrants rather than narrow craft interests.

EARNINGS AND WORK HOURS

Exploitation of immigrant labor became a concern and a subject of considerable debate among contemporary labor leaders and reformers. Declining wages meant that operators worked punishingly long hours in order to earn a meager livelihood. It was sometimes even alleged that immigrants invented long hours. Some observers, like Jacob Riis, considered such hard work as being motivated by greed rather than the desperate need to earn a basic livelihood. Newcomers were also criticized by labor commentators for supposedly accepting work at lower wages, thus displacing older and better paid labor and becoming instrumental in employers' quest for higher profits through speedups.[63]

The sewing machine, in particular, became a symbol of the exploitation and oppression of newcomers. Extolled by employers, who "got their work quicker, and it was nicer," the machine, the worker soon learned, had the power to depress piece rates. And it was the sewing machine that enabled unskilled immigrants to adapt and learn how to earn their living quickly. Without it, "this class of people could not do it," maintained a New York cutter.[64] Although they usually were victims, rather than perpetrators, of the system, the vast majority of unskilled workers were viewed as being responsible for the decline of tailors' wages. The immigrants, their contractors, and subcontractors, who were referred to as the "cheaper element" or "a very ignorant class of people," appeared responsible for the tailors' woes.[65]

The 1870s marked a turning point for skilled labor. The process of declining wages and increasing hours had begun with the depression of 1873 and continued through the rest of the decade, following years of expansion during and immediately after the Civil War. Trends discernible before the mass entry of East European Jews into the industry became its hallmarks. Skilled tailors' weekly wages had risen in the years from 1864 to 1873 to $20 to $25, but declined to $8 to $9 in 1882. Charles Miller, a veteran of the cutting trade in men's suits, the most skilled and best paid among the tailoring jobs, reported that his weekly earnings plunged to $15, or $640 annually, in the early 1880s. Skilled tailors, like Conrad Carl, therefore joined the ranks of workers in mass-produced garments, earning only $8 to $9 weekly at the going piece rate, although they were turning out two to three times more work than before the Civil War.[66] Although the pre-1873 economic expansion was profitable for skilled workmen, the tailoresses', seamstresses', and other needlewomen's wages did not increase at the same rate. Women workers continued to be paid subsistence wages; they had obtained smaller increases during the expansion period. By the 1870s they, too, were back at the 1860s levels.[67] In the early 1880s, tailoresses who were engaged in the production of cheaper goods, such as boys' wear, earned only $3.81 to $4.50 for a full seven-day week, or half the amount earned by tailors.[68] With the influx of Jewish immigrants, the wage differential between men and women grew. According to a study by the U.S. Industrial Commission, the concentration of women in the least skilled aspects of manufacturing, particularly the finishing tasks, explains why they earned only one-half to two-thirds of the rates of machine operators.[69] The disparity in earnings reflected the exclusion of women from the better-paid occupations, even when they were employed on exactly the same tasks as the men. Although this was possibly because women were slightly slower, it was, above all, due to the fact that wage bargains were agreed on an individual basis, and only on rare occasions were women able to obtain what they demanded.[70]

It should be noted, however, that the data gathered by the New York State Bureau of Labor and published in its annual reports beginning in 1889 and, after 1897, in more detailed quarterly reports, relied on information supplied by unions. Yet, in 1900, union membership represented only one-fifth of the total workforce in garmentmaking.[71] Moreover, while unionized workers tended to represent labor employed in larger shops, immigrant labor found employment in tenements. The latter category was therefore only partly reflected in the information collected. These economic realities make meaningful comparisons for immigrant labor more difficult. Furthermore, wide wage differentials within the same industry and for the same jobs make average figures even less accurate.[72] Even among organized workers, there were wide differentials: Some coat makers earned as little as $1 weekly, while others earned $15. Tailors, mainly samplemakers, could earn anything from $3 to $50 weekly.[73] Seasonal employment fluctuations present further obstacles in accurately assessing newcomers' wage levels. Spring and fall were the busiest seasons, while many workers were unemployed during the winter and summer. In 1897, for example, the average number of days worked fluctuated between 217 to 255 for men and between 228 and 272 for women.[74] Thus, although the slack season did not mean complete inactivity, the shops' payroll tended to drop considerably, and on average, workers in the industry lost three to four months of work a year. While some found temporary employment at much reduced wages, others spent their unemployment period with no earnings.

Little is known about the length of the working day among tenement and home workers. However, it is likely that immigrants and women, who were the majority among such workers, worked between twelve and eighteen hours, while the workday in larger manufacturing establishments averaged eight to ten hours daily.[75] Despite the limited data concerning wages and hours, the information gathered for the 1880s and the 1890s demonstrates certain characteristic trends. Thus, the United States Industrial Commission found that despite the fact that productivity in New York increased by two thirds, coat workers' earnings dropped by 6.2 percent, piece rates fell by 50 percent and work hours increased by 20 percent. Similarly, pressers' wages fell by 10 percent, the piece rate having declined by 40 percent, but their work hours rose by 20 percent.[76] These trends indicate that only by working increasingly longer hours, with their wives and children supplementing their earnings, could garment workers secure a minimal income.

Long hours and the intensification of work were issues that separated old labor from new. Henry White, the General Secretary of United Garment Workers of America, a leading garment workers' union, testified in 1899 that "old tailors" had it in "their nature to get a fair compensation or not to work, and take their chances," while among the Hebrew tailors, "such a consideration does not obtain at all; it is a matter of work, and that is all. They take no chances. If they cannot make a living working twelve hours a day, they will make it working fourteen or sixteen hours. They will go to any limit in order to live by working, and it is just because of that he is enslaved." In other words, immigrant workers were regarded as responsible for the new mass-production system rather than as its victims. In fact, far from being inspired by greed and "deliberately" starving themselves, they desperately needed to work long hours not only to earn more but to acquire skills and speed.[77]

By contrast, veteran tailors viewed a long workday as an infringement on their rights. The assault on traditional work habits began with the use of the machine at home, when the tailor was forced to intensify his work pace to compensate for the falling prices the manufacturers paid.[78] Gone was the satisfaction with work that had been enjoyed in the golden age of craft. The skilled artisan's fate and the quality of his life under the system of mass production was summarized by Conrad Carl: "We work now in excitement—in a hurry. It is hunting; it is not work at all; it is a hunt."[79] A questionnaire sent by an unidentified tailors' union in the early 1880s reflected some of the grievances shared by many tailors. The survey asked about Sunday work, children's schooling, and leisure pursuits such as "time and the means to visit Central Park or any other places of pleasures."[80] The answers confirmed the deteriorating status of qualified tailors. Their struggle for an eight-hour day was a response to encroachments on their way of life, including time off work. The survey concluded that a shorter day would avoid overproduction, reduce unemployment, and increase wages, while also providing "greater opportunities for intellectual growth, more comfortable and healthy living apartments, through greater command of time for living at a distance from place of employment." According to the New York chapter of the Journeymen Tailors' Benevolent and Protective Union, increased leisure time "would raise the moral and social condition of the people," make them better citizens, and "thereby add to the general peace and prosperity of all."[81] These struggles for an eight-hour workday appeared irrelevant to the mass of Jewish immigrants. As chapters 5 and 6 will show, Jewish immigrants' collective action followed paths of industrial action that were somewhat an enigma to the American public because of their often illegal and violent nature.[82]

In the short term, whatever the price, immigrants gradually gained some benefits from their hard work. Usually, improvements in their situation occurred after five years of residency. One-fifth of Jewish workers who had less than five years' residency earned less than $7.50 a week, but only 4 percent earned so little after five to ten years in America. Those earning at least $15 weekly doubled after five years.[83] The immigrant workers gradually benefitted economically by becoming familiar with the new economy. Joseph Dyenson became a "greened out" immigrant—that is, one with experience—after ten years of eking out a living in the garment industry. Having first been a worker and then a contractor, in 1902 he decided to look for a position outside the industry, because being in a garment shop meant "remaining a greenhorn." His first job as a collector of payments for a furniture shop brought "no great fortune, but I greened myself out a bit," he remembered. His new position provided him with contacts within the Jewish community and with immigrant organizations, and later, by starting a landsmanshaft, he gained respectability.[84] Others became small manufacturers, like A. Gumner, who accumulated enough experience and a network of connections that enabled him to establish an independent business. Other small contractors, for example, advanced by using their skills and their contacts with uptown suppliers to enter the world of manufacturing. Especially successful were those who were quick to discover the growing demand for women's clothes, like Samuel Cohen, who produced wrappers and kimonos in his home.[85] These small manufacturers believed that their modest beginnings would eventually lead to success. Louis Borgenicht, who began by peddling homemade aprons in the neighborhood, remembered, "We were starting from scratch, yet almost at once we understood that there were no boundaries to the progress we could make." Sarah Reznikoff was an enterprising young immigrant who lived alone and survived on piecework by making collars and belts. Subsequently she set up a household and homeworking partnership with her cousin and future husband, Nathan Reznikoff. She got work for them both making wrappers, which were delivered to the apartment by a subcontractor, and she engaged her lodgers' daughter to sew on the buttons. Eventually Sarah and Nathan saved enough money to send for her mother.[86] Those immigrants who remained workers learned through experience to demand their due. For example, Abraham Solomon Melamed, who became a cutter, stipulated his wage instead of leaving it to the boss. Others did likewise.[87] However, wage bargaining on an individual basis was confined to the more skilled and higher paying jobs such as cutting and patternmaking. The vast majority of the less skilled and unskilled, including machine operators, pressers, finishers, and button sewers, were in no position to rely on their bargaining power as individuals. Once they became familiar with the waged economy, taking collective action was their best option. The garment industry, with its links to the community based in a specific neighborhood, played a leading role in the evolution of Jewish collective identity. The large concentration of immigrants in one urban setting

Figure 3.2 Division Street, New York City, 1905. ©Collection of the New-York
Historical Society.

and one industry reinforced their awareness of economic "enslavement"
and "tyranny." These phrases, evocative of a common historical past, frequently were used both by immigrants and in the labor movement. Despite
workers' divisions along skill lines and wage differentials, their common experience and shared grievances against declining wages, speedups, increasing tasks, and bosses' power in the workplace all inspired a rhetoric of solidarity. This collective experience ultimately contributed to their ability
to make economic demands. On the other hand, the contracting system

made individual advancement on a small scale possible. However, these two channels, the one collective and the other individualistic, were not mutually exclusive and together they mobilized the immigrant population of the Lower East Side. The community's economic base cannot alone explain how the world of work merged with the wider community and created an "enmeshing" of the economic and political dimensions, giving rise to a uniquely Jewish working-class culture. The immigrants shared concerns about work but also about rent and food prices and, ultimately, about issues that touched upon the individual's relations to society. Complex webs of community linked civic associations to other aspects of the public sphere.[88] The language of work suffused public actions, as did the Jewish community's dynamic cultural traditions.

CHAPTER FOUR

Making a Home and Earning a Living on the Lower East Side

He whom God has not blessed with sons, daughters, and a large household where all can contribute by doing their own work; he who will not turn his small house into a boarding home for twenty workers and peddlers, subsisting on their leavings and taking upon himself to sleep on the earth . . . such a one will never see an extra cent in his purse.

—Rabbi Moses Weinberger

The Lower East Side's Jewish community occupied a new type of urban space. The newcomers were almost its exclusive inhabitants in numbers and concentration, which had no precedent in modern Jewish history. The population density contributed an explosive element to the quality of mass demonstrations and social actions, as well as to their meaning and purpose. The fact that individuals lived, worked, and socialized in close proximity facilitated the establishment of a wide range of organizations and institutions. Such associational organizations as landsmanshaftn, fraternal clubs, synagogues, and trade organizations provided public arenas for popular participation where social actors "with overlapping identities as legal subjects, citizens, economic actors, and family and community members form a public body and engage in negotiations and contestations over political and social life."[1] These associations, which were democratically structured and open to popular participation, developed a corresponding political language. Here, newcomers could voice citizenship rights couched in a new idiom and using a mixture of old-world and new-world symbolism. Although the movement toward secularization and the struggle for democratic rights within the

---

Sarna, ed., *People Walk on their Heads*, p. 58.

community itself had begun in Russia, the American political context led to the development of new social demands within the larger society.

In the tightly defined area, where life was identifiably Jewish and separate from the rest of New York, private and public spaces merged, to the considerable consternation of outsiders. Contemporary photographs of Hester and Orchard Street markets show tumultuous, active crowds. Local residents used streets, marketplaces, and institutions as if they owned them, mounting social protests and celebratory marches as well as displays of public grief. At the same time, living spaces in tenement blocks were used as workshops and were therefore open to the comings and goings of outworkers and subcontractors. They were also used for such public transactions as informal prayer meetings during the working day, the educational activities of a *cheder* (religious school), and neighborhood meetings. In a framework of such blurred distinctions of public and private space, individuals could express private grievances in public and receive spontaneous support from strangers. Social, economic, and political concerns were aired in the "workplace"—which may in reality have been home to a family and lodger/workers—in meetings of landsmanshaftn, synagogues, shops, and marketplaces.

The street was where both sexes and all classes coexisted. Jewish women participated more in street politics than women from other immigrant communities. Women in the Italian neighborhoods, for instance, although highly visible in the streets on religious holy days such as the Madonna festivals, were observers rather than participants in other street events.[2] In contrast, descriptions of strikes and demonstrations in the Jewish community testify to the participation of Jewish women in public events. Ella Woolf enthusiastically described her sense of freedom in experiencing street life and ascribed it to her attendance at the Baron de Hirsch school: "My memory of it is very sweet because of the freedom I had. It was so different from the hard life I had on the other side. I wasn't allowed to go here. I wasn't allowed to go there. . . . I felt as if I were born here. And that was the school that made me feel that way."[3]

On the Lower East Side, popular concerns relating to aspects of private and public life permeated all communal networks. This, in turn, facilitated the mobilization of sympathizers to workers' causes at times of strikes, boycotts, or campaigns of ostracism. The blending of the public and private spheres promoted a particular kind of bonding that ultimately led to the formation of a new ethnic awareness. The experience of shared waged work and the proximity of work to synagogues, schools, and public halls led to a virtual takeover of the Lower East Side by its Jewish residents, thereby emphasizing their separate political culture. This brought immigrants into conflict with mainstream American social and political values, as expressed by American labor unions and the law.[4] The community's occupation of public spaces contravened widely accepted notions of social behavior as sanctioned by the law and civil society.

As with many other immigrant concentrations, the Jewish community's settlement on the Lower East Side constituted a means of displaying the distinctiveness of its ethnic identity in relation to the host community. In the words of a recent article on the subject, the process of forging ethnicity "involved a dialogue between majority and minority cultures."[5] The dominant society's perception affected the immigrants' self-definition. Participating in the "dialogue" between minority culture and the dominant groups were, on the one hand, the immigrant Jews, and on the other, German Jews, progressive reformers, and labor unionists such as the Knights of Labor. The immigrant community's control over a virtual "off-limits zone" posed an implicit challenge, especially to the authority of more established Jewish institutions and their representatives, the German Jews. From the very beginning of the migration wave, German Jewish welfare organizations assumed a degree of responsibility for immigrants but denied unconditional support to the recipients. In particular, German Jewish charities, which had set up an office on Eighth Street, were critical of the "occupation" of the Lower East Side by people whom they were intent on sending out of New York City. They also saw it as their charitable mission to rid the community of unruly elements, particularly the anarchists and socialists. Their policies, as later examples will show, indicated a clear bias against political activists.

From the beginning of the migratory wave, German Jewish philanthropists had promoted a policy of Jewish immigrant dispersal that conflicted with the community's wishes. The Baron de Hirsch Fund adopted this policy as early as the 1880s, but in 1900 it became intent on counteracting the community's cohesion and militancy. Similar mistrust of the immigrant workers existed among American labor activists. Craft-oriented labor unions of New York in the 1880s shared little in common with Jewish workers, whose social practices and strategies for communal actions were seen as deviant from the unions' notions of propriety and respectability.

DEMOGRAPHY AND ECONOMY

The Jewish East Side of the 1900s was an area of one and a half square miles, stretching from the East River to Third Avenue and the Bowery on the west and from 14th Street on the north to Monroe Street on the south. It had been formed over a period of twenty-five years by Jewish immigrants from Eastern Europe in a neighborhood previously inhabited by the German and Irish middle class and, in some parts, by the Irish poor. By the 1900s, this district was the most populous area in the city, if not the world. The Jewish population of the Lower East Side started to grow in the 1880s, when New York boasted only a few thousand Jews, to approximately 168,750 in the early 1890s; it climbed to 290,000 in 1900 and reached a peak of 542,061 in 1910.[6] According to a report of the University Settlement Society, the Lower East Side's overcrowding surpassed that of the most congested sections of Bombay.[7] The congestion, however, did not deter newcomers, who sought refuge among their compatriots and made it their first stopping place. Although by the 1890s and 1900s new Jewish settlements in Williamsburg and Brownsville as well as in Harlem attracted newcomers, the Lower East Side remained their main entry point to American life.[8]

Gross overcrowding resulted from widespread penury. Jewish families, which averaged six persons, also took in lodgers to help with the rent. According to George Price, who served as health inspector on the Lower East Side in the 1880s, one unit consisting of three rooms could house a family of husband, wife, their six children, and thirteen lodgers.[9] One newly arrived immigrant wrote that his new home of two rooms was shared by six boarders and a family of eight. The apartment also served as a shop to one boarder, a shoemaker, and to the landlord's two daughters, who did sewing at home. The father of the family, a *melamed* (teacher) by profession, used the apartment as a classroom, and it was occasionally converted into a synagogue. Though crowded "like herrings in a barrel," each one had enough space, "this being one of the miracles which happen to our brethren, the children of Israel, in this country."[10]

Responsibility for the family economy was shared by members of the family. Although according to one source, "it was by no means typical of immigrant life that wives should continue to be or become the breadwinner," Jewish women supplemented household income by doing piecework and finishing work.[11] Force of circumstance led married women to work, particularly if they had migrated alone. Pearl Halperin, who came to the United States in 1908 with a child of eighteen months, learned blousemaking and worked for $5 a week until her husband joined her from Archangelsk. She spent $6 monthly for rent and $3 for childcare services by her landlady.[12] On the whole, however, taking in boarders was probably the biggest single occupation for married women, more respectable than homework and consistent with domestic responsibilities. It had been practiced in the old world, where young female and male apprentices lived and ate with master-artisans, but grew immeasurably in the United States, where a constant stream of immigrants provided a source of income. Earnings from renting living space and services, which were usually women's responsibility, brought in additional income ranging from $3.12 to $8 a month in the 1880s and 1890s.[13] Running a store or family business was also more respectable for married women than working outside the home as wage workers. The growing metropolis offered possibilities for women. As a cursory glance at contemporary pictures of Hester Street and other market streets of the Lower East Side suggests, women pushcart peddlers were a common sight.[14] As with women in the shtetl, who were often actively engaged in commercial activities, especially those who were widowed or had husbands engaged in scholarship, immigrant women engaged in selling a variety of goods at market stalls.

The teeming humanity enclosed within one and a half square miles shared some distinctive demographic characteristics. Women were present in large numbers; according to one estimate, from 1886 to 1898, women over age sixteen constituted 41.6 percent of the population, and 44.03 percent of the Jewish immigrants from 1899 to 1914. Only the Irish immigration had a higher proportion of women (51.29 percent from 1899 to 1914).[15] A second characteristic of the East European immigrants was the number of children below fourteen, which averaged 24.9 percent of all Jewish immigrants between the years 1899 and 1910, 26.5 percent in 1902, and 28.4 percent in 1906. Among other immigrants, such as the Poles, Russians, Hungarians, and Rumanians, children averaged only 12.3 percent of the general population. Moreover, according to a study conducted in 1903, Jewish families in New York had the highest birth rate of any ethnic group. While Catholic families averaged 2.03 children and Protestant families 1.85, Jewish families headed the list with 2.54 children.[16] The number of elderly people was insignificant among Jewish immigrants during the years 1899 to 1914, with only 5.8 percent of immigrant Jews over the age of forty-five. In contrast, the same age group among non-Jews represented 17.8 percent of immigrants.[17]

Jewish families presented a classic example of how large households and high birthrates helped make financial survival possible. Families had to survive seasonal unemployment as well as provide for relatives left behind in Europe. It was calculated that in 1890, a family of six required a monthly income of $40.[18] Children contributed their share to the family economy, earning as little as $3 per week in buttonsewing and basting, for instance, in the sort of shop where Rose Cohen's father was a piece worker. Rose, who joined her father in America at the age of twelve, was initiated to the life of work in a coat shop to help earn the money needed to bring the rest of her family from Europe.[19]

The estimated number of children attending schools was surprisingly low. Jewish children stayed at school for the required four years between the ages of eight and twelve, and the mandatory six years after 1903, but usually they did not attend longer than required by law and began working soon after fulfilling the legal requirements. A 1908 survey confirms that Jewish parents recruited their children to work. Over half of the Jewish children in school that year were in grades 1 through 3. The numbers, however, declined considerably after third grade, and most children left school after the mandatory sixth grade.[20] Following the enactment of the Compulsory Education

Law in 1903, Jewish parents preferred to send their children to classes offered by the Educational Alliance, where a shorter school day made work possible.[21]

The entire household, with wives, children, and relatives, as well as lodgers, could form a production unit in clothing manufacture. Establishing such a venture was relatively easy; a small capital of $50, a few sewing machines that could be obtained on easy credit, and a kitchen or bedroom that could be used as a shop were the basic requirements. Although many wanted to be contractors, this existence was precarious; the work brought only minimal financial gains to many of those who tried to raise their standard of living in this way. Contractors had to work late into the night and did not earn much more than ordinary workers.[22] But the idea of independence spurred those who tried this route. "Since I was twelve I've been working for others. Now it's time to start on my own. That's why I came here," wrote Louis Borgenicht, who went into contracting and later into manufacturing. Samuel Cohen, describing his fifteen-hour workday, a total of eighty-two hours a week, explained why he became a contractor: "At least no boss to nose around about my work." Isidore Kopeloff, an anarchist, summed up the situation: "Everybody had the drive to become independent and they all tried hard. Everybody was tormented and suffered and wanted to succeed."[23]

The path to contracting and, possibly, manufacturing was difficult. Unpredictable demand and slack seasons often made the realization of the dream of upward mobility a two-way street, with many finding themselves slipping back into wage work. The contractor's own precarious status made him sympathetic to the workers' plight. Small contractors complained at being called exploiters: "We work harder than you. We earn sometimes less than you, in any case never more than you. We suffer from the hands of the manufacturers; what kind of exploiters are we?" Isidore Kopeloff confessed that "I didn't have an answer to their argument. . . . Because of my anarchistic principles, I couldn't admit that employer is right vis-a-vis the worker. But deep down I felt and clearly saw that not all those who are called 'bosses' are exploiters."[24] Kopeloff's accounts of his work in a shirtmaking shop illustrate the blurred lines of distinction between workers and small bosses, particularly when the two often exchanged places and developed a sense of camaraderie reinforced by common experience and collective memory. Noteworthy is his description of the singing of Russian songs in a shop, where the majority of workers were young, educated Russian Jews with only a few elderly workers:

> We were all inspired and joined in and sang: the boss, his wife, and their grown children all sang with gusto and with feeling. Even the old Jews hummed and tapped with their feet to the rhythm. . . . All those who were choking with sorrow sang their hearts out. Often the whole crowd sang a long time into the

night. And when we ended singing, we began talking and discussing. The discussion was then something completely new. We felt a special liveliness and a new strange tenderness. It was a true unity and togetherness. Not only all the workers—women workers as well as the old workers—it was a unity that included the boss, his family, and also me, an outsider.[25]

Shared memories and culture and the common immigrant fate imbued the relationship of workers and contractors with ambivalence. The contractor, unlike the large employer, was a person who lived in the community, was seen in the streets and synagogue, and was the person who hired the operators in the labor market, known as the *chazer* or "pig" market on Hester Street near Ludlow, pork being the only item not on sale.[26] Many within the labor movement considered small-scale contractors as much a part of labor as workers. Israel Barsky, employed as a tailor in men's clothing and one of the first union leaders to emerge in the 1880s, called for all those involved in the garmentmaking industry to create one general union consisting of all grades, from the lowliest baster to the highest-paid cutter, as well as the contractor, whom he also regarded as being exploited. Only real bosses, those who "do not put their hand in cold water and like to put out the fire with other people's hands," had no place in the union, according to Barsky. Affinity of interest and a common enemy—the manufacturers—sometimes brought together contractors and workers.[27] The socialist leadership in the larger unions, however, saw these attempts as a diversion from union ideals. During a shirtmakers' strike, for example, when contractors wished to join workers to fight their "common enemy," the union warned against the "wolflike nature" of contractors who, at the first opportunity, allegedly, would always try to exploit their workers, depress their wages, and increase their hours.[28]

Despite the ambiguous relationship between workers and small contractors, new waged-work hierarchies upset old-world ties. As the reefermakers' strike of 1905 suggests, conflict between employer-contractors and workers occurred despite landslayt connections between them. During that strike, workers rebelled against the Weinstein Brothers, important reefer (cheap coat made entirely by machine) manufacturers who preferred to employ their landslayt, especially newcomers, in a branch of work that required only minimum skills. The Weinstein Brothers' attempts to resolve the dispute by organizing parties and promising benefits were rejected by their workers, who persisted in their demands for an end to a sixteen-hour workday and other abuses.[29]

SELF-HELP AND SOCIAL ORGANIZATION

In addition to economic hardship, immigrants on the Lower East Side faced the hostility of American public opinion, organized labor, and the German

Jews. Communal and religious resources such as synagogues, landsman-shaftn, and other mutual-aid societies became, therefore, essential tools for community welfare. Although the associations were not politicoeconomic organizations like labor unions and concentrated instead on mutual help and respectability, they responded to new social and economic needs and ultimately adopted new goals.

To outsiders, all inhabitants of the Lower East Side appeared as "Russian Hebrews." In reality, however, the Jewish community was characterized by cultural and ethnic differences and a proliferation of organizations and institutions. Hungarian, Russian, Rumanian, and Galician Jews clustered in distinct ethnic neighborhoods. Hungarian Jews, for example, settled in the area north of Houston Street; Russian Jews huddled in the southern parts of the Lower East Side, south of Grand Street to Monroe Street; and the Galicians occupied a smaller area between Houston and Grand Streets. Ethnic divisions also encroached upon the workplace. Jews from Hungary and western Poland were employed in making better garments, while work on rougher goods was done by Polish and Lithuanian Jews.[30] Young intellectuals from Russia found employment in shirtmaking, which did not demand much physical strength, while the stronger Rumanians worked as pressers and pantsmakers.[31]

Contemporary critics claimed that religious observance had declined. To the regret of traditionalists, America symbolized a spiritual wilderness where old and cherished values were abandoned, scholarly and religious codes dissolved, and spiritual values replaced by a growing materialism. Even traditional spiritual leaders forsook spiritual matters: "They concern themselves with affairs of the stomach. . . . They sink up to their necks in a torrent of present-day banalities and material possessions, just like all the rest of their Jewish brethren in this city and land."[32] Sabbath observance was the first to go, due to economic necessity. The majority of immigrants worked on that sacred day, since most businesses were open, which was anathema to the newly arrived.[33] A carpenter who settled in Pittsburgh was bewildered by the liberated ways of his brethren in America:

> My first Sabbath in America made a most painful impression on me. My brother-in-law arrived home from work Friday. . . . He made *Kiddush* (a ritual of wine blessings on Sabbath eve), my sister-in-law prepared a good, Sabbath, home-like meal. . . . Everything was fine and pleasurable that evening. On the morrow, on the morning of Sabbath, seeing my brother-in-law dress in his overalls, take his saw and leave for work, the entire Sabbath eve of America turned sour for me.[34]

Another newcomer to New York in 1888 conveyed a similar experience. Not wanting to transact business on the Sabbath, he was warned by his sister-in-law, "If you feel that way about it, you'd better take the first steamer back. We do things differently in America." When the same immigrant asked why some synagogues were well-attended, his sister-in-law retorted that the worshipers were rich Jews and that "landlords like them can afford to waste time."[35]

Despite everyday pressures, most immigrants retained much of their cultural practice, which traditionally had been linked to life in East European communities. Synagogues and communal organizations proliferated on the Lower East Side. However, the former served not only as places of worship but also as meeting places for landsmanshaftn and unions and even as places of work. Only sixty to seventy out of the hundreds of Lower East Side congregations were located in buildings designated as places of worship; others were housed on the premises of landsmanshaftn meeting places or workshops. Benjamin Rabinowitz, who came in 1899 at age sixteen, described what happened in his place of work: "On Friday we would move the machines aside and cover them, and the *shames* (caretaker of a synagogue) . . . would set up the benches and sweep the shop, and we used to come and pray."[36] Immigrants from the same localities often established their own congregations, which provided a forum for meeting acquaintances, making contacts, and finding jobs or lodgings, among other functions.[37] Synagogues on the Lower East Side also served as nuclei for various civic institutions that traditionally were linked to places of worship, such as burial societies, charities, study groups, and schools. In some synagogues, affiliation was based on skill and occupation; often the worshipers not only came from the same locality in Europe but also were employed in the same trade and were members of the same union. Bernard Weinstein, a secretary of United Hebrew Trades, described a membership meeting in a synagogue on Norfolk Street of bearded, elderly pressers wearing skull caps, all of whom belonged to the Children's Jacket Makers' Union and to the same synagogue.[38]

The hallmark of associational life of the Jewish community, catering to a variety of needs and traditions, was the new type of mutual benefit societies—the landsmanshaftn. Typically, landsmanshaftn were based on the old-world geographic region or locality of their members. Membership in societies bearing the same town's name might differ according to social, religious, and age differences, as well as ideological factors. Whether secular or linked to synagogues, landsmanshaftn provided practical help in the areas of employment, health, burial, and emergency financial needs. They were an invaluable resource for newcomers, particularly workers. According to the available data, the number of immigrant members in landsmanshaftn peaked between the years 1903 and 1909, the high point of immigration, but there is no reliable evidence about the levels of workers' membership during these years. Much later on, in 1938, 75 percent of members were working class, while 15 percent were small businessmen and 10 percent were professionals.[39]

The landsmanshaftn were more successful than unions in providing for immigrant workers' needs, demonstrating the usefulness of practical organizations based on common roots and familiar institutions. These civil associations were founded on participatory, democratic principles that contributed to ethnic and working-class solidarity through the provision of mutual aid.[40] They became key players in Jewish communal politics and in Jewish labor unions and were instrumental in consolidating Jewish working-class welfare. In the landsmanshaftn, unlike the German Jewish charities, reciprocity and solidarity were core values. They were mutual-benefit societies, which served as arenas of popular participation that articulated and promoted a developing political culture.

The failure of contemporary trade unions in the clothing industry to provide for workers' needs during periods of hardship may explain the swelling ranks of lodges and benefit societies.[41] Some historians have argued that workers' preference for mutual-benefit associations based on hometown links retarded successful unionization. Moses Rischin wrote, "While Jewish workmen paid respectable dues to landsmanshaftn and benevolent societies, unions melted away from lack of funds."[42] This view is based on an understanding of labor organizations as exclusively workplace-oriented, with secondary importance being ascribed to less direct processes of working-class formations within the wider sphere of civic participation. Union organizations that brought improvements to some American workers in the nineteenth century offered a model that was largely inapplicable to the garment industry. By contrast, the landsmanshaftn offered opportunities for multilayered alliances independent of day-to-day employment issues but concerned with material welfare. They were effective in harnessing the working class in a broad spectrum of participatory social politics without detracting from working people's impulses to organize around work issues, as the widespread and frequent industrial unrest showed. Israel Barsky considered unions divisive because they were organized along occupational lines. In contrast to this narrow perspective, he envisaged a comprehensive industrial union, where workers from all branches of production would be welcome. Every member would feel that "he belongs to one large family and will never go under. In the times of greatest misfortunes, he will know that there is someone he could lean on."[43] His vision of a union was that of an enhanced mutual-aid society, quite similar to a landsmanshaft, or to the later Workmen's Circle, which would work cooperatively and pay benefits to those who were sick or out of work.[44]

The role of landsmanshaftn in providing material benefits and a modicum of economic security reinforced their "mostly male character," observes historian Daniel Soyer.[45] Some of the more progressive and radical societies included both males and females as full-fledged members. Some associations consisted entirely of women. Although these societies offered benefits identical to those in men's societies, many had male presidents. Thus, although landsmanshaftn were inclusive organizations with equal membership privileges, including the vote, open discussions, and access to leadership positions and to honorific disinctions, they remained male preserves.[46] A particularly striking change from the old country was the new freedom and unlimited right to express one's opinion. Customary deference, especially in religious matters, was replaced by a more democratic impulse. Spiritual leadership in landsmanshaft congregations was no longer the exclusive privilege of a learned elite. Synagogues broadened their leadership to include a new class of spiritual leaders and preachers from their own ranks. Even Moses Weinberger, a conservative critic of the new community, considered the new orators, often simple and "meek" tailors and shoemakers who spent most of their days in the shop or the factory, qualified to address the congregation. Although they had no formal education, their experience and oppression at the machine and the suffering they had undergone qualified "tailors, shoemakers, and tanners" to deliver meaningful commentaries on the Scriptures.[47]

The new social institutions reflected contemporary community concerns and conflicts. In his authoritative study of landsmanshaftn, Daniel Soyer demonstrates that some developed a distinct working-class character and ethic. This was the case not only when a landsmanshaft was closely linked to strikers through membership ties, but also when direct landslayt ties to specific labor causes did not exist. For example, one such organization, the Progressive Slutzker Young Men's Benevolent Association, denied membership to strikebreakers.[48] Other landsmanshaftn often granted valuable assistance to strikers, as in the case of reefer workers in 1905 and 1907, fur workers in 1907, and the mass strikes of 1909 and 1910. Occasionally, they even were known to send financial help to non-Jewish strikers. In some cases, bitter struggles over strikes tore apart the membership, as in the case of the Melnitzer Benevolent Society, which decided in 1907, under the influence of employer members, to expel striking fur workers for nonpayment of dues.[49] Splits reminiscent of old-world ideological disputes sometimes occurred. Abraham Cahan, the editor of the *Forward,* wrote about two apparently identical mutual-aid societies set up under the auspices of one landsmanshaft. A split had taken place when one landsmanshaft required all members to declare their belief in God. This alienated workers, as well as "free thinkers," who founded an alternative mutual-aid society. Ideological rifts in the community, reflected also among landsmanshaftn members, led to the founding of the Workmen's Circle (Arbeiter Ring) in 1892, a national secular federation of workers' benefit societies, which ultimately came to represent working people's needs. As the umbrella federation of numerous landsmanshaftn and other immigrant organizations, it appealed to the "worker and citizen" in its declaration of principles. Red banners, socialist hymns in Yiddish, and festivals celebrating world socialist events, such as May Day and the Paris Commune, were substituted for traditional landsmanshaftn symbols.[50]

GERMAN JEWS AND THE IMMIGRANT COMMUNITY: GEOGRAPHY, ECONOMY, AND IDEOLOGY

The battle lines between German and East European Jews were drawn around the economic, cultural, and highly politicized question of what constituted being "American." The powerful German Jewish community's definition was unacceptable to the immigrants, because it infringed upon their autonomy, customs, freedom of movement, choice of trade, and even education. Despite being poor and rootless in America, immigrants had their own concept of what constituted being American. It was, for them, a land of liberty, citizens' rights, and evolving goals, articulated through their own cultural vocabulary. It was a vision that inspired early immigrants, such as those in Elizavetgrad in 1881 who sent a petition to the Alliance members in Paris, asking them to compel Jews to immigrate to America, which they described as "most civilized and offers most guarantees of individual freedom, freedom of conscience and security for all property and endows everyone of her inhabitants with both civil and political rights."[51] The Lower East Side's population epitomized a group distinct from other American Jews. It stood for everything that was alien and even non-American, a community ripe for transformation, whose degradation was graphically described by Progressive writers such as Jacob Riis.[52] Separated by geography and culture, the Jewish East Side offered an alternative vision to the dominant culture through its unique communal institutions and activities. It was an ethnic ghetto that attracted the concern and disapproval of the German Jews as well as the American public and its reformers, while the Jewish labor movement was criticized by its American counterpart.

From the beginning of the great wave of immigration, German Jews had embarked on well-publicized efforts to assist their less fortunate brethren. They aimed to relieve the immigrants' misfortunes through the tried and tested methods of other social reformers, by transmitting to them their own values: the spirit of individualism, industry, and competitiveness. Their philanthropic activities were motivated by the impulse to protect the immigrants from the hostility of Americans. Using charity as a means of Americanizing its recipients, however, was no less motivated by a need to regulate and dominate a distinctive workers' class and culture. Jewish immigrants from Eastern Europe were not welcomed by most of the press or the public. Unlike German Jews, who adapted readily to this country, their Russian brethren seemed to be a mixed blessing. A contemporary Jewish immigrant, George Price, an inspector of the New York City Health Department, agreed: "Immigration is a good nourishment for this land, but too much of it, particularly if it is of an inferior quality, as the recent immigration is, becomes unassimilable and is apt to upset the American stomach and is likely to become very dangerous."[53] Waves of immigrants who "looked exactly like the Polish riff-raff" confirmed the worst fears of German Jews.[54] They looked servile and "despondent," and their low status was attributed to their life in Russia, which had not prepared them to understand the privileges and obligations "of a resident of America or Western Europe."[55] They were poor, allegedly incapable of earning a living because of their unproductive occupations, devoid of skills, and not used to the new freedoms bestowed by the "great Republic." In short, they presented a threat to American Jewish life. Consequently, German Jews initiated a cultural and economic campaign to transform this East European community into an acceptable and respectable minority.

Among their policies was "normalization" through dispersal. The density of tenement life and work received widespread publicity in the 1890s in the writings of reformers concerned with hygiene, sanitation, and child labor. German Jews also focused on the social dangers stemming from such a high concentration of the poor in a closely knit community, which fostered rebellion, strikes, and other forms of resistance to values cherished by German Jews. According to them, the ghetto was a disgrace, which reflected negatively on all Jews. It was a barrier to becoming an American, a place where an immigrant continued "his unsavory habits, his jargon, his manners, his association, his modes of thought."[56] They viewed the Lower East Side as providing cohesion "so often harming the interest of the needle industry, carried on among the dense Jewish population of our city."[57] Resettlement of Jews in uncongested rural areas, where settlers would take up agriculture, was one of the German Jewish philanthropical projects. They hoped that dispersion would not only bring immigrants in touch with more "American" surroundings but also moderate anti-immigrant sentiments, alleviate labor market competition, and raise wage levels in the city. German Jews, including many business leaders from the clothing industry, had a particular interest in preventing unhealthy competition from immigrants who could undercut larger entrepreneurs. They hoped that immigrant dispersal would ensure a better regulated industry by eliminating their East European competitors, regarded as even more dangerous than the specter of native anti-Semitic agitation.[58]

Charitable projects were in part economically motivated but were also prompted by other considerations. The belief that charity would pauperize its recipients strongly inspired these programs.[59] Traditional charity, based on giving "without a system, without accounts, and without investigations," was considered harmful and wasteful. German Jews initiated a different kind of philanthropy, described as a system "conducted like a business, a railroad, or a clearing house."[60] The givers believed that charity should be given only if it had the educational goal of instilling American values and controlling cultural and economic life. True to American aspirations, Jewish charitable institutions followed the principle of "aiding those who aid themselves." They opposed donations that "fostered a habit of relying upon individuals and congregational institutions, and in proportion weakened the instincts of manliness, self-reliance, and honor."[61] Instead of putting resources into supporting people on the dole, German Jews decided to teach them that "to earn a living in this country means nothing more nor nothing less than hard, very hard work."[62] One example was the Baron de Hirsch Fund, which was run and managed by a roster of prominent German Jews to help immigrants who had been in the United States for more than six months and less than two years. "Alms-giving" and charitable relief were excluded by the de Hirsch Fund, as well as by other philanthropic institutions, so as not to "cripple the tendency to self-aid."[63]

In this spirit, the Fund's grants were given only to those who, during a brief residence, have "already demonstrated their capacity for existence and progress in this country." Thus, the philanthropists refused to support an agricultural colony in Meridian, South Dakota, which was founded by the idealistic Am Olam group. This experiment was considered "undeserving" because its members were "persons who have immigrated to the United States as long as seven or eight years, and who have failed as agriculturalists." Similarly, because of the philanthropists' belief in business principles, money for settlers in Woodbine, an agricultural colony in New Jersey, was advanced as loans, rather than as grants.[64] One charitable organization summarized this policy as follows:

> The word *charity* could be stricken from the language, for it covers a multitude of sins. . . . It is a matter of common belief, for instance, that it is a deed of charity to give anything to any person who, from necessity or a vicious instinct, will accept it, and this notion leads to the encouragement of mendicancy and pauperism.[65]

The same report recommended substituting the principle of "social improvement" for that of "charity."[66] Education became central to this philosophy as "the new charity" deserving investment.[67] The goal of turning immigrants into productive citizens was intertwined with the idea of "uplift" and Americanization. The charities planned to educate and train immigrant children, to raise them "above their surroundings . . . giving them a taste for manual work, promoting self-reliance and industry . . . towards developing their moral nature and also fitting them for technical and mechanical fields of work."[68]

The success of Americanization through education was hindered by the popularity of the cheder. Viewed as a dangerous rival to the American school, it was described as "filthy, ill-regulated and hurtful physically, morally and mentally."[69] Its greatest danger was its closeness to home, family and traditional values. Conducted "in the sleeping, eating and washing room of the teacher" and using traditional teaching methods in the "hateful lingo" and "ireful gesticulation," this traditional religious education reinforced the very values that Americanized Jews intended to eradicate.[70] German Jewish philanthropists envisioned an alternative school system that would be managed along professional lines and would remove children from parental and ethnic influences. Public schools would introduce young immigrants to new, American ideas:

> From the moment our cheder pupil has marched to the sounds of the piano from the assembly room to his classroom, he cannot help comparing the American methods of teaching with the Polish. The spacious schoolroom, with its high windows . . . the dignified bearing of his lady teacher, her decorum, her un-*rebbe*like, gentle manners, everything must vividly strike the child's imagination. In the course of a few weeks he will begin to understand and to speak English. He will speak it in his school, at play, he will even use it, much against the wish of his parents, when addressing them.[71]

The German Jews hoped that, ultimately, children would reject not only the use of Yiddish but also their parents' lifestyle and culture. German Jews viewed alienation of the children from their surroundings as a desirable goal and an effective means for successful Americanization. The superintendent of one school for immigrant children boasted, for example, that "through my daily inspection in the classroom I have cured many a mother from the dread of water, discharging her dirty offspring from school, and re-admitting it only on her promise that she would keep it clean."[72]

The charities thus embarked on schemes to finance English classes for children and adults alike, with special teaching for children that included some Biblical and religious instruction, to counteract the cheder's attraction.[73] No less than 60 percent of the well-endowed Baron de Hirsch Fund was to be invested in educational institutions. Special English classes were also offered to *melamdim* (religious teachers). Their curriculum included English, American history, political history, history of American institutions, DeTocqueville's *Democracy in America,* and the Book of Psalms in English translation.[74] According to the educational board, the schools were well attended except on Fridays, when children were kept home by their parents to help prepare the Sabbath. To rid them of "this evil habit," some children

Figure 4.1 Talmud School in a Hester Street tenement, ca. 1890. The Jacob A. Riis Collection, Museum of the City of New York.

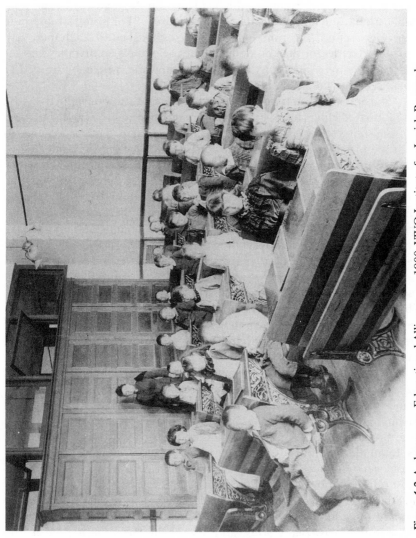

Figure 4.2 A classroom, Educational Alliance, ca. 1900. YIVO Institute for Jewish Research.

were expelled on the following Monday.[75] The success of the free English classes and the sight of the Americanized pupils were a source of satisfaction to the German Jews: "The little immigrants with their pile of books on their way to the Public School thoroughly Americanized even to the fashion of wearing the cap on the back of the head, and on the high road to an honorable, useful, and let us hope prosperous future."[76] For young adults, trade classes were set up. Vocational schools were established to teach men "easily acquired trades, or the knowledge of the use of tools, so that they may become 'handy men' in shops." Women, meanwhile, would be trained as "house servants, cooks, children's nurses."[77]

The best known among German-sponsored educational efforts was the Educational Alliance, founded in 1893, the site of numerous activities ranging from sports to English and civics.[78] The manifest goal of the Alliance, to teach the blessings of American citizenship as conceived by "the Guggenheimers, the Strausses, the Schiffs" who "grew rich and fat upon the labor of immigrants," did not escape the ire of the pro-labor press. For example, a forerunner of the Alliance, the Hebrew Institute, though founded for the purpose of educating the young, was accused by the *Forward* of waging a war against socialism and being used as "a place for befogging and embittering the Jewish masses." The leaders of the educational efforts were identified in the socialist press as "well fed, rich managers" whose hatred of trade unions and the socialist movement was well known.[79] Israel Zangwill, the author of *The Melting Pot* and a champion of Russian Jews, questioned the Educational Alliance's aim of Americanizing the newcomers. Accusing the German philanthropists of trying to form a Jewish "four hundred" group of premier families, he suggested that "perhaps the Russian Jew is needed to civilize the American Jew."[80]

Education remained an arena where the struggle between two opposing cultures for the minds of immigrants and their children was waged. Suspicious of the uptown Jews' intention to Americanize the "downtowners," the immigrants and the Socialist leadership promoted their own version of education and Americanization, no less bent on transforming the newcomers. In an effort to introduce the Jewish masses to universalist concepts of social justice, revolutionary struggle, and solidarity, those sympathetic to socialist causes, led by Jacob Gordin, a leading dramatist of his day, founded the Educational League, where students took English, social studies, and literature from a socialist perspective. Above all, it was the Yiddish press, writers, orators, poets, playwrights, and, eventually, institutions such as the Workmen's Circle that championed the cause of the secular socialist education so widely accepted by the Jewish immigrant masses.[81]

Other aspects of charity welfare programs also provoked criticism among labor circles. Trade schools and trainee programs were said to exploit low-skilled immigrant workers. For example, products manufactured in workshops by trainee carpenters and metal workers were sold at below market price, and trade schools set up by the charities were considered "scab schools."[82] During the height of immigration, when the influx of new-comers strained all available resources, the Baron de Hirsch Fund's management admitted that local charities were compelled to teach the immigrants garmentmaking, a skill that could be acquired quickly by special arrangement with employers.[83] Consequently, "greenhorns" were sometimes sent to work in factories in New York and New Jersey at lower wage rates, where they remained contracted to an employer until they mastered simple skills.[84] It is no surprise that these practices drew indignation from Benjamin Feigenbaum, a well-known contributor to the early Socialist press, who referred to the charitable givers in a lengthy article entitled "The Slave Dealers of Eighth Street," published in 1892 in the *Arbeiter Zeitung*.[85]

Clearly, the largesse of the givers was colored by political considerations. Jewish philanthropists openly exercised political judgment in their distribution policies, refusing assistance to a vast category of the "nondeserving." Applicants for assistance were scrutinized; "socialists" who "do not go to the synagogue" were denied assistance, as were those with links to strikers and unions. "If they strike on account of their union, let them suffer for it . . . let them starve," was reportedly said by a United Hebrew Charities official during an 1890 cloakmakers' strike.[86] The residents of the Lower East Side resented and resisted these criteria. The Jewish labor press attacked the "pseudo philanthropists" who "exploit their brethren mercilessly" by demanding obedience to the new ethic of free competition and individualism.[87] The anti-union and pro-business attitude of Eighth Street charities provoked frequent attacks in the Jewish labor press. The German Jews' disdain and contempt toward the people they were supposed to help was resented: "They seem to imagine uptown that all those downtown Jews are a herd of Hottentots who must be civilized in the mould of the uptown, just as Europe wants to civilize the Chinese," commented the *Forward*. The same report accused the "cream of the uptown Jewish capitalist society" with its "bediamonded hands" and "alabaster fingers" of viewing the downtown Jews as "poor, corrupt, dirty and sinful."[88] Rose Cohen described how her unemployed father "started for Eighth Street. He returned in the evening empty-handed and sick with humiliation." No wonder that German Jewish charity giving met with the response, "Better the whip of *fonye* (the czar) than the charity of Eighth Street."[89]

THE ORIGINS OF JEWISH LABOR ORGANIZATIONS

The cultural and economic life of the Lower East Side separated the Jewish community from its New York neighbors and made it an object of local hostility. Many Irish residents, for example, resented the encroachment of Jewish settlement and openly attacked those who dared cross the geographic boundaries between the two areas. Areas bordering on the East River and Catherine Street and nearby sections were danger zones for Jewish peddlers because of the Irish "loafers" who "sat in the sun or brawled on the docks."[90] Pulling of whiskers was a form of harassment familiar to many Jewish peddlers. Irish policemen, never tolerant of Jews, demonstrated their bias openly during the famed Rabbi Jacob Joseph funeral riot of 1902, when they did nothing to protect the mourners from attacks by Irish workers at the R. Hoe and Company factory. On the contrary, a commission of inquiry showed that there was anti-Jewish sentiment among the police and the employees of R. Hoe and Company. "I am as much afraid of the police as any other citizen in this neighborhood," testified one resident of Grand Street, while another witness quoted a manager employed by the company as having declared "I don't care for you sheenies a particle."[91] Adolf Held, an activist in the Socialist movement and a trade unionist, remembered that Corlear's Hook Park was particularly dangerous for Jewish children and that one could only visit the Pitt Street and Hester Street Parks in large groups.[92]

Geographic separation was matched by scanty contacts between Jewish workers and American labor, especially during the first years of Jewish settlement. The practice of using newly arrived immigrants as strikebreakers exploited the prevailing ethnic insulation, as in the case of New York Jewish immigrants brought in as scabs in the freighthandlers' strike of 1882. The Jewish ghetto's insular character was evident, for example, during the events of 1886 in Chicago. Abraham Bisno, an immigrant tailor who was later to become a factory inspector in Chicago and later still a real estate agent, noted that striking cloakmakers were completely unaware of the dramatic events at the McCormick Harvester Works in the adjoining neighborhood, nor did they know about the fateful Haymarket events which had taken place a day earlier. The marching strikers eventually learned of the events after being chased and ferociously beaten by the Chicago police.[93]

In general, ideological, social, and cultural differences separated the immigrants from the Knights of Labor, the dominant labor organization of the 1880s. The Knights, initially a secret society of workers that achieved its momentous rise as a national labor organization in the 1880s, was founded on the principle of inclusivity. Its motto, "An injury to one is the concern of all," launched the Knights as a broad-based organization that unionized workers "beneath and around existing craft unions."[94] Its wide appeal coincided with the growing number of workers who were "factory operatives," whose previous status as skilled workers was rendered meaningless by structural changes brought in by mass industrial production. Alliances between the surviving artisanal class and the new class of semiskilled workers, based on organizational principles across gender, skill, race, and occupation, became the hallmarks of the new organization.

Although the Knights of Labor upheld the principle of solidarity and cooperation between all producing classes, local assemblies followed varied organizational paths. Some were open to all employees in one industry, others organized workers in specific crafts or occupations, and still other locals or "mixed assemblies" were open to all producing classes. Thus, while District Assembly 49 of New York fought for the inclusion of unskilled, mainly Bohemian, cigarmakers, not all locals considered the less skilled as desirable members.[95] Not surprisingly, new immigrants had few ties with the Knights. The growing wage differentials between the skilled and the less skilled, especially immigrants, discouraged truly broad-based organizational campaigns. Residential separation and systematic subdivision of the workforce along lines of ethnicity, race, and language, initiated by employers, further undermined the option of an inclusive labor organization in this period.[96]

Among Jewish workers, it was the cutters, the most skilled among clothing workers, who had some contacts with the Knights of Labor. One of its constituent organizations, the Cloak and Suit Makers' Union, became a local of the Knights of Labor with a membership that consisted largely of more westernized Jews from Austria, Galicia, and Germany, as well as American-born women.[97] Generally, attempts by the Knights of Labor to organize Russian Jews were frustrated by economic, cultural, and ideological differences. In Chicago, for example, Bisno and fellow cloakmakers did not become active supporters of the eight-hour movement adopted by skilled American labor in the 1880s. Jewish cloakmakers, who were mostly piece workers, were ready to work all hours; even a ten-hour workday would have seemed a desirable, though unattainable, goal.[98] Moreover, when it came to union organizing, the principle of communitywide organizing embraced by the Knights was anathema to Jewish labor leaders. "It was common talk amongst our people that storekeepers, bricklayers and blacksmiths don't know anything about clothes," observed Bisno, referring to a Knights of Labor committee made up of a diverse membership rather than workers in one industry, which was intended to negotiate with the cloakmakers' employers in 1886. Conversely, German and Irish cutters declared that they would not work with "Columbus tailors" and "funny Jews."[99]

The masonic customs of the Knights further discouraged links between the new Jewish immigrants and the Knights. Although the organization abandoned secrecy and became public in 1882, its practices of "ritual fraternalism" marked by high drama remained central.[100] For example, Abraham Rosenberg, who immigrated in 1883 and became an active union member and president of the ILGWU from 1908 to 1914, was suspicious of the initiation ritual and the secrecy practiced by the Knights of Labor. At the ceremony inaugurating the Dress and Cloak Makers' Union as an Assembly of Knights of Labor, the District Master-Workman and several other Irish members delivered speeches in English to an uncomprehending audience of Jewish greenhorns. The ritual that followed split the two groups even further. To the cloakmakers' amazement, one of the Irish Knights drew a large chalk circle on the floor, instructing those present to stand around it, while another deputy put a small sword on the table and hung a globe over the door. Wrote Rosenberg, "Many of us, on seeing this sword, feared that either we would be slaughtered or we would be turned over to military service. . . . Many of us believed that our end had come."[101] Few of those present understood the ceremony's symbolism, that of a pledge to avenge disloyalty to the working man.[102]

Christianity, deeply rooted in the Knights' culture, drew the two camps further apart. Christian beliefs imbued the organization's philosophy and its imagery. Christ's humble origins as a carpenter's son and the emphasis on Christian principles of true justice were familiar symbols to the organization's members. Similarly popular were notions of American patriotism and nationalism. While patriotic occasions were fully endorsed by the national leadership, May Day celebrations did not meet with Terence Powderly's approval. In a Chicago parade in 1887, the Knights carried only the American flag and not the red flag of socialism.[103]

Ideological differences compounded the cultural gap. The prevailing socialist ideology within the Jewish unions, which modeled themselves on the German-speaking socialist unions in New York, clashed with the Knights' ideology on the issue of inviting employers, mainly small manufacturers sympathetic to labor's cause, to join the unions.[104] Differences concerning strikes also set the two groups apart. Knights' locals and immigrant workers favored strikes, but Powderly opposed them. "Strike at the boss and hit yourself," he warned Maryland miners who staged a walkout in 1882.[105] Ideological conflicts became intense throughout the 1890s. The Jewish socialist leadership identified with the American Socialist Party and waged campaigns against both the Knights of Labor and against Daniel De Leon, who had gained ascendancy in District Assembly 49. Jewish unions that joined De Leon were ostracized by rival Socialist groups and later expelled.[106]

The possibilities of cooperation between Jewish unions and the Central Labor Union of New York faltered because of similar cultural and social reasons. The Central Labor Union, the city-wide labor organization of the 1880s and the 1890s, cooperated with the new United Hebrew Trades to organize immigrants and membership recruitment. CLU, for example, sided with the cloakmakers' strike of March 1886, which demanded the abolition of contracting.[107] Conversely, Abraham Cahan reported that several powerful delegates opposed the Jewish membership, arguing that Jews were incapable of full union participation because they came from countries where they were used to a low standard of living and low wages.[108] Communication with the CLU also failed because of cultural and language differences. Isidore Kopeloff, for example, described his experience in 1886 as a worker in a factory making cigarettes. When the workers struck, they could only receive help from English-speaking CLU representatives, whom Kopeloff and his fellow immigrants did not understand.[109] Moreover, according to Bernard Weinstein, the secretary of the United Hebrew Trades, the CLU was an ultra-conservative organization, with strong ties to the old working-class community and to Tammany Hall politics, which were both alien to the unskilled and socialist Jewish workers.[110]

Not surprisingly, Jewish workers wanted to form their own unions; as one immigrant in the building trades said, "They wanted their own people on whom they could rely, who will be able to protect them, and that was because they were greenhorns and strangers in the land."[111] The founding in 1888 of the United Hebrew Trades, an umbrella organization of Yiddish- and Russian-speaking socialist members of the United Labor Party, reflected this need. Its goal was to unify existing unions and "progressive labor societies" into one central body.[112] It resembled the Central Labor Union in constituting a coordinating organization instead of separate trade and labor unions. United Hebrew Trades proclaimed its commitment to "mutual protection against the oppression of capitalism" and to an active struggle to achieve "a truly human society, where each individual shall receive the full value of his labor." American labor leaders resented the establishment of separate "Hebrew" trade unions. Samuel Gompers warned that it "will have evil consequences." He favored affiliation through a skill or craft rather than a religious or ethnic identity. Gompers hoped that Jews would gain knowledge and experience in labor organizing through "mingling with the working men in those trades of other religions and nationalities."[113] But New York's labor organizations were willing to grant only limited recognition to the growing presence of Jewish labor. One example of cooperation was that of Yiddish speakers attending, along with their English and German counterparts, the citywide May 1st celebrations, the one and only day when diverse labor groups were united and marched together under one flag.[114]

Despite such occasional alliances, the differences between the two camps persisted. In a citywide Labor Day parade of 1894, a year of a severe depression, all trades "marched well, they were dignified and orderly, they were well dressed and self-respecting looking; they were true specimens of American labor," according to a contemporary report.[115] The Horseshoers' Union made a particularly fine appearance, commented the same report: "They are a sturdy lot of men . . . and yesterday they looked particularly well in uniform aprons, shirts and caps. Their only ornament was a red horseshoe painted on a leather apron."[116] Nothing could have offered a more striking contrast to the colorful parade, than the Jewish coatmakers on strike, as observed by one reporter. Although some of the strikers were "robust looking," others appeared "famine stricken."[117] The strikers were buttonholemakers, fellers, operators, and finishers, new slaves to the system of mass production. They clearly were not in a position to share the proud tradition of the New York mechanics in the official parade. The contrasting appearance of the two groups symbolized their different goals, strategies, and rhetoric and emphasized the Jews' distinctiveness and insularity, as well as the altogether different system of production they were involved in. The prevailing view in socialist circles reaffirmed this distinctiveness. Although opposed to Jewish parochialism and a strong advocate of socialist internationalism, the *Zukunft,* an influential literary and political journal expressed the following sentiment:

> We are not patriots of a separate "Jewish Labor Movement." We want Jews to be members of American unions. Yet we cannot ignore the fact that, under present circumstances, Yiddish-speaking labor unions are a necessity, that without them, the Jewish workers will not begin to enter the American organizations.[118]

The remoteness of contemporary labor from Jewish workers, and the absence of permanent organizational contacts between American labor and immigrant labor, characterized the 1880s and the 1890s. Throughout these critical years, marked by ever-growing numbers of new immigrants from eastern and southern Europe, the newcomers and American labor grew farther apart. In the years following the decline of the Knights of Labor in 1887, craft unionism became the dominant force in the American labor movement. Seeking strength through business unionism, disciplined membership, and secure strike funds, craft unions found little in common with the unskilled newcomers. Growing anti-immigrant sentiment in the ranks of American labor as well as among the general public further undermined the possibility of solidarity and unity of American labor.

Its continually changing ethnic composition has been singled out as the most characteristic aspect in the formation of the American working class.[119] New groups of immigrants experienced the transition to industrial society in new and unique ways, and continuous adaptation shaped the behavior of diverse working-class populations. The disynchronization of the process is mirrored in the case of the Jewish immigrants who entered American society at the cusp of the Knights' rise in the 1880s. The political culture of the Jewish newcomers and the character of the clothing industry encouraged labor strategies that diverged from those embraced by the Knights. The characteristically anarchic strike patterns among the newcomers distanced them considerably from the business unionism of the

AFL. Little effort was made to incorporate nonskilled workers, whether Jewish or not, into the labor movement.[120] Not surprisingly, even after their organizational successes, the ILGWU and ACWA remained marginal to the mainstream of American labor. As Robert Asher argues so persuasively, the Jewish unions and their Socialist leaders were viewed as too militant and therefore were denied access to the power structure of the AFL. Only in the 1930s, when the AFL began to support government intervention and government-sponsored social insurance programs, was the ILGWU admitted into the AFL's power structure.[121]

The clothing industry's unique character reinforced the marginalization and insularity of the Jewish community and Jewish labor. This isolation contributed to the formation of the newcomers' cultural and social identity. Ethnicity, culture, and religion helped create a unique bond of mutuality between Jewish immigrant workers and their community. The Lower East Side thus became the arena where labor unrest merged with other community actions without union organization to reinforce its goals. Jewish workers freely evoked commonly held values and experience while developing a new language of struggle. The political culture kept labor concerns alive, without formal structures.

CHAPTER FIVE

Themes of Collective Action

So one fine day, or was it a miserable day, we got a notice in our pay envelope saying "From today on, the price of the button hole will be three cents instead of 3½ cents." My ire was aroused. I said to the girls, "are we going to take it?" At the time I knew nothing of unionism but it was that rebellion of the injustice towards the workers that was awakened in me. We all went into the wash-room and we decided that we won't take the cut. I didn't know whether I was the spokesman, but I was pointed out as such.
—Rebecca August, an immigrant (1905)

Collective actions, caused by labor grievances, erupted regularly, and sometimes violently, on the Jewish Lower East Side. Strikes were about economic issues but at the same time provided an arena for expressing demands that surpassed a narrow, material focus. They mobilized not only workers but other community members who were not in the garment trade. Numerous strike actions were initiated to redress specific grievances in an endemically unregulated industry, in scattered workplaces and "kitchen and bedroom shops." The garment trade was in a constant flux of slump and boom according to season and in a spiral of ever-decreasing earnings. The hiring of scabs was normal practice because the work was unskilled, and even successful strikes had, at best, a temporary ability to protect jobs. The Jewish working-class community took up broader employment issues in addition to wages and conditions, issues such as job protection and the generalized pauperization of their class. Verbal or physical abuse and hiring and firing procedures were among the issues that impelled popular protest. Workers

Rebecca August, YIVO, RG 102, no. 266, p.1. Rebecca August was born in 1883; at the age of seven, she and the family joined her father in London. In 1904, she joined her father in Chicago while the rest of the family stayed in London. In Chicago, she and her father worked in the clothing industry, hoping to save money to bring the rest of the family to the United States.

wanted greater pay uniformity, improvements in employment practices modeled on larger factories, and the abolition of the prevailing contracting system, which increased competitiveness among middlemen through wage cutting. In an industry that thrived on cutthroat competition and the subdivision of the production process, contemporaries were understandably critical about labor's over-ambitious goal of transforming industrial relations.

The major characteristic of Jewish working-class unrest was its tendency to mix "bread and butter" employment issues, such as wages and hours, or grievances specific to the garment trade, like closed shop, with demands for workers' political and economic rights. This type of militancy, which was not unique to Jewish labor, was condemned by the American press for its "anarchic" opposition to the market system and for addressing the larger issues of "political economy."[1]

THE CULTURE OF COLLECTIVE ACTION

Economic grievances and labor struggles were the sparks that periodically ignited social unrest on the Lower East Side. These communitywide collective actions offered broader opportunities for participation than communal associations such as landsmanshaftn, prayer meetings, and more formal organizations from which some community members, including women, might have been excluded. Economic conflict triggered a variety of responses from beyond the confines of the workplace. These public displays of participatory democracy, such as parades, street protests, and clashes with the police, could not be identified as either social or economic. As the *New York Tribune* commented, the Lower East Side strikes were actions not by a group of workers but of a race and a nation.[2]

Collective actions that aimed to redress social injustice were based on the shared political and cultural values of a community living in a familiar economic and cultural universe. Jewish immigrants interpreted economic injustices through a solidaristic, reciprocal perspective, based on a long, shared history of opposition to tyranny. However, immigrants absorbed both traditional European and American symbols. Their newly acquired expectations and their interpretation of American democracy, together with a new analysis of general exploitation, guided working immigrants in their actions.[3] Jewish employers and bosses also invoked American symbols of liberty and citizenship to legitimate their policies. The language of citizenship was a malleable instrument in political struggles between the opposing sides of labor and capital.

Strikes and other collective actions provided occasions for using these symbols to legitimize the demand for power and rights. Sidney Tarrow has interpreted collective action as representing both "old meaning" and "the stage in which new meanings are produced."[4] In initiating strikes, immigrants combined the "old meanings" of their familiar culture with a new freedom, as citizens entitled to economic as well as social and political rights. Contemporary political commentators commonly ignored the activities of non-union, cultural institutions that aimed to improve working-class conditions, considering labor organizations to be the only means of achieving social benefits. Far from being anarchic, as they had been described by contemporary observers, Jewish workers learned how to act collectively around common social, economic, and political concerns through a variety of collective activity, including street meetings, theater, the synagogue, and mutual-benefit societies. Historians of the Jewish working class have treated labor struggles in this period as a prelude to later organizational trade union activity. They have tended to portray the Jewish working class as "immature" and as an anarchic proletariat "engulfed in darkness" that only later learned how to organize effectively.[5] This view provides only a partial understanding to the springs of collective action, since it is based on the conviction that workers are concerned exclusively with union activity and economic relationships with employers.

Jewish militancy flourished in the world of community action, where religious tradition, residential closeness, and old-world ties brought individuals together. The garment workshops were part of the neighborhood and never far from places of worship or educational institutions. The community lived largely by one trade. Contemporaries marveled at the unique links that caused outbreaks of "strike fever" to spread like wildfire, at a moment's notice, throughout the Lower East Side and later to other Jewish centers, such as Bayonne, Astoria, Brooklyn, and Long Island.[6] Strong community ties transcended categories of trade and craft, particularly when divisions of skills were not yet clearly established among immigrants who had been newly introduced to garmentmaking work. Switching trades was common. Israel Barsky, a leader of United Brotherhood of Tailors, commented, for example, that "pantsmakers, cloakmakers, vestmakers, shirtmakers, all should belong to the same union. . . . We see very often that a cloakmaker becomes a vestmaker, a pantsmaker becomes a jacketmaker, a shirtmaker becomes a pantsmaker, and the other way around."[7] When one member was in trouble, the others pitched in to help out, despite the fact that trade union organization did not exist. Julius Gershin, who immigrated in 1904, described how the boss hired gangsters and scabs, but despite these difficulties; "If there were 20 people and 10 were committed, the rest would also get up to strike. . . . If there was a collection for a strike, everybody went as one. . . . The ones who didn't belong did not take the opposing side, they also went on strike."[8]

The cloakmakers' strike, during the severe depression of 1894, also involved peddlers, expressmen, and even liquor merchants. Strike solidarity transcended barriers of trade, craft, and class. The strikers were enthusiastically supported by the community with food and other services.[9] Violence, boycotts, and communal ostracism faced those who transgressed the working-class code, thereby transforming these eruptions into communal, rather than trade actions. In 1901, for instance, during a strike of coatmakers, two expressmen who sympathized with the strikers were indicted by the authorities and held on $500 bail for "malicious mischief." They had led a crowd of seventy-five striking coatmakers on a violently destructive foray against coatmaking boss Abraham Samuels, whose employees refused to join the strike.[10]

The communal-residential links that bonded the workers with their sympathizers drew further strength from their common cultural heritage. The historical memory and language of enslavement, whose meaning was almost exclusively derived from the Bible, continued to inspire socialists, anarchists, and trade unionists alike. The popularity of Jewish speakers, with their alien "haranguing" oratorical style, puzzled the American public. East Side meeting halls were filled to capacity during strike actions, with audiences apparently oblivious to the unbearable heat in packed halls but fascinated by the speakers.[11] Large crowds surged from one meeting place to another to attend every event, squeezing onto staircases or standing outside after being turned away for lack of space. The speeches resonated with familiar idiom and imagery drawn from historical and religious experience. The predominantly male strikers would huddle in a manner similar to the traditional Jewish way of praying or studying. Egyptian slavery became a symbol for the toiling garment workers, while the Pharoah's enslavement of the Jews was used as a metaphor for the attempts of autocratic employers to subdue the workers by imposing inhuman conditions.[12] "Fellow slaves" was Joseph Barondess's greeting to striking cloakmakers in 1894, while Meyer Schoenfeld, the coatmakers' leader, reminded his audience that their forefathers were also enslaved by Egyptian taskmasters and likewise had to throw off their yoke. John Swinton reminded them that they were living in the Land of Egypt, "in the house of bondage, WANTED, A MOSES."[13]

The collective historical memory legitimized rebellion and rendered the industrial experience highly intelligible. The story of deliverance from Egypt was a particularly evocative, recurring theme among Jewish workers. Jewish coatmakers struck regularly in the months of July and August, marking the significance of another milestone in Jewish history, that of the ninth day of the Hebrew month of Av. On that fast day, according to one coatmaker, when Jews mourned the destruction of the Second Temple and their enslavement by the Romans, the memory of that tragedy assumed a new urgency and became a call for rebellion:

> We shed tears on that day, we lament the loss of our independence and glory, we sigh over the fate of the women and children who were outraged and tor-

Figure 5.1 Protest against child labor in a May 1st labor parade, 1909. Library of Congress. Courtesy of Beth Hatefutsoth, Tel Aviv.

tured by the brutes of Rome. Well, it often happens that while we are at it we also weep over our own misery and utter groans for our wives and children, who are starved and tyrannized by those brutal bosses of ours.[14]

It was hardly surprising, therefore, that in 1899, on the symbolic 9th of Av, the day which marked the destruction of the Temple, 20,000 determined and united coatmakers began a strike.[15]

Synagogues represented a natural base for labor organizing in this cultural context of shared Biblical and historical heritage. At a meeting in their synagogue, a group of old pressers from Galicia decided to set up a union. Bernard Weinstein, secretary of the United Hebrew Trades, reported that the president of the local delivered a union speech evoking religious and historical symbols and traditions. To the question Who was the first walking delegate? he answered, "The first walking delegate of the Jewish people . . . was Moses, and the Elders of the Sanhedrin were the first executive board."[16]

A more secular interpretation was offered frequently by invoking black slavery and czarist oppression to describe industrial misery, in contrast to the immigrants' vision of America as a land of the free. Joseph Barondess urged the strikers from Jonasson's factory, one of the largest employers in the garment trade, to rebel against "slave wages," which were allegedly lower than the "wages" paid to black slaves. Some labor activists compared Jewish industrial workers to new American slaves who "took [the] place of the Negroes who with great effort had won their freedom from slavery." On another occasion, a speaker referred to Jewish laborers as "white slaves," whose conditions he described as "worse than soldiers in Russia."[17] The *Arbeiter Zeitung* attacked employers in Baltimore for demanding character references from previous bosses. "Are we in dark Asiatic Russia or in free America?" inquired the reporter.[18]

Jewish workers' meetings were open to all and were run with minimum formality and no set agenda. At the strike gathering of 1901, for example, "every now and then a speaker would get up and talk to the meeting in Yiddish," which was the older generation's language, while the younger ones spoke only in English. Meetings were also attended by nonworkers with an interest in community matters or close involvement with strikers, such as wives and children.[19] For example, in 1894 during the cloakmakers' dramatic strike, "a remarkable meeting" took place in a hall filled to capacity with cloakmakers and their wives. A suggestion to return to work was put to a vote. "Do you want your husband working under the guard of Pinkertons?" asked Barondess. The rhetorical question was rejected overwhelmingly. Scabs were denounced, and some who had returned to work were physically attacked.[20]

No less puzzling than the "remarkable meetings" and the oratory observed in the Jewish quarter by the contemporary public were some walkouts and strikes that appeared unspecific in their objectives and aimed at redressing a "multitude of grievances." Occasionally the socialist leadership and union committees succeeded in controlling strikes by insisting specific demands be made. Other strikes were criticized by union leaders as wasteful and meaningless, for they apparently did not have any concrete goals.[21] Strikes in general, especially those which appeared to be unplanned and without stated objectives, had a typical holiday air. Strikers organized dances and outings to Central Park, and these, along with the crowded meetings, were celebrations of successful, if short-lived, escapes from industrial discipline. This holiday atmosphere was criticized in labor circles. Union leaders condemned the so-called beer strikes, or unplanned walkouts from small workshops, which happened without prior warning to either union leadership or bosses. Employers became familiar with this pattern of stoppages, which they sometimes succeeded in defeating by bringing the strikers a keg of beer and getting them back to work a few hours later. Some contemporaries even reported that both bosses and workers were glad to have a day off.[22]

The cloakmakers' strike of 1894 also impressed observers with its festive spirit, which pervaded the East Side. A "crowd of men, many wearing greasy outing shirts, some of them carrying their coats on their arms, poured through the streets, moving from one hall to another to hear their speakers 'haranguing.'" Women also participated in these celebrations. When seamstresses went on strike in 1895, they dressed in holiday clothes and danced in Congress Hall to music provided by the union. A Sunday-like atmosphere also had marked the beginning of a strike of twenty-five hundred women shirtmakers a year earlier. The *World* reported that traditionally timid women dressed in white dresses and wearing yellow bonnets with green and red ribbons, gave a resounding "yes" when asked to vote for strike action. In 1901, five hundred women pledged to stand by male cloakmakers who had walked out on strike, and then celebrated their decision by dancing for several hours with the striking men. Three years later, tailoresses met to celebrate and dance when they went on strike for a closed shop.[23] Theresa Malkiel's diary of the famous 1909 shirtwaist strike testified, "It was funny to see the few men among us but I give them credit for coming out." Although she was sardonic about the initial scorn poured on the striking women by her suitor and the public at large, she was nevertheless staunchly loyal to her class: "The pity of it is that us working people don't really realize what a power we are. . . . Our bosses couldn't get about without us working people."[24]

The larger local community consistently participated in the garment industry struggles, ignoring the hard-and-fast rules set down by the union. Despite the fact that Jewish workers did not always control strike funds, industrial unrest relied on support built on the strong solidarity that linked the garment workers on the Lower East Side. This was also true in other working-class communities, such as the Slav miners in Pennsylvania.[25]

Attempts at orderly unionization were often frustrated by these spontaneous outbursts. Formal structures, with power vested in committees and elected officers, conflicted with the more egalitarian ethos based on participatory democracy. In the Jewish community, cultural ties, the absence of craft loyalty, the mobility from status of employee to contractor, the proliferation of small or home workshops, all, in their different ways, were at odds with the accepted ways craft unions organized.[26]

The efforts to organize more effectively through union drives ran concurrently and sometimes in conflict with the complex but informal community networks involving neighbors, friends, relatives, and landsmanshaftn through which jobs were found. Both the cutthroat character of the industry and the Jewish garment workers themselves, whose living depended on being available at any time and any place for work, resisted any restrictions imposed by unions. Above all, traditional union policies divided labor along craft lines, which would ultimately have fragmented labor into separate, self-contained units built on trade and craft. The close links between the community and the trade made Jewish labor notorious among contemporary commentators, who accused Jews of being inherently capitalistic and individualistic and thus unable to establish or maintain labor organizations.

INTERPRETATIONS OF LABOR UNREST

The culture of industrial unrest was founded on Jewish immigrants' interpretation of the condition of labor. In many instances, as this chapter shows, minor incidents escalated into major disputes and engulfed the community in social turmoil. Every hint of injustice was met with a broad show of loyalty. Struggling trade union leaders, however, condemned what they saw as sabotage of the normal process of trade union organizion and collective bargaining.

During the 1880s and 1890s, the decline of the Knights of Labor provided a space for the growth of the AFL, which initially supported a political interpretation of the conflict between labor and capital. However, as a result of the Haymarket affair, this was also a period of union persecution, which encouraged a tendency to seek accommodation with employers, rather than risk defeat in a hostile climate. The AFL was organized along traditional union lines, based on the centralization of authority for collective bargaining and the establishment of stable organizations providing member benefits. This type of union exerted a discipline opposing strike actions or other disruptions of orderly negotiations.[27] The sort of Jewish immigrant labor unrest labeled as "indiscipline" illustrates the conflict between capital and labor and also between grassroots militancy and labor organizations. Both the social and organizational conflicts illustrate a fundamentally divergent perception of social and political justice. Table 5.1 indicates the contested terrain between organized labor and capital on the one hand, and Jewish rank and file and trade unions on the other.

Table 5.1 illustrates some of the divisions between the aspirations of the rank and file and the more pragmatic goals of labor organizations, as well as conflicts between labor and capital. These structural differences indicated underlying tensions between the two, relative to the reform of the industrial system. It is in light of these tensions that historians and writers of the period described immigrant workers' skeptical attitudes to unions as backward looking and destructive of viable labor-defensive organizations. Observers at the time and later commentators alike have criticized the Jewish workers' apparent inability to unite and maintain a solid proletarian movement that could negotiate and deliver results. The view that Jewish workers were too militant, misguided, and undisciplined, or, on occasion,

Table 5.1 Industrial Relations in the Clothing Industry: Employers' Practices, Trade Union Strategies, and Jewish Immigrant Workers' Responses

Employers' practices	Power over jobs (hiring & firing)	Abusive language & behavior	Subcontracting Employment of strike breakers	Task system & speedups Sweatshop system Wage reductions Increase in working hours
Trade union strategies	• Orderly collective bargaining • Control over labor supply • Pragmatic solutions	• Irrelevant to collective bargaining	• Closed shop • Reorganization of industry	• Negotiation toward defined goals
Jewish workers' interpretation	• Injustice	• Humiliation • Harassment • Victimization	• Unethical	• Wage slavery • Profiteering • Exploitation
Jewish workers' responses and tactics	• Militancy • Spontaneous walkouts • Confrontations • Industrial unionism • Inclusivity of all workers	• Legitimate grievances	• Communal ostracism • Violence • Refusal to compromise with strike breakers	• Demand to abolish contracting system • Industrial action • Community involvement • Mutuality

apathetic and lacking in class consciousness, dominated the thinking of labor leaders and reformers, whose aim was to improve the anarchic conditions in the needle trades. Although competition was fierce among the workers, it was at least as strong among employers, who vied with each other to drive down wages, thereby increasing their profit margins.

Bosses imposed strict discipline, inducing isolation and fear on the shop floor.[28] When work was available, workers were rivals for more and better quality goods so that they could save up for the slack periods. In this competitive atmosphere, employers exacerbated competition among workers through their own brand of favoritism. The contractors or foremen in charge of distributing work sometimes took advantage of their powerful positions by demanding "loans," which in fact were bribes, never to be repaid. Everyone seeking work was "deep into his own problems and troubles and had to worry about sending some money to his parents. I had to send some money home and that is why everyone also was for himself and worried about his own troubles," reported one immigrant. Rebecca August, a buttonmaker employed by Hart, Schaffner and Marx of Chicago, explained why she worked so hard: "The more money I made, the sooner we could send for my mother and her six children."[29] Another immigrant remembered that "you didn't tell fellow workers how much you made, and therefore one worker would rush the others, hoping that the boss would give him a raise." Piecework, the major cause of speedups, promoted a climate of hostility and suspicion and "made us each other's enemies." Joseph Guterman subsequently described the isolation of working in the trade by saying that "everybody was a world for himself." A sense of joint decision making emerged only gradually.[30]

The absence of a cooperative spirit and of stable unions led some to believe, simplistically, that the immigrants were "stupid, uninformed and enslaved people without education and without working class awareness. We even had to teach them how to read a newspaper. They fell into a stupefying and enslaving atmosphere of the shop where they were not considered human."[31] Moreover, many contemporaries subscribed to the observation made by labor historian John Commons that "the Jew's conception of labor organization is that of a tradesman rather than that of a workman."[32]

The tendency of Jewish workers to call for strike action was praised, but the unruly membership of their short-lived unions was criticized by contemporary commentators. "It was difficult to hold everybody together," according to Abraham Rosenberg, who recalled how new members who were won over to the union cause at the height of the 1888 strike lacked the patience to negotiate concessions and opposed their leaders' advice to proceed cautiously.[33] In 1901, Henry White, the general secretary of the United Garment Workers, a trade organization of workers in men's garments, voiced his disapproval of an impending tailor-coatmakers' strike, which aimed to mobilize 25,000 to 50,000 workers:

> We do not think that these strikes do any good, for the reason that they origi-
> nate from organizations which grew up overnight, so that when they are vic-
> torious they are not in any position to reap the benefit of their victory. They
> cannot enforce their contracts and the union goes to pieces soon after their
> victory is assured.[34]

This seemed typically cautious advice from a responsible labor leader, but observers regarded mass walkouts as yet another sign of Jewish workers' sup-posedly anarchic character. Strikes were declared on the basis of an inter-minable list of grievances that lacked coherence and focus. Stoppages of this type were unpopular with the general public and labor leaders alike because they appeared impulsive, "angry and vindictive," and they involved an en-tire ethnic community and not just a part of the workforce. The *Tribune* warned its readers to expect a "strike of a race" and not that of a union when reporting on the impending walkout of Jewish tailors during the depression of 1893.[35] In 1885, John Swinton, a non-Jewish labor commentator and ed-itor of *John Swinton's Paper,* warned Jewish strikers to be less violent: "These poor fellows must learn how to conduct strikes."[36]

Militant cloakmakers, however, did not take labor leaders' advice for long-range planning and well-coordinated, strategically organized actions. In 1897, thousands of tailors demanded the abolition of the task system, without heeding their executive's advice to affiliate to a central labor or-ganization. Even Joseph Barondess, once the cloakmakers' fiery leader, counseled delay, warning militants that their strike would fail. On one oc-casion, while the leadership was preparing a walkout and drafting demands, impatient tailors held a vigil outside Walhalla Hall, threatening to break down the doors to the room where the United Brotherhood Cloakmakers' Union's closed Executive Committee meeting was being held. "Have you no pity for our wives and children who are starving?" cried the men in the street. Eventually, when the crowds broke into the room, the Executive Com-mittee agreed to the strike.[37] Similarly, on the eve of the mass strike of 1910, hundreds of workers "beleaguered the offices of the union clamoring that the strike be called at once" and accused the hesitant leadership of exploiting the promise of a general strike in order to build up membership.[38] Union leaders became increasingly critical and weary of militant members, who only joined the union when they wanted to call a strike. When three hun-dred skirtmakers employed by John Bonwit applied to join the ILGWU, it was suspected that they were already on strike. Some regarded stable union-ism as a priority; among them was the *Arbeiter Zeitung,* which applauded eight

hundred kneepantsmakers who met to discuss strike funds, athough there
was "no strike nor slack. It was a real business meeting."[39]

Union leaders wanted to build up strong organizations and used strike
rhetoric as an incentive to recruit. In planning the 1909 cloakmakers' walkout, the ILGWU abandoned traditional propaganda in favor of recruitment
drives and strike agitation. To organize the union among shirtwaistmakers,
the leaders decided to exploit the fact that "the trade was surcharged with
restlessness and that a big venture [a strike] might catch the fancy of the
workers."[40] Traditionally, however, leadership wanted to maintain control
over industrial actions and opposed spontaneous or unauthorized walkouts,
insisting on a more bureaucratic approach. For example, the United Pants
Makers' Union decided in 1892 that "No strike in any shop will be recognized without first being sanctioned by the executive committee." Likewise,
the International Cloakmakers' Union of New York and Brownsville declared that no shop had a right to strike without permission from its local.
In 1896, the New York cloakmakers decided that "when a shop or a firm go
on strike without the approval of the union, the union will not be responsible for such strikes."[41] This divide between official and unofficial practices
originated from a working-class political tradition that prioritized economic
interests above other cultural and social perspectives. However, a meaningful interpretation of Jewish labor requires a wider cultural reading to include the impact of community issues on labor actions and vice versa.

The fact that Jewish garment workers were prepared to take action on
behalf of themselves and other victimized members indicates strong feelings
of solidarity despite the apparent competitiveness of the market system. The
tension between the need for organization and the militancy of the rank and
file, despite the fact that there were no strike funds, was a pervasive theme
of labor unrest.

STRUGGLES FOR CONTROL OF THE WORKPLACE

A variety of issues, apart from wages and hours, inspired labor struggles.
These included control over time, closed shop, and a demand to be treated
with dignity. In the needle trades, many employers were themselves newcomers to the production system and to subcontracting. They came from a
social class similar to that of their workers, but they behaved toward them as
masters might have behaved toward servants, using abusive language and
meting out physical punishment and dismissals for insubordination. Workers in turn challenged their bosses' unlimited power in the workplace
through spontaneous rebellions. Experienced American labor leaders, the
press, and even Jewish Socialists often deplored these demands for immediate redress of minor irritations and advised workers instead to focus on

the major issues of wages and hours. In fact, the unions sometimes preferred to formulate demands dealing with concrete issues such as wages, hours, and closed shop, although the friction may have originated from employers' unacceptable behavior. The 1893 strike of three hundred cloakmakers employed by Julius Stein, for instance, was triggered by a superintendent's "lowly and degrading treatment," an issue omitted from the settlement although an agreement on wage levels was concluded.[42] Plain harassment, even what would now be called sexual harassment, took a backseat in negotiations with employers about material conditions, as Pauline Newman noted in a letter to Rose Schneiderman in 1911. She considered it bad strategy to raise issues of morals when negotiations over wages and hours were at stake.[43]

Abusive behavior was a fact of life. Max Pine, later secretary of the United Hebrew Trades, recalled receiving a beating from his boss as a penalty for joining the union. When other workers tried to restrain the angry boss, he shouted, "I will kill the green pumpkin. He wants to make revolts here? I will show him what America is!" In a dramatic display of their anger, Pine's co-workers unscrewed their sewing machines and carried them out of the shop. The demands presented later to the boss included recognition of the union, an increase in pay, the refusal to carry bundles of unmade clothes from the contractor's storage to the shop located on the fourth floor, and regular paydays every two weeks. And, as part of the agreement, the boss himself had to carry the machines back to the shop, while his wife was to cease cursing and insulting his workers.[44]

The first celebrated strike of mainly Jewish cloakmakers in August 1885, began as a protest against abuse, but the leadership proceeded to formulate more traditional union demands, including shorter hours, increased wages, equal pay rates, and consultation about new styles, rather than being dictated to by the superintendent. They also demanded the dismissal of scabs, reinstatement of all strikers, and a closed shop.[45] Although some contemporaries perceived this strike as a "revolt for bread and butter," others noted that the strikers "have been very roughly dealt with by their employers in the past" and made a specific demand "to be treated with politeness and consideration."[46] In 1905, in a smaller strike, pressers staged a walkout in defiance of a hated foreman. Their action was triggered by the dismissal of a worker who had protested against compulsory overtime by threatening the foreman with a heavy iron. This led to a walkout of the independent union of "old pressers."[47]

In 1901, women shirtwaist workers at Goldsmith and Co. walked out in protest against an employee's unjustified dismissal. The circumstances of this strike were not about hiring procedures or employment rights but about control over their own time in the workplace. The firm's women workers complained that when there was little to do, they had a right to do their own sewing, since they were on piecework and therefore were not infringing on their employer's time. One Saturday at noon, when there was nothing for them to do, they walked out, but when they came back on Monday, they were fired.[48] This incident defined a contractual code, which rejected the imposition of industrial time, discipline, and bosses' claim to power over workers' time on the factory floor, even when they were not working. Rose Schneiderman described a comparable incident when, as secretary of her local in 1903, she won an agreement on behalf of a group of women who demanded to be paid at noon on Saturdays, after they finished work, instead of waiting for the men who went off at 4 P.M. This comparatively insignificant incident symbolized, nevertheless, the value put on employees' rights to their own time.[49]

In subsequent periods, employer abuse and victimization of workers remained sensitive issues but were difficult to codify within the legal process of collective bargaining even after the signature, in 1910, of the Protocol of Peace, which laid down a procedure for settling disputes through established channels. Despite the compulsory arbitration mechanism, fifteen workers in the shop of J. C. Stratton, joined by comrades from other shops, refused to obey the Board of Grievances, which called on them to return to work within a specified period. John Dyche, the Joint Board's Chief Clerk and the signatory to the Protocol, retaliated against the unruly workers by sending substitutes.[50]

STRUGGLES FOR CLOSED SHOP AND AGAINST SCABS

Theresa Malkiel, who published a fictional diary based on her own experience of the women shirtwaistmakers strike of 1909, expressed her deep disdain for scabs, or strikebreakers—a sentiment shared by most members of the working community: "I wonder who was the first to use the name scab? By Jove the right one at that; nobody clean could be mean enough to step into somebody else's shoes."[51] The 1890 cloakmakers' strike demonstrated how the issues of substitute labor dominated workers' struggles and revealed important differences between the struggles of old craft and the new unskilled labor militants. There was unremitting friction because employers refused to countenance a closed-shop system. The strike of 1890 was one of the period's most famous and effective industrial actions.[52] The 1890 cloakmakers' strike began at the firm of Meyer Jonasson, one of the largest cloak manufacturers. It was caused by the employer's refusal to employ union members. All employees, including the cutters, retaliated by going out on strike and were locked out. Cloak production in New York came to a virtual halt. All sections of the workforce were united temporarily, under the leadership of the Consolidated Board, against the Manufacturers' Association,

Figure 5.2 Striker argues with a strikebreaker in New York City, 1905. Photograph by Lewis W. Hine. Courtesy of George Eastman House.

with its ample resources, which represented the thirteen largest cloakmaking manufacturers.[53]

Divisions soon appeared in the workers' previously united front, between the cutters, the aristocrats of the cloak industry (many of them German or Irish), and the Jewish cloakmakers. The latter were largely unskilled workers, led by Barondess, the cloakmakers' leader. With Thomas H. Garside as the strikers' representative at the Consolidated Board, the cutters demanded the dismissal of scabs, insisting, to a lesser extent, on the restitution of time lost during the lockout. The issue of scabs was ultimately settled through a compromise whereby the manufacturers agreed to fire the scabs on a Friday but reinstated them on the Monday after.[54] But this agreement did not end the strike. The major opposition to a comprehensive settlement came from the Jewish cloakmakers, who vowed to stay out forever if need be, "before they would work with scabs."[55] They insisted that all hands employed in cloakmaking during the strike be discharged and "left for the union to dispose of as it sees fit," and that only union labor be hired, which the manufacturers refused to accept. Had it been a question of wages, they noted, the issue would have been settled, but yielding to cloakmakers' demands would have been tantamount to a surrender of "all they have stood for," wrote the *World*.[56]

Not all sections of the workforce supported the cloakmakers. The skilled cutters were willing to settle with the Manufacturers' Association, on the basis of a compromise on the issue of scabs. Dion W. Burke, the cutters' representative, directed the six thousand Jewish operators to agree to the manufacturers' terms and to return to work; otherwise "every labor organization would be arraigned against them and the Operators' Union be entirely broken up."[57] Garside also wanted the operators to settle and admonished the workers for making excessive demands, destroying the union, and achieving nothing. Similarly, the Socialist *Arbeter Zeitung* preached caution when strikers demanded dismissals of all scabs and withdrawal of charges against two strike leaders. The paper cautioned, "A strike is a battle against capital under the control of capital. In a revolution one can achieve anything, in a strike one must want only that which is possible to achieve." But the cloakmakers remained unmoved, drew a barrage of insults about anarchist infiltration, and faced a smear campaign against Barondess—known as their "czar." "Every man familiar with the labor movement in this country knows that the concessions made by the cloak manufacturers gave all three of the unions a sweeping victory," argued Dion W. Burke, accusing Barondess and even Garside of anarchism, inciting to riot and bomb throwing "as they did in Chicago," a pointed reference to the Haymarket affair of 1886.[58] Such critiques fell on deaf ears as a contemporary, thinly disguised novel about Barondess showed. A fictional account of the 1890 strike portrayed the workers declaring, "Down with the Socialists! They can give us nothing but advice. Joseph, our Joseph, will give us bread."[59]

Unskilled operatives' fierce opposition to scabs had both a practical and a moral significance. In contrast to cutters, unskilled workers were easy prey for instant substitution that the Consolidated Board had no power to prevent. The outcome of the 1890 strike proved that unskilled labor was right to have little faith in the ability of the Consolidated Board to represent them. In the end, the cutters signed a separate agreement with the manufacturers and contractors and returned to work. In contrast, the operators voted 1,536 to 20 to continue the strike. The community was solidly behind them and showed it by donating whatever valuables they owned. Despite the violence and the warnings that the operators were "cutting their own throat," the pressures of the busy season brought some gains. The strikers had won a battle—demands for closed shop and minimum weekly wages were granted—through Barondess's masterly handling of the dispute.[60] Gabriel Schwab, the manufacturers' representative, summed up the proceedings by noting that Barondess "made the manufacturers give him what he wanted, ran the whole meeting, licked them thoroughly and . . . is laughing in his sleeve." The victory was celebrated on the Lower East Side with red flags and a band playing the Marseillaise. The community stamped its identity on the strike's successful outcome by legitimizing its demand for equitable economic rights. Even critics like John Swinton had to admit that Barondess was "able and accomplished."[61]

The strike of 1890 indicated how cloakmakers on the one hand and veteran and skilled cutters on the other adopted widely differing tactics in their labor struggles. The cloakmakers used force against their enemies—scabs and employers—which confirmed an image of anarchism "stained by blood." This was reinforced by Barondess's threats against press criticism; he had allegedly declared that capitalists would be "swept out of existence" by abolishing private property and reversing the mistakes of "the heroic forefathers of this country."[62] Significantly, Jewish immigrants interpreted the American system as protecting working people's civil rights and not as prescribing accomodation and compromise, but American public opinion and trade unionists alike were hostile to the belligerent strikers. "You are not an American citizen . . . but you assume more authority than a native would. If you were in Russia, you would be sent to Siberia for this," Judge Duffy of the Essex Market Police Court admonished Max Abrahams, a cloakmaker arrested in 1890 for calling workers out on strike. Arthur Dale, chairman of the Consolidated Board representing the strikers, criticized the strike's violence: "As American citizens we are not accustomed to such dictions or threats."[63]

The cause of the 1891 strike, like that of the preceding year, originated in a disagreement over employment rights, "who shall and who shall

not be employed." It was precipitated by the dismissal of about thirty workers by an employer who claimed that they were insufficiently trained to do
the work. Barondess, however, demanded that the workers be reinstated and
employed "in the same capacity." One employer alleged that Barondess ordered him to reinstate a worker who demanded time, rather than piecework, which became the immediate cause of the strike.[64] Barondess and the
defiant strikers continued to hound scabs and their employers. Workers'
demands for control over job security were accompanied by that for a
closed shop. These twin issues became a repeated trigger for cloakmakers'
and coatmakers' industrial actions on an almost annual basis. As Albert
Hochstadter, president of the Clothing Manufacturers' Association remarked in 1901, "The question is not now primarily one of wages, hours or
sanitary conditions of labor, but a question of union or non-union shops."
Attacking the unions' demands for a closed shop, he stated that employers
"are not willing to have their business run by labor unions."[65] The most celebrated shirtwaistmakers' strike of 1909 provoked similar reactions. The
walkout at the Triangle Waist Company, which began over dismissals, was
another example of a sympathy strike that had nothing to do with conven-
tional union demands. "It is the most astonishing strike I ever knew. The
wage demands mean nothing. We are actually paying more than the union
asks," declared one employer. Women strikers walked out during the slack
season, demanding to know how many hours' work they would have the following day, so they could attend to their daily affairs. They also asked for
equal pay, the abolition of piecework, and weekly remuneration.[66]

Even after the signature of the Protocol of Peace in 1910, which supposedly ushered in a modicum of regulation in the garment industry, labor
continued to contest the control of employers.[67] Jewish immigrants, although they were new to the industrial experience, perceived employers'
power as encroaching on their rights as workers. A system of closed shop was
the only means whereby employers' prerogatives could be curtailed. As Rebecca August so vividly put it, when she went on trial in 1912 for infringing
the law in the course of her union activity, "They asked me why did I inter-
fere in their [the bosses'] business, didn't I know that they had their capital invested there. I said, yes I know that, but we have our labor invested
there, so you see capital and labor must go hand in hand."[68]

In 1910, the demand for the union shop, declared by the *New York
Times* as "un-American," became again an inflammatory issue, when cloakmakers walked out and were soon joined by six thousand shirtwaistmakers.
Most strikers rejected the new idea of the preferential shop proposed by
Louis Brandeis, although the formula had previously been approved by
strike leaders as a compromise alternative to the closed shop. Preferential
shop was a settlement whereby employers agreed to give priority, though not
exclusivity, to union members on condition that they were as well qualified

as nonmembers, a definition which was wide open to biased intrepretation. The rank and file continued to demand closed shop and even laid siege to the *Verheit* offices on East Broadway in protest against the journal's support for the Brandeis settlement. A court injunction against picketing did not put an end to agitation.[69]

Although the strike was ultimately settled on the basis of the preferential shop, the agreement's shortcomings soon became apparent. Some strikers were never rehired and substitute workers retained their jobs, while loopholes within the agreement continued to cause conflict.[70]

STRUGGLES AGAINST SWEATSHOPS
AND THE CONTRACTING SYSTEM

The contracting system, which prevailed in the garment industry, was a source of continued conflict between capital and labor. It was based on continual undercutting through the task and piece system, as well as other irritants and indignities, such as tool hire, payment for electricity, and abysmal working conditions. The organization of production in small workshops, "kitchen and bedroom" shops, meant that work was unregulated, hours long, and wages, which unscrupulous bosses often failed to pay altogether, low. In 1888, the editors of the *Yudishe Folkszeitung* described the contracting system in graphic terms: "Willingly or not, they [the contractors] are forced to play the role of leech number two. They are parasites who suck whatever leech number one has left the worker."[71] By going on strike, workers hoped to bring about a reform in work conditions, which were scandalous in small shops.

Strikes against the contracting system broke out regularly. In 1890, shirtmakers demanded a minimum shop size of fifteen sewing machines, hoping thereby to eliminate the worst abuses in small establishments. Four years later, vestmakers demanded that every shop have at least three sewing machines without the contractor doing any sewing. Many small-scale actions were aimed at regulating work and the process of production. In one strike, a modest but important objective was the installation of a clock to stop exploitation.[72] Similar strikes in small shops aimed to agree on a more precise job definition and thereby establish employment rights. For instance, in 1892 employees demanded that bundles of cut material be brought to the shop so that they did not have to spend time fetching and carrying, that sewing machines and free electricity be provided, and that pay be regular.[73]

Other strikes aimed beyond single-shop settlements to eliminate the system of contracting. "Bosses, little bosses and tiny bosses" were a plague on the trade.[74] Workers demanded the abolition of the entire system of contracting, subcontracting and sweated labor. Their aim was to bring the

process of production out of tenement rooms into larger factories super-
vised by employers and accessible to public scrutiny. They campaigned for
a greater concentration of production to eliminate the evils of unrestrained
competitiveness and achieve better pay and regular hours, which, in turn,
would put an end to competition among workers.

In 1886, striking cloakmakers demanded that manufacturers provide
workshops instead of the contractor-owned rooms and lodgings. The manufacturers rejected this demand, and Meyer Jonasson responded that "it
would be absolutely impossible to allow them to work in buildings owned by
the manufacturers as there would be no room for them." The firm also
claimed that Jewish immigrants, particularly observant ones, were better off
working in small workshops where Sunday laws did not apply. In the end,
manufacturers, eager to settle the strike, promised the arbitration committee to give assistance to cooperative shops, and some even supported the
suggestion to "do away with the contract system entirely."[75] But they soon
reneged on their agreement, calling it unrealistic and reiterating their earlier refusal to dispense with contracting:

> They demand us to completely revolutionize our business before July 15 by the
> abolition of contract work and the establishment of factories. The question is
> not one of prices. Had they demanded that, the question would have been set-
> tled long ago. . . . The system [of contracting] is a necessity, having been an
> adjunct of the cloak trade for fifty years, and it would require much time to
> change it.[76]

Clearly, more was at stake than just money. Abolishing the contract system
and initiating some sort of cooperation would have compromised not only
sweating and other forms of cheap labor but would have redefined the control of the system as a whole. The strike of 1886 concluded with a weak compromise by employers to cease using tenement sweatshops and provide a
minimum of five machines. It specified that "we will do what we can to control the contractors," but they did not undertake to terminate the sweatshops. Labor leaders at the time blamed the strike's failure on bad timing
(it took place during a short season), on lack of coordination with a central
labor organization, and, more significantly, on its over-ambitious objectives.
Above all, the strike's main goal, the abolition of contracting, met with opposition from labor organizers. John Swinton, for example, criticized Jewish workers for their ill-advised attempts to reform the very core of the industry.[77] Other commentators noted that the strike ended with thousands
of workers returning to work for the very contractors they had hoped to put
out of business. Nevertheless, the struggle itself had elicited much support
among workers determined to abolish the hated system. To celebrate their

victory, crowds poured onto the streets of the Lower East Side carrying brooms symbolizing the extinction of the sweating system once and for all.[78]

Repeated attempts to eradicate both contracting and the task system continued into the twentieth century. In 1901, a mass strike of twenty-five thousand workers, mainly tailors, demanded the abolition of the contracting system, negotiations between manufacturers and workers, a fifty-nine-hour work week, and work by the week.[79] The strike was opposed by many labor leaders, particularly Henry White, general secretary of the United Garment Workers (UGW), the parent organization of the Brotherhood of Tailors, a traditional supporter of tailors' strikes.[80]

Under the pressure of the UGW, the tailors dropped their original demand to abolish contracting, postponing it until the following year. Instead, they advocated that all contracts be negotiated with the manufacturer and not the contractors, thus making the former responsible for work conditions in the latter's shops and demanding a commitment from manufacturers to deal with noncomplying contractors.[81]

STRUGGLES AGAINST THE TASK SYSTEM

The efforts to abolish contracting were but one path toward the goal of regulating the industry; battles for the abolition of task and piece systems were a route toward uniform and equitable wages.[82] The daily "task" was the embodiment of exploitation. It was especially practiced in the men's garment industry, where it enabled contractors to increase the quota of work without paying any more for it, forcing workers to work faster, and for longer hours.[83] Significantly, calls to abolish the task and piece systems included demands to reduce pay differentials and regulate hours. However, attempts at reform met with opposition from manufacturers and contractors alike.

In 1886, tailors, largely employed in the men's garment industry, demanded the abolition of the task system and went on strike for weekly wages to be determined "by what the men's services may be found to be worth." Contractors, claiming that the new wage scale would drive them out of business, were quick to reject these demands. However, under pressure of the busy season, some agreed to abolish the task system. They promised to employ union members, working ten hours a day for five days and nine hours on a sixth and pay them weekly. The 1886 agreement was a temporary expedient that was quickly revoked. Employers set tasks ever higher, and by 1894, during a period of severe depression, they demanded production of thirty-eight coats a day, a task unattainable even by the fastest tailor whose daily limit was twenty coats.[84] Exploitation grew, especially in smaller shops employing five to twenty workers. The average weekly pay in 1894 was $9, although contractors claimed that tailors could earn $18 to $19 weekly. According to one coatmaker, in 1894 it took him two days to earn a day's pay, although he made one hundred coats within four days working eighteen hours a day: "They called me lazy," he indignantly reported. "A fair living wage for a fair week's work" was the slogan of thousands of strikers in 1894.[85] The Lower East Side became charged with strike activity that temporarily united rival unions and different trades. It witnessed violent outbursts by strikers against employers and scabs; their aim was to abolish the sweating system and piecework. Wages were falling, hours increasing, and new tasks being imposed on the workforce, especially in small contracting establishments. Meyer Jonasson demanded a $2 deposit to be forfeited if workers went on strike, and a deduction of $2 a week over the next nine months, even if they returned to work.[86]

Employers, both large and small, adamantly refused to surrender any part of the organization of industry to labor or to labor representatives. They denounced the strike, its leader, Barondess, and other "unscrupulous agitators."[87] Jonasson declared that the concessions that the workers demanded "would be equal to giving up our business to our workmen" and threatened to move his enterprise from New York to another part of the country or even abroad. Henry Seligman, of Seligman Brothers, echoed, "I do not think that the day is at hand when we should stoop to treat with the labor organizations which now affect our trade." Daniel Richman, chairman of the Manufacturers' Association, accused labor leaders of being "more rum-besotted and whiskey-soaked than the leaders of any other trade union." The coatmakers, unlike the cloakmakers, settled the strike, but the employers rejected their demands and called in the police to protect strikebreakers and property.[88] The 1894 strike ended in defeat and a return to work at reduced wages, because of utter destitution. During a particularly cold winter, many had to rely on charity from settlement societies and jobs in street cleaning to survive. The defeat worsened work conditions, especially for tailors. During these struggles, even the *New York Sun* showed sympathy for the plight of the people on the East Side and advocated an end to sweating.

In July, 1895, at the height of the depression, the Brotherhood of Tailors, with a membership of fifteen thousand, went on strike against tenement sweatshops.[89] This was a "model strike," which won the sympathy of a public alarmed by the risk of the spread of infectious diseases through garments manufactured in homes with poor sanitary conditions. The *New York Tribune*, for one, found that "public welfare is commonly invaded and universally menaced by the system" and argued for the workers' demands. The *Tribune* also applauded the strikers' exemplary conduct and their refusal to be associated with the anarchist leader Emma Goldman. However, an agreement signed in mid-December was rejected by employers who reserved the right to hire and fire workers and refused to observe a ten-hour day.[90] In 1896, another coatmakers' strike against the task system was concluded without an agreement regarding the task or contracting system.

As in previous years, the violent unrest of 1897 provoked John Swinton to plead with the workers for patience and perseverance. Like many of his contemporaries, he regarded attempts to establish a time system in the place of the task system as unrealistic. Using traditional metaphors, he compared the struggle against the coatmaking bosses to that of the ancient Israelites against their traditional enemies, the Amalekites, the Jesuits, and other oppressors. But, like the Israelites who suffered forty years in the desert, "there are very few lentils to eat at present. . . . The men must have patience."[91]

Simultaneous with industrywide demands for greater workers' control over the system of production, some segments of the garment industry, sometimes even workers in individual workplaces, strove for agreements regulating pay, hours, and wages between a manufacturer and his contractors, rather than tackle the contractor-worker relations in the industry as a whole.[92]

Attempts to transform the system of production achieved only short-term results. The small-shop system of garment production, which led to price and wage undercutting, proved remarkably resistant to change. Unlike conditions in the steel industry, where centralized capital could successfully impose a uniform system of production, the garment industry became increasingly fractionalized.[93] The efforts of larger employers both to control the labor force and to eliminate cutthroat competition were repeatedly frustrated by smaller manufacturers. Paradoxically, larger employers gained from the subsequent establishment of the ILGWU, a broadly based union that succeeded, ultimately, not only in establishing standards for the industry but also in protecting employers' profits.

CHAPTER SIX

The Politics of Morality: Jewish Workers and the Ethnic Community

> In Russia for the mass gathering one had to go to a forest, one had to be on the lookout for the police, but in the United States we sang the Marseillaise when we walked the streets . . . the Russian Marseillaise. . . . There is a French Marseillaise . . . that was the symbol of the workers' movement. And when we walked in the street and sang the Marseillaise, we felt in heaven.
>
> —Julius Gershin, immigrant

Public protests by the urban Jewish community demonstrated its new and evolving social code, its sense of identity and autonomy. These actions reinforced a political culture of collective goals and loyalties by overriding individual objectives. The community's social code expressed working people's right to act collectively against their adversaries and to demand social, economic, and cultural change. Workers turned to the neighborhood for support in their struggles, and the community imposed economic boycotts, provided financial assistance during strikes, ostracized enemies such as scabs, and defied employers and other transgressors of the workers' code of ethics. Outbursts of violent protest also revealed a broader critique of the economic and social order. Such actions were inspired by the historic understanding of a long-embattled community, which had been transplanted into a new political system offering new opportunities. The participants in these struggles—Jewish workers and their allies—all belonged to the same ethnic community, occupied the same area on the Lower East Side, and for the most part shared the same trade.

Julius Gershin, YIVO, RG 113, p18.

Although inspired by material considerations, industrial actions generated a new political language for other social conflicts. In the period when the boundaries between public and private, community and work, were more fluid, the language used had distinct roots in material struggles and was freely applied to other community affairs. The women who in 1902 began a meat boycott against rising prices referred to themselves as "strikers" and called the nonboycotters "scabs," a term that gained rapid currency in situations unrelated to strikebreaking.[1] For example, it was applied to tenants who continued to rent rooms from a landlord against whom a boycott had been declared for ruthlessly evicting nineteen families.[2] In another case, a perplexed reader sent a query to the "Bintl Brief" section of the *Jewish Daily Forward,* asking whether it was ethical to buy cheaper coal from a new coal merchant who had been called a "scab" for undercutting a more established competitor.[3] Thus, the language of workplace rights supplied familiar metaphors for many other kinds of social conflict.

Crowd behavior has long been central to the writings of social and cultural historians. E. P. Thompson, for example, described the English eighteenth-century food rioters as defenders of traditional rights, noting that they based their demands on the historic custom by which justices of the peace determined the price, weight, and content of bread.[4] In contrast, protesting crowds on the Lower East Side did not put their trust in established institutions of the state. In the instance of the meat boycott, some women called for a rabbi to fix the price of meat for the entire Jewish community of New York, following a custom brought from the shtetl. The majority of women, however, did not appeal to the paternalistic authority of traditional leaders but embraced the principle of participatory democracy as a means of empowerment in political action.[5] They used streets, homes, and synagogues to legitimize their campaigns and all available means to stigmatize and punish those who infringed an unwritten community code. The ultimate realization of their goals depended on the interaction of tightly linked, familiar, communal networks. The workers' proximity to and use of buildings such as synagogues, meeting halls, schools, and manufacturing shops created a space defined as uniquely theirs and distinctively working-class Jewish. This unique intertwining of the social, political, and cultural arenas forged an all-inclusive sociopolitical framework, where all members could exercise full participatory rights, regardless of whether they were men or women, workers, synagogue members, tenants, or consumers.

In this context, women were central to communal life and fully integrated into the militant community of working immigrants rather than relegated to assigned activities or spaces. Although women remained concerned with the traditional role of feeding their families, gendered divisions emphasizing men as breadwinners or "providers," a concept integral to American labor, were not reflected in Jewish experience. Jewish women assumed the role of providers for their families as much as Jewish men. As Paula Hyman has so convincingly shown, women were the dynamic force behind the kosher meat boycott of 1902, when they mobilized Jewish meat consumers throughout Manhattan, Brooklyn, and the Bronx. Organizational strategies adopted during the 1902 boycott relied heavily on women's networks to mobilize support. Central to its success was the use of force, so characteristic of this and similar struggles on the Lower East Side, which placed women at the center of these dramatic events. Women participated in attacks on scabs and police, as well as on those who breached unwritten community laws, behavior largely condemned by the American public, American unions, and the judiciary. Women defended their forceful, sometimes violent, strategies in the name of their obligation to provide for their families. In contrast, American courts invoked the legal language of keeping the peace and following the rule of law and American institutions. Jewish women were labeled as criminal lawbreakers who should be "handled in a way that they can understand and cannot forget . . . let the blow fall instantly and effectually," according to the *New York Times* in 1902.[6]

Women's participation in labor and community matters changed with the rise of structured unions.[7] In 1909, leading unionists insisted on a turning from what they viewed as the militant, disorderly behavior that traditionally characterized Jewish strikes. Samuel Gompers and others applauded examples of more orderly and disciplined picketing during the shirtwaistmakers' strike of that year. Moreover, women's inspirational and uncompromising role in the strike was extolled as contributing to the organizational achievements of the ILGWU. In retrospect, however, it appears paradoxical that, despite being the historic icons of the struggles of 1909, women were excluded from leading positions in the union.[8]

The mass of Jewish workers demanded that a rule of "fairness" be applied to social and economic relations in the workplace and the marketplace. They took up positions against the market economy by initiating industrial action against employers and against exploitation by landlords, shopkeepers, and the long arm of the law. The new format of community politics, which they envisaged as encompassing all these spheres, inspired a new moral language forged through public protest and debate. The conflict involved the Jewish working-class community and its adversaries: the employers, landlords, and traders. These schisms caused splits in the community and even in families, with daughters known to denounce fathers and brothers as "traitors to the cause." The flashpoints for these conflicts were not only the streets and public meeting places but also private spaces, which were invaded by protesters, flouting all conventions. In contrast to the expectations of the American middle class, the public forum and the crowd, rather than elected representatives, became the guardians of the emerging morality.

AGENCIES OF CULTURAL TRANSMISSION

Broadly shared notions of justice and rights gradually cohered into an explicitly socialist vision. A group of Jewish intellectuals, editors, writers, orators, poets, and organizers contributed significantly to formulating that vision and in articulating the community's ideology. Through the medium of newspapers, street-corner poetry gatherings, marketplace encounters, and theatrical productions, the people of the Lower East Side constructed an ethnic identity with a socialist character.

Although the Jewish intellectuals were of diverse cultural and social background and political beliefs, they held a widespread aspiration to overthrow the capitalist system and construct a new social order along socialist principles. The group's intellectual origins were formed in the secular and revolutionary atmosphere of the Jewish Pale in the second half of the nineteenth century. Some members of the group were born into russified families that did not speak Yiddish and did not have much exposure to Jewish tradition and learning, including Philip Krantz (1858–1922), who became the editor of *Arbeiter Zeitung*, and David Edelstadt (1866–1933), the well-known Yiddish poet of the Lower East Side. Others, including Abraham Cahan (1860–1951) and Morris Winchevsky (1856–1932), grew up in traditionally Jewish homes and received a traditional Jewish education. Cahan learned Russian in secret against the will of his parents.[9] Upon their arrival in the United States, these young intellectuals experienced conditions no different from that of other immigrants. Many had to work in the clothing industry. Morris Hillquit, for example, later a lawyer and a leading socialist, became a shirtmaker and immersed himself in the life of the Lower East Side, where he acquired fluency in Yiddish and joined others in a commitment to the cause of revolutionary change.

Initially, the exiles from Russian political movements emphasized their internationalism. At annual conventions of the Jewish section of the Socialist Labor Party between the years 1891 and 1895, a banner was displayed reading "We are not Jewish socialists, but Yiddish-speaking socialists." Although politically shaped by their Russian experience and internationalist in their outlook, whether Marxist, anarchist, or socialist, many intellectuals ultimately became fully involved in the Jewish community and its concerns.[10] The Dreyfus Affair in 1897 and even more the Kishinev pogroms of 1903 and 1905 prompted a growing debate between the internationalists and those concerned with Jewish issues. Significantly, in 1905, the English-language newspaper *The Worker*, an organ of the Social Democratic Party, declared, "Homestead and Coeur d'Alene were battles of the twentieth century . . . Kishinev of the sixteenth century."[11] Similarly, following the 1903 outburst of pogroms, the *Zukunft* observed that "'Jewish Socialists' are quite a new species of humanity" who should not be taken too seriously, since the new identity is but a "temporary emotion." Reality, however, proved to be different with the growing ranks of those identifying with the "Jewish feeling" gaining ascendance in Jewish socialism.[12]

Affirmation by leading intellectuals of their Jewishness was above all due to the pragmatic need to gain an audience. That made the intelligentsia re-evaluate Yiddish as a means of political education and debate.[13] The lingua franca of the community, Yiddish, was a language that in the past had been disdained in favor of Russian culture and politics. Yiddish, reinvigorated by the American experience, was used by the intellectual vanguard not only to establish links to the Jewish community but, in the words of the historian Paul Buhle, to symbolize "a sort of realm of imagined liberation—a mental homeland."[14] The political content of that homeland was communicated powerfully through the Yiddish press, oratory, poetry, political activism, and the Yiddish theater.

The everyday living experience was transformed through the artistic expression of major poets, whose work was indissolubly linked to the community by virtue of its subject matter and its use of language. Both David Edelstadt and Morris Rosenfeld, unlike Morris Winchevsky, who made his living as a writer, worked in the garment industry and wrote about their experience. Addressing the world with a distinctive voice of common experience, these poets spoke for the people, striving to represent more than just their own feelings. Truly working-class poets, they were the interpreters of plebeian realities who created an "imaginary homeland of a people who could not imagine a secure home without the victory of world socialism."[15]

The Yiddish press, above all, was a premier medium of education and communication on issues concerning Jewish workers. The *Arbeiter Zeitung*, founded in 1890, the first Yiddish socialist paper of significance in America, was published under the auspices of the United Hebrew Trades and the Socialist Labor Party. Its credentials as the newspaper dedicated to the concerns of the working immigrants were soon established when, in the year of its founding, it provided its readers with a full and dramatic report of the nine-thousand-strong May Day march demanding an eight-hour workday. No less important to the paper's standing and popularity was its support for the numerous strikes, especially the cloakmakers' strike of that year.[16] The ability of the editors to communicate its political priorities and socialist principles using familiar and often traditional idioms in simple Yiddish, assured its growing popularity. The paper's founders, Abraham Cahan, Morris Hillquit, Louis Miller, and Bernard Weinstein, were soon joined by Philip Krantz, the poets David Edelstadt, Morris Winchevsky, and Morris Rosenfeld, Joseph Barondess, the well-known leader of the cloakmakers, and a host of orators, speakers, and teachers who preached and fought for unions, social justice, and socialism. Many of these activists were also the founders of the *Jewish Daily Forward* (1897), which promoted its own unique brand of socialism to an ever-growing readership.

The rising circulation of the socialist newspapers and journals—*Di Zukunft* (1892), best known as a socialist literary journal, and the daily *Abend Blatt* (1894)—all published under the auspices of the Arbeiter Zeitung Association, outstripped the readership of the anarchist *Freye Arbeter Shtimme* and, eventually, of the *Yudishes Tageblatt,* considered a bourgeois and orthodox paper. The success of the Yiddish socialist press reached new heights with the growing popularity of the *Jewish Daily Forward,* headed by Abraham Cahan.[17] Evidently, the socialist Yiddish press, with its commitment to unions, workers' struggles, and the education of its readership, successfully conveyed important and broadly accepted messages and political interpretations of the American experience. Commentaries in the *Arbeiter Zeitung* by Benjamin Feigenbaum and Morris Hilkowitz (Hillquit), for example, expressed timely concerns and successfully communicated the indignation and rebellion felt on the Jewish streets against the class of new despots and "slave dealers."[18] Exploiters among contractors and scabs had their names publicized, and special ads warned the public about their misdeeds.

The primary goal of the socialist press, to educate worker-readers, was central to the aspirations of the intellectual leadership. They wished to enlighten and westernize the Jewish masses. As noted by Hutchins Hapgood, Cahan's "career as an east side writer was primarily that of a teacher. He wished not merely to educate the ignorant masses of the people in the doctrines of Socialism, but to teach them the rudiments of science and literature." Cahan's aspiration to educate the masses was rooted in the Russian populist tradition of "going to the people," now transferred to the New York proletarians.[19] The widespread conviction that only enlightened workers would seek the goal of true socialist liberation inspired the educational project. Bringing to the Jewish masses the rudiments of secular learning with a universalist and socialist message through the medium of journalism was to become the main project of the socialist leadership. The monthly *Zukunft* undertook a mission to teach the worker "how he is oppressed economically and swindled politically" and to show him the road to liberation. Biographies and the teachings of Marx, Darwin, and a long list of heroes of the struggle for liberation of the human spirit filled the pages of the journal. Moreover, the papers printed reports of political unrest, especially the news of the 1905 Russian revolution, all news of interest to the readership and leading intellectuals.[20] Of no less value in the educational project was the role assigned to literature for its didactic value. "We always try to provide novels that ignite the minds of ordinary readers but are also good and realistic literature," proclaimed *Arbeiter Zeitung* in 1897.[21] Publication of realistic novels aimed to instruct readers and to bring them closer to the goal of socialism. Readers be-

Figure 6.1 Title page of the *Jewish Daily Forward,* 2 May 1897. The forces of Social
Democracy, carrying a banner calling for an eight-hour workday, charge
"Forward" against the fortress of capitalism to liberate its victims. YIVO
Institute for Jewish Research. Courtesy of Beth Hatefutsoth, Tel Aviv.

came familiar with Chekhov, Tolstoy, and Gorky in Yiddish translation. As Morris Raphael Cohen, the philosopher and teacher, remembered, he turned to *Arbeiter Zeitung* for intellectual stimulus, which he found in Abraham Cahan's articles on socialism, and also to learn about world literature, such as Flaubert's *Salammbo,* which he could read in translation.[22]

The ability of the editors, writers, and poets to convey the gospel of socialism; to express succinctly, in poetic language, sorrow and misery; to agitate and to arouse to action were legendary. Abraham Cahan's gift to communicate socialist ideas in plain style under the pen name *Der Proletarishker Magid* (the working-class preacher) made him a hero and a leader. Although considered by later critics as "coarse and primitive," the style and the simple explication of economic and political issues, especially when combined with Cahan's respect for religious and traditional sentiments, were effective tools of education.[23]

A similar ability to create an emotional bond with the Jewish audience was shared by the orators of the day. Cahan observed a new Jewish oratorical style when reporting in 1898 on an open-air Socialist meeting addressed by an Irishman, a German, and a Jew. The latter scored the biggest success, as Cahan noted: "Our people are so fond of public speeches and debates, and anybody who can make himself understood and has the knack of holding our attention is sure of an overcrowded meeting."[24] The packed meeting halls and the "haranguing" style of the speakers became a phenomenon remarked upon by the *New York Times,* which noted the large crowds following speakers from one hall to another. The oratory was interspersed with familiar references to enslavement and oppression, as in Barondess's greeting to the striking cloakmakers in 1894 as "fellow slaves."[25] Evoking Talmudic epigrams in his exhortation to action, Barondess's dramatic gifts were lost neither on his listeners nor on his critics.[26] Israel Barsky was another popular orator. In his political message, Barsky decried the narrow goals of unionism, advocating the inclusion of contractors in a broad-based labor organization. Like Jacob Gordin, the writer and theatrical producer, he also saw the theater as "irresistible" in attracting all members of the community, and therefore a powerful teaching weapon.[27] Barsky was frequently seen addressing large crowds in the Pig Market on Saturdays, where workers gathered to seek employment for the following week. Equally ubiquitous as a speaker and agitator was Benjamin Feigenbaum, whose special talent, in the words of Abraham Cahan, was to make a "socialist concept graphically clear" with a passage from the Bible or the Talmud.[28]

Like public meetings, which were often attended not only by workers but also by wives, children, and other members of the community, the audience would crowd into one of the many Lower East Side theaters to see realistic portrayals of their lives. In Hutchins Hapgood's description, "The sweatshop woman with her baby, the day laborer, the small Hester Street shopkeeper, the Russian-Jewish anarchist and socialist, the ghetto rabbi and scholar, the poet, the journalist. The poor and ignorant are in the great majority, but the learned, the intellectual, and the progressive are also represented."[29] Because of the popularity of the theater, Jewish intellectuals were passionate about its educational purposes. Jacob Gordin, for example, the best-known playwright, used to come on stage between the acts to deliver political commentaries on his plays. Abraham Cahan criticized the popular diversionary melodramas as *shund* (trash) and called for more realistic plays as part of his educational campaign of "teaching, leading, elevating the masses." According to Cahan, theatrical realism was fundamental to political activism in offering a social critique.[30] Consequently, all Socialist newspapers formulated a high-culture definition of good and bad theater and waged a war against the romantic melodramas of the period.

Contemporary observers of the Jewish community noted the importance of realism and the direct influence of the Yiddish theater on the community. Edward King, a novelist and playwright close to Abraham Cahan, remarked upon the phenomenon in his novel *Joseph Zalmonah*. The main events revolve around Zalmonah, a thinly disguised Joseph Barondess. The cloakmakers' struggles, which he led, are represented in the theatrical productions central to the book. The novel describes how contractors and sweatshop employers who attended a play dealing with exploitation were compelled to flee the theater, fearing the audience's wrath.[31]

The agitator, the speaker, the writer, the union organizer, who were sometimes one and the same, attracted admiration in the Jewish neighborhood.[32] Committed to the mission and the duty of enlightening the masses, the educated among them were revered as leaders and guides. It must be said that, for the most part, socialist leaders viewed the Jewish workers as "uncultured," childlike, and lacking in class consciousness. This clash between theory and practice was portrayed in *Joseph Zalmonah*, with striking cloakmakers distrusting socialists whose goal is the "Grand Revolution."[33] Nevertheless, these public figures successfully conveyed a political message sympathetic to immigrant aspirations. One newcomer's reaction to the socialist message is particularly telling:

> One Friday, going home from work (in children's jackets) and considering what paper to buy, I noticed a Yiddish paper with the name "Arbeiter Zeitung." I bought it and began to read it, and remarkable, this was the thing I wanted. . . . Although till then I never heard about socialism and its doctrine, still I understood it without any interpretation. I liked it because its ideas were hidden in my heart and in my soul long ago; only I could not express them clearly.[34]

A street culture of which strikes, boycotts, and campaigns were a part drew inspiration from many of the universalist notions expressed by socialist intellectuals like Abraham Cahan. Moreover, the oppositional culture redefined these abstract ideas into activism, which developed its own logic in the struggle against the "system." Landlords, employers, scabs, and shopkeepers became the targets of opposition, the focus of communal scrutiny, and they were penalized for breaking an unwritten moral code.

APPROPRIATING THE POWER OF THE LAW

The market economy divided the Lower East Side community. Battle lines were drawn between those who pursued individual financial gain and those who mobilized against what they perceived as injustices against working people, consumers, and other citizens. Employers and scabs, as well as profiteers such as butchers and landlords, were targeted for popular action. During their struggles to enforce the communal code of social justice in the workplace and marketplace, workers flouted old social norms: "Women don't count in times like these," shouted the strikers on one occasion, shoving aside the contractor's wife who was protecting his shop, thereby implying a concept of the greater social good overriding the rights of the individual.[35]

Strikes and other public actions, such as boycotts, parades, and demonstrations, symbolized a new, implicitly "ideological" politics. Sympathy strikes, though impromptu and sometimes poorly organized, and campaigns for victimized workers were often more effective in getting support than official actions. Strike leaders, who were the spokespeople for solidarity struggles, held unusual authority over the crowd, although they were not always official union appointees. "Two hundred ill-dressed men marched down Rivington Street and through Suffolk 4 P.M. yesterday," the *New York Sun* reported during the first known strike of Jewish cloakmakers in 1885. This strange contingent, headed by "a small man with a roll of paper," which was presumably a petition or declaration, was a scouting committee appointed by the strikers to inform cloakmakers of the strike and to call for a work stoppage. "Brothers, get up and stop work," announced a similar group of cloakmakers, who went from one shop to another in 1891, followed by bands of men, armed, according to one boss, with "long knives and shears," instantly recognizable tools of their trade.[36] These colorful parades were more than calls to strike action; they also enabled immigrant workers to organize collectively and to proclaim the validity of their symbolic code. Knives and shears were tools, but they also symbolized powerful weapons.

The 1886 cloakmakers' strike showed that the message of solidarity and identification with a new working-class code of behavior was addressed not only to workers in the same trade, but also to other members of the working class. Charles Katzenstein, an expressman whose job was to transport materials and finished garments, was threatened with a boycott for cooperating with employers working for manufacturers who refused to settle with the strikers. He was told to appear before the strikers' executive board: "In case you do not appear before this Board by 2 P.M. we will take suitable action to set a boycott on your business." Katzenstein appeared and was duly charged by the cloakmakers "with aiding their employers by carting materials and manufactured goods." The board also informed him that unless he paid a $1,000 fine, a boycott would be imposed, apparently because he had previously been guilty of a similar infringement for which he had been fined $100. In 1886, however, Katzenstein brought an action before Judge Duffy of the Essex Market Police Court, charging the members of the executive board with blackmail. Duffy issued a summons against three members of the board but eventually dismissed the charge because of insufficient evidence.[37] A similar example of workers' enforcing people's justice occurred during the 1891 cloakmakers' strike, when a contractor brought charges of harassment against two cloakmakers. A committee representing the union informed him that he had been fined $200 for prosecuting the men, and that unless he withdrew the charges, the union would blacklist his company.[38] Employers began to counter such tactics by calling on state institutions for legal redress against bribery and blackmail. Perhaps the best-known case of this kind occurred when the firm of Popkin and Marks had Joseph Barondess arrested for extortion, in retaliation for a $500 fine the union imposed after the 1891 cloakmakers' strike as a penalty for not abiding by the terms of the settlement.[39] Such worker-initiated measures against employers were not always effective and, at times, were even detrimental to labor's interests and were soon abandoned.

Other sorts of rough justice, such as machine sabotage, proved more effective. In 1885 and 1886, the cloakmakers walked out, carrying with them the main screw or other parts of sewing machines, effectively bringing work to a halt.[40] Similarly, "messing up" or strewing uncut pieces of garments, as well as more extreme acts of destruction and damage to goods, were successfully used to disrupt production. In one case, two hundred striking cloakmakers destroyed a batch of finished jackets produced in the shop of Billet, a contractor for Benjamin and Caspary, a firm that continued working after the strike was declared.[41] However, the tactic of outright destruction was abandoned after an 1891 incident that led to a series of legal charges against Barondess and ten other union leaders.[42] The ensuing trials and prison sentences did not damage Barondess's reputation, but the bad publicity the cloakmakers received did result in both a change of strategy and a desire for greater respectability, thus putting an end to organized sabotage.

To avoid confrontations with the legal system, strikers turned instead to a sympathetic community, with whose help they succeeded in intimidating their adversaries. Workers brandishing scissors, flatirons, revolvers, clubs, and old European bayonets would invade workplaces and assault bosses and scabs, sometimes pursuing them into neighborhood streets to attack and abuse them in public. Usually, neither scabs nor unpopular employers, many of whom had connections with the neighborhood, could escape popular revenge, despite police protection. The 1894 cloakmakers' strike, like many others, was charged with violence. Scabs hired by Jonasson were confronted daily by demonstrators, many of them women, who gathered in front of the factory to "greet" the strikebreakers as they arrived or left work. They attacked the working girls, "tearing their hair and clothing and endeavoring to maul their faces." Male strikebreakers received a similar "welcome" from the women who, ignoring the police, attacked them and tore their whiskers.[43] Zetta Bloomberg, one of the women arrested following the attack, had a record of similar assaults. When asked, "Why did you engage in such an affair as this?" she answered passionately, "How can I help it? My children cry for bread, I ask my husband for food to give them. He says, 'Can I take the flesh off my bones to feed them? What else have I when my place is taken?' So I go out to fight for him."[44] Another group explained their attacks on women strikebreakers: "Those women had no right to take our places, and the only way to stop them is to frighten them."[45]

Although anonymous crowds played a central role in punitive forays against scabs and employers, occasionally attacks were more personal. For example, striking workers sometimes followed and tormented former employers who hired strikebreakers, or vented their anger on scabs, who were held responsible for taking away their livelihood.[46] Sometimes scabs had their homes invaded and their lives threatened. Strikers claimed the right to use moral and physical force against their foes, without making any distinction between public issues such as pay and prices or the private spheres of home or individual behavior. The Lower East Side was entirely appropriated by the working community during protests. Strikers could easily locate and identify strikebreakers—as in the case of a 1896 work stoppage, when they identified fellow cloakmakers who wanted to return to work—put them under house arrest, and kept them incarcerated. During the violent strike of 1894, two workers broke into the home of two women strikebreakers and beat them "severely." In a later incident, during the 1910 waistmakers' strike, the workers initiated an intimidation campaign against a scab by calling on his wife four or five times a day, demanding to know her husband's whereabouts and threatening to kill him "on sight."[47] During the same strike, a scab's wife reported that two women and a man forced their way into her apartment, threatening to kill her and her four children unless she persuaded her husband to return from Philadelphia.[48]

It was difficult to escape the community's censure. When employers, trying to evade the constant threat of attacks by strikers, attempted to pass work on to subcontractors, word got around and their shops were duly attacked. Paradoxically, occasionally even scabs were known to help strikers. In one case, despite the prompt arrival of the police on the scene, the strikers, who were about to attack the scabs, were joined by the strikebreakers so that all escaped arrest.[49] Some contractors thought that removing their business from the Lower East Side would give them greater freedom of action. Those who attempted to escape the reign of terror, the frequent strikes and struggles, hoped to find a safe haven in Brooklyn, Queens, Yonkers, and Long Island. Strikers, however, continued to hound their traditional adversaries—scabs and exploitative employers—pursuing them relentlessly wherever they went. The 1891 cloakmakers' strike became notorious because of the strikers' forays from the Lower East Side against employers such as Greenbaum and Billet, who had moved to Jamaica, Long Island. On another occasion, scabs working in Jamaica were forced against their will by a group of forty strikers to go to New York to listen to "incendiary speeches." During the same strike, police were alerted to a group of one hundred defiant cloakmakers who reportedly were leaving Manhattan "to do some persuading" in the Brownsville shops.[50] Yet another incident that year involved the contracting shop of the Vogel brothers, who got round the workers' demands by moving uptown to 157th Street and hiring thirty scabs. Eight strikers, all former employees, went to the shop with a bulldog at closing time and attacked the owners who, "holding each other's hands for courage," shook "like leaves in the wind."[51] In the same year, at the height of Joseph Barondess's popularity, Meyer Jonasson threatened to open a factory in Berlin, "where there will be no Barondess to keep our people in turmoil."[52]

Violence was also used against those who profiteered through the workings of the market economy, especially in cases where shop owners could raise prices substantially because of a predictably high demand. Butchers and landlords who charged prices beyond an "acceptable" level became targets for reprisals. The 1902 kosher meat riots were the most dramatic of these community protests, which encroached not only on the shops but also on the homes of consumers who violated the boycott. A 50 percent increase in meat prices triggered the riots.[53] Although small butchers attempted to mount an opposition against the meat trusts, they soon settled their dispute by reaching a mutually satisfactory agreement with the wholesalers. Lower East Side women, who were determined to reduce the exorbitant prices to a previous, more acceptable level, engaged in a highly successful and well-publicized struggle.[54] As one protestor stated, "Our husbands work hard. They try their best to bring a few cents into the house. We must manage to spend as little as possible. We will not give away our last few cents to the butchers and let our children go barefoot."[55]

The charged language used in boycotts, with words like *strikers* and *scabs,* had no obvious connections with the workplace. Demonstrators engaged in the widespread destruction of meat to punish those butchers who cooperated with the meat trusts. The issue of meat was of key public concern. The struggles spread from the Lower East Side and other parts of Manhattan to Brooklyn as boycotters attempted to rouse the public against butchers and their patrons. The boycotting women and their sympathizers, who described themselves as community "soldiers" and "strikers," brought terror to those who did not join the struggle, denouncing them as "scabs." Even sabotage was used as a tactic during the kosher meat boycott. Women besieged butchers' shops, pouring kerosene, oil, and carbolic acid on the goods.[56] In Brooklyn, as in Manhattan and the Bronx, enraged consumers went from shop to shop determined to close down businesses. In one instance, angry boycotters in Brooklyn dragged huge sides of meat from their hooks and trampled upon them, while others threw the meat into the street, using it to play football. In another incident, chunks of meat were hurled at the police who were trying to keep the protesters at bay, while other demonstrators impaled the meat on painted sticks, carrying it around "like red flags."[57] Meat purchasers "met with the mob's fury." When spared from violent attacks, they were followed through the neighborhood and forced to surrender what they had bought. According to one report from Brooklyn, after crowds of protesters finished sacking butcher shops, they entered private homes, "picking up whatever meat they could find to throw on the street where it was caught and pitched about and trampled upon."[58] When asked by a judge, "What do you have against a woman who has bought meat?" one woman who had been arrested for disorderly conduct defended herself by citing the indissoluble bonds between the individual and the community. She argued that meat consumers ignored the community's welfare: "It doesn't matter to me what others want to do. But it's because of others that we must suffer."[59]

Just as riotous was the kosher bakers' strike of 1905. Although it was initiated to achieve strictly industrial targets of a ten-hour workday (to replace the oppressive twelve- to twenty-hour workday), closed shop, and a new wage scale, the battles that ensued involved strikers and sympathizers from the community. Despite the severe shortages of kosher bread, especially the favorite pumpernickel bread, forays against bakers who continued to work occurred daily.[60] Strike sympathizers stuffed the chimney of one shop that refused to comply with old quilts, and in another poured oil into the ovens, thus effectively stopping production. Workers who were found kneading dough despite the strike were "dragged out and disciplined." The dough was drenched in kerosene or thrown about. Sympathizers, among them many women, took part in these disciplinary actions. When a rumor spread that a pushcart full of freshly baked bread concealed under blankets was making its way through the neighborhood, "word flashed around to the strikers and a yelling mob soon filled the street, smashing the cart and trampling upon it." Those in charge of the cart were stripped of their clothes and their bread

Figure 6.2 Members of the Hebrew Bakers' Union vote to continue their strike. *New York Herald*, 10 August 1905. General Research Division, New York Public Library, Astor, Lenox and Tilden Foundations.

thrown into the street.[61] Not surprisingly, retailers, fearful of retiliation, refused to buy bread brought over from bakeries in other locations.

The tenants' movement of 1907 and 1908 provided another important example of community action. Initiated in opposition to high rents, the movement questioned the right of landlords to unlimited profits. A forerunner of the 1907 to 1908 action was a similar incident in 1894, when striking cloakmakers opposed the payment of rent on principle while they themselves had no income. That year, some landlords had sympathized enough with tenants to agree to forego the collection of rents, but in 1895 they were encouraged by employers to reject any compromise.[62] The frequent rent increases, on the Lower East Side and in other Jewish neighborhoods, fanned public protest. In 1905, antilandlord posters in English and Yiddish were displayed frequently, and several demonstrations were organized against landlord-speculators who bought buildings and then raised rents. In one instance, angry crowds besieged a landlord's apartment, throwing stones and mud at his windows, because he had increased the rent and served dispossession notices on forty families who refused to pay it. On the day of the scheduled evictions, the entire block was in an uproar and a large, stone-throwing crowd gathered again outside the landlord's apartment.[63]

From 1907 to 1908, a period of economic depression and unemployment, an all-out war against landlords flared up. A rent strike mobilized one hundred thousand people and spread to Harlem, Brooklyn, and Newark.[64] The community became the main base for action and won the support of the Socialist Party and the Eighth Assembly District, as well as of several unions.[65] Yet, while the strike fever spread rapidly, the walkout was initiated at block level. As Pauline Newman remembered, "We lived so close together we knew each other. And everybody agreed that they really could not give the landlord the increase in rent. And so by word of mouth you got everyone from the same street and from the next street and we called a meeting."[66] At one meeting organized by the strikers, landlords received a rough reception. One, who had argued that the houses he owned were his property and that "he had the right to ask whatever he wants for his merchandise," was shouted down and forced to leave the platform. A resolution was passed to compel landlords to decrease rents "to an affordable level," followed by a demand to decrease the rent by 20 to 30 percent. Openly defiant tenants, who hung red flags and posters from their windows and fire escapes, called on others to boycott landlords who evicted tenants. These acts in turn provoked violent confrontations with landlords, who had the full support of the police and the help of hired East Side thugs.[67] Rent strikes like those of 1894 and 1907 to 1908 were partly caused by structural economic crises during depressions that heightened financial hardship among the poor, but these revolts also expressed popular notions of fairness and justice. Communal demonstrations of moral outrage against the power of the profit motive expressed the dynamic character of local politics.

THE JEWISH COMMUNITY AND ESTABLISHED JUSTICE

The Jewish community's ethical code clashed with profit-based principles when it came to struggles between employers and employees. The community counterposed its own code against the courts, police, and other law-enforcement agencies, which were regarded as natural protectors of employers' rights rather than upholders of impartial justice. The small-time employer, trying to counter the violence of the East Side crowds, resorted to such weapons as scissors, shears, and, on occasion, guns, but the bigger manufacturers turned to either the police for help or hired protection by Pinkertons. During the 1894 cloakmakers' strike, for example, Police Superintendent Thomas Byrnes promised the manufacturers full cooperation in protecting factories from attack. Policemen guarding scabs became a common sight. The strikebreakers employed at Friedman's, a large cloak manufacturer, had to be escorted to their homes or the streetcar by the police. Similarly, during the 1896 tailors' strike, policemen were stationed near the workplaces of contractors who resumed work.[68] "The police, who are the bosses' partners in every strike, stand ready to break the heads of strikers," thundered the *Forward* during the bakers' strike of 1905.[69] However, police presence did not deter crowds; on the contrary, the sight of a "hostile policeman on guard" was sufficient to provoke the demonstrators. Crowds exploded against the police, who sided with employers and rarely troubled to protect the Jewish population when it was attacked by local thugs or Irish "loafers."[70] In 1891, policemen who had tried to arrest strikers harassing scabs entered a cloak factory on Broadway and provoked the rage of "a small mob who swooped down upon a policeman to recover their comrade" and beat the policeman badly. Although the strikers were ultimately deterred by the threat of force, the hostile throng marched with their arrested comrades to the police station. In a similar incident, during an 1894 tailors' strike, the crowd fury turned on a Jewish policeman who tried to disperse strikers assembled near the tailors' headquarters on Suffolk Street. A crowd of people who "seemed to rise out of the ground" began pushing and hitting the policeman to free the prisoner. The policeman was finally rescued by a reserve force who arrived on the scene. During a cloakmakers' strike the same year, an off-duty policeman who tried to prevent the assault of 150 strikers on a tenement at 316 Delancey Street, which housed a large number of scabs, was clubbed and beaten mercilessly by an angry crowd shouting, "He is a policeman, do him up."[71]

The 1902 meat boycott, although primarily directed at butchers, was also accompanied by public outbursts against the police. Officers who came to protect butchers and their property were greeted with flying pieces of meat. In one case, a policeman who tried to make an arrest faced a furious crowd that "tore his clothing to rags, broke his helmet and tried to pull him down on the ground, when they would have made short work of him." He finally managed to escape under a shower of rocks, vegetables, eggs, and meat. Another time, a policeman using force was attacked by a crowd that took away his helmet and club and paraded them as trophies.[72] In a related incident, a large-scale battle against the police ensued after several officers, under the pretext of clearing the street, began clubbing boycotters "below their waists." On the following day, a huge crowd of three thousand gathered in front of the Essex Market Police Court, hissing and shouting at policemen who were protecting the butchers.[73] Demonstrations near the law courts became a regular civic spectacle of hostility against the police and the judicial system. Arrests provoked hostile crowds that followed those arrested through the neighborhood to the police station. When five striking cloakmakers were arrested in 1885, a "mob" of three hundred strikers marched to the police station and demanded either their release or imprisonment for the entire group. During the 1896 tailors' strike, "a howling crowd" of five hundred followed those who had been arrested. After being dispersed, they reassembled in a more peaceful mood.[74]

Those who sought the protection of the law and used it to press charges against workers, strikers, and other offenders were singled out for particular hatred. Crowds assembled in front of the law courts and police stations to hurl insults and threaten and attack such individuals. During the 1886 coatmakers' strike, striker Calman Klein was arrested for entering a shop and resisting removal. He was later charged and released on $300 bail and instructed to keep the peace for one month. The verdict infuriated the strikers, who followed him to the courthouse and taunted the contractor who had pressed the charges with cries of "Hang him! String him up!" The plaintiff had to resort to the protection of police, who escorted him to safety. A similar form of intimidation convinced Bernard Steague, a coat contractor, not to press charges against the workers who stormed his shop.[75] During the 1909 coatmakers' strike, Hyman Horn, also a contractor, pleaded with the magistrate not to send the seven offenders to jail "as it might tend to injure him." The men were duly discharged.[76] The police were equally unsuccessful in other attempts to press the law or prevent violence on the Lower East Side. Police Inspector Byrnes, well known for his brutality and friendly relations with the underworld, confessed that he was unable to prevent riots but argued that he was applying moderation tactically. He declared that unlike the New York longshoremen or carmen, Jewish cloakmakers were incompetent and lacked the courage for "a decent riot" and that they "wiggle about like so many eels, and it's the hardest thing to get your hand on them."[77]

Rank-and-file militancy contrasted with moderate union leaders' more respectable strike tactics aimed at avoiding harsh prison sentences or fines. The 1910 strike instructions, for example, advised workers: "Pick no argument and enter into no discussion with employers, with members of the firm or with other employees. . . . Show the world that you are an organized, disciplined, well-behaved body who know your rights and are law-abiding citizens."[78] However, the cloakmakers disregarded the new strike rules, although the penalties for doing so, which included fines and committal to a workhouse, were unusually harsh. A vigil by a crowd of four hundred near Joseph D. Wein's factory, which took place in contravention of police warnings, was accompanied by shouts of, "We have killed generals in Russia and may be able to do better in this country." The same strike witnessed assaults on employers and scabs, as well as the destruction of property. Ultimately, some cloak manufacturers were forced to close their businesses rather than risk more violent confrontations involving scabs, strikers, and the police.[79]

The contested terrain, both geographical and political, was expressed in the activities of the crowd. As in so many other historical examples, the much reviled mob behavior gave a concrete reality to the political aspirations of the Jewish community. Group actions not only expressed the immigrant needs for work, food, and shelter, but also proclaimed a distinctive value system. They called into question the allocation of power, whereby the rule of law inevitably was on the side of the "big battalions" of business. Their leaders noted that violence had often succeeded in restricting the power of those in authority.

COMMUNITY AS AN ECONOMIC AND SOCIAL WEAPON

The clashes with the courts and police reinforced the community's traditional mistrust of state institutions, brought from Eastern Europe, where autocratic rule denied citizens access to the political process. On American soil, Jewish immigrants were able to make political gains by extending their range of civic participation. Through strikes and other public acts, their ideological perspectives evolved in relation to the American legal and political system. Their power lay in organic community institutions such as synagogues and mutual-aid societies, as well as labor unions. Jewish immigrant workers distrusted the legal and executive agencies of the state and, unlike their American counterparts, rarely took up the option of lobbying local or state political offices. Instead, they turned to broad-based neighborhood support to bolster their cause.[80] It was evident to members of the Lower East Side community that they had to rely on their own institutions for help during periods of prolonged privation. This mutual loyalty and support was reinforced through political acts such as strikes and boycotts, which were often accompanied by violence, contravening against the law, and rough justice against public enemies. They could not call on either the state or welfare organizations, such as Jewish charitable bodies organized outside the community.

In contrast, the more established, Americanized skilled workers looked to political institutions for redress. The 1890 cloakmakers' strike illustrates how the cutters, who represented a more settled craft section of the garment workers, appealed to the law and the institutions of the state, using language based on republican ideals.[81] The strike began after two large cloak manufacturers discharged some of their workers because of their union activity. Soon operators, and later, cutters, employed by Meyer Jonasson joined the strike. The members of the Manufacturers' Association followed suit and locked out all their workers. At the strike's outset, Charles Miller of the Clothing Cutters' Union submitted a resolution condemning the Manufacturers' Association as a capitalist organization that sought to destroy the workers. According to Miller, the Association was not to be tolerated in "a civilized Commonwealth" because it caused the destitution of women and children.[82] His union sent a petition to the mayor of New York demanding his support and the abolition of the Association. During the same strike, James P. Archibald, secretary of the Central Labor Union, alleged that politics and republican ideals had been corrupted and demanded that honorific functions be reserved for deserving "fathers of the City." A union-sponsored mass meeting called upon the mayor to remove Abraham Schwab, a prominent manufacturer and a leading member of the despised Manufacturers' Association, from his position as trustee of the Brooklyn Bridge, and to replace him with "a gentleman of more humane feeling and disposition than is shown by Mr. Schwab toward his underpaid and underfed slaves."[83]

The cutters invoked the aid of the grand jury, which repeatedly sided with the employers. As the strike continued, the locked-out cutters tried to indict the Manufacturers' Association for conspiracy on the grounds that it prevented them from pursuing their trade because they belonged to a union. However, to the dismay of the cutters and the general public alike, a grand jury refused to indict the Association. "These skilled cloakmakers came to America in order to better their condition, and having learned by experience what a republican form of government meant" had an absolute right to unionize, remarked the *World,* adding pointedly that members of the grand jury included William Rockefeller and other officials representing corporations and trusts.[84] The public's support for the strikers was further underscored on July 12 when, in an editorial entitled "The Rights of Man," the *World* expressed the widely held critique of the grand jury's verdict. Other allegations of corruption by business interests followed, including the accusation that the jury system had been transformed from a "bulwark of liberty to a fortress of injustice in the hands of capitalists, and is now used in administration of criminal law against the poor and in favor of the rich."[85] The grand jury's failure to indict the Association, along with the antilabor remarks of the jury foreman who openly stated, "I am not in favor of unions," caused fury in labor circles and encouraged further protests. It also prompted appeals for a more impartial system of justice, where labor and capital could compete on a more economically and legally equitable footing. These appeals, which exemplified labor's general strategy, criticized business for corrupting state institutions and republican ideals. At a mass meeting of strikers attended by Samuel Gompers, a resolution was passed calling for the abolition of the grand jury system "as a relic of English feudal barbarism which should have no place in our American judicial system." The cutters also resolved to call upon the state of New York to "aid and defend the life and interest of its citizens who are the backbone of the republic."[86]

However, the bulk of the Jewish strikers, who did not belong to the elite cutters and who showed plainly the "pinch of hunger," expressed their militancy in community-oriented actions. Rather than appeal to the city's institutions, every Friday night, the beginning of the Jewish Sabbath, the strikers would hold mass meetings vowing to begin the strike "anew." The immigrant cloakmakers refused to follow the example of the cutters and enthusiastically voted to reject their settlement because it did not include the firing of all strikebreakers. The scene of the vote was unforgettable for Abraham Rosenberg, according to whom all those participating in the meeting, whether strikers or not, donated all they could afford—earrings, watches, rings—for the benefit of the strikers.[87] Similar differences in strategy were underscored during the 1902 struggle against the rocketing prices of the meat trusts waged by Lower East Side inhabitants and many other working people throughout New York. The issue became the concern of the general public, even the city's Board of Aldermen—who at one point condemned the trust, which worked "to enrich the greedy corporations" and to weaken "the strength of the working men." Furthermore, the board demanded that the federal and state authorities stop the "unlawful conspiracy for private gain in a food which is an actual necessity for the working classes of the city."[88] Copies of its resolution were sent to the U.S. president, the U.S. attorney general, the governor, and the New York state attorney general.[89] Initially, Jewish meat boycotters also appealed to the district attorney, but through direct action, besieging his home and ringing his bell incessantly until late at night. The boycotters believed that the district attorney would listen to the pleas of women consumers, since he lived on Rutgers Street and was also a member of the neighborhood community. But their petition went unanswered; instead, the district attorney accused the protesters of "proving themselves bad citizens."[90] This failed attempt to get redress by means of democratic lobbying was followed by the full-fledged war declared by women against butchers and meat consumers already described. Jewish tenants also began the rent strike of 1905 and 1906 in a remarkably restrained manner, by bringing the dispute to the attention of their alderman in the 12th district assembly. Soon, as with the meat boycott, this action escalated into more violent community agitation and defiant protests against the landlords.[91] During the kosher bakers' strike of 1905, the strikers, who had been attacked by thugs of the notorious Monk Eastman gang hired by employers, decided to petition the city's mayor. They moved to do so in light of the clear favoritism of the political establishment to the employers; they demanded to be given police protection equal to that provided to the employers.[92]

Strikes and militancy depended on the community's generosity and financial support, which provided crucial help in the absence of stable unions with large strike reserves. Often in ideological rivalry with each other, Jewish unions hardly were in a position to extend more than symbolic help to strikers. Appealing to workers in other trades to send contributions, as well as imposing payments on those workers whose firms had already settled, were two ways to ensure minimal financial help.[93] Sometimes the support elicited was pitifully small. In 1892, for example, Jonasson's cloakmakers received a relatively large contribution of $580.15 from other unions and cloakmakers. The employees in Jonasson's Woodbine branch, on the other hand, received only $32.50. The Shirtmakers' Union of New York gave an even smaller contribution of $5.15 together with $2.85 to striking tailors in Baltimore.[94] Direct appeals to those who returned to work brought more substantial results, as in the case of tailors who donated 15 percent of their earnings to the 1895 strikers and an additional countrywide assessment of 25 cents per worker. This strike was officially led by the United Garment Workers (UGW), a national organization that included numerous trades in the men's clothing industry.[95] Assistance from non-Jewish unions, however, was mostly unavailable. Even the famous 1891 cloakmakers' strike, led by Barondess, did not succeed in eliciting a positive response. And in 1894, a year of great privation among striking cloakmakers, United Garment Workers refused to help on the grounds of alleged "bad [strike] management" and the strikers' failure to organize properly. The 1894 strike and its leaders were denounced by the Central Federation of Labor as "a farce" because workers in non-union shops had been illegally enrolled onto union registers.[96] The meat boycotters in 1902 were equally unsuccessful in rallying support from New York unions. At a meeting of the Amalgamated Sheet Metal Workers' Union, one delegate proposed a resolution calling on workers to stop buying meat. In response, the socialist leader of the Cigar Makers' Union claimed that working men could not live without meat, and so the motion was defeated by socialist supporters.[97] There was no certainty that the officially designated charitable societies, a potential source of help, would support Jewish strikers on the Lower East Side. Maintained and financed mainly by German Jews with ties to the clothing manufacturers, these philanthropies proved unwilling to furnish "the sinews of war to the enemy." Thus, they subjected all applicants for assistance to rigorous scrutiny during the punishing strike of 1894. Labor activists were denied help and must "be held responsible for their own suffering," maintained the charities' spokesmen.[98]

At the grassroots level, members of the Jewish community were more generous toward the strikers, providing their main source of support during times of need. Their assistance often was unstinting. "The neighbors on the East Side in strike affairs are not stingy," was one contemporary's impression in 1904.[99] Throughout the aforementioned 1890 cloakmakers' strike, the non-Jewish public also showed its support by taking up collections in churches and asking for donations in the city's newspapers. A Jewish congregation offered cheap dinners to cloakmakers with union cards.[100] During the 1893 economic crisis, the United Hebrew Trades (UHT) channeled relief in kind to the hungry and unemployed through members of the community. Many butchers, doctors, bakers, and restaurants provided free food or services to anyone presenting a ticket from the UHT, or about as many as four hundred families daily. Similar community support existed in Brownsville, where individual donations of food were distributed through workers' groups, which called upon all those who were in need and too embarrassed to beg to come forward for assistance.[101] In 1894, the second consecutive year of depression and during a prolonged cloakmakers strike, the local Jewish community again provided assistance to the impoverished strikers. In contrast, the AFL and Samuel Gompers disapproved of the strike and did not offer support to the cloakmakers. Although the UGW approved the financial assistance to strikers, it eventually reversed its decision after hearing an adverse report on the strike's outcome. Eugene V. Debs was the one dissenter who supported the strike and compared it to the American Railway Union strike.[102] Refused help by the UGW as well as the AFL, and with a steadily diminishing strike fund, the workers depended on the many restaurants that distributed dinner tickets, as well as on the barbers, owners of Turkish baths, and doctors who provided free services.[103] The cloakmakers themselves established a relief depot, distributing flour, potatoes, sugar, herrings, and coffee contributed by sympathizers. Even some Lower East Side contractors contributed money to strikers.[104]

Landlords' attitudes toward strikers who owed back rent varied. Those facing eviction because they owed one to three months' back rent were sometimes shown leniency by sympathetic landlords and judges. However, other landlords formed a protective association against defaulting and militant tenants. Members each contributed $25 to the organization and agreed that no landlord would rent an apartment to tenants who could not show receipts for their last rent payment. It became clear by January 1895 that emergency funds and gifts of food from the community, which itself had been suffering from the strains of economic depression, could not meet the strikers' needs.[105] Support for the long strike eventually dwindled as the winter ended, when all hope of reemployment was lost. The defeated workers were only saved from destitution thanks to the Society for the Improvement of the Condition of the Poor, a non-Jewish charitable society that spent $10,000 to pay hundreds of strikers to clear snow.[106] The original plan of channeling payment for public works, to be performed by needy Jewish workers, through the United Hebrew Charities was abandoned quickly. Revealingly, the community preferred to be beholden to a non-Jewish society rather than the United Hebrew Charities, whose links with employers in the garment industry were well known.[107]

In addition to providing essential, if limited, financial assistance, the Lower East Side community was an invaluable ally in political battles. On numerous occasions, in contests with employers or against profiteers, groups resorted to the weapon of public censure. Labor newspapers, unions, local networks, public demonstrations, and violent protests were among the tactics used to shame the transgressors. Workers were able to publicize their grievances and thus mobilize the community's public opinion. In 1898, thirty-three striking families from Brownsville cooperated to publish their grievances against their employer and to "blacklist" him. People who did not heed such warnings were described as having "sold out their brothers" and were branded in the labor press as shameless scabs.[108] Employers' malpractices were advertised far and wide as a warning to others. One employer, who had embezzled wages, was branded in the press:

> Brothers and sisters, do not fall into the claws of a tiger! The boss who took your wages wants you to forget that he took $250 from our poor workers and he opened a shop in Newark and he wants to open another shop in Bayonne. Shirtmakers, be warned and don't go to seek work there![109]

Appeals to boycott employers were supplemented by admonitions to shun their other services. Underpaid buttonholemakers, on strike in 1886, issued an appeal to boycott a bakery and grocery owned by their employer. This threat prompted the employer to write in a letter to the *Sun* stating that although "he didn't care for labor organizations," he could prove that he paid his employees as much as $25 to $30 a week and not $6 to $7 as was alleged.[110] In 1892, strikers called for a boycott of a restaurant owned by a "scab suspender boss" if he didn't recognize the union. Boycotts against shops and also against theaters and music halls in 1891 and 1893 were widely advertised and publicly supported.[111] However, if labor reprimanded its enemies, it also rewarded its friends. For example, during the 1886 cloakmakers' strike, expressmen Goldberg and Siegler received strikers' praise and thanks for withholding their services from the manufacturers.[112] Some boycotts were extremely effective. In 1904, a landlord who owned two buildings on East 12th Street increased rents and evicted nineteen families. Although he was successful in reletting the apartments to "scab" tenants, a community boycott of his grocery store was so successful that ultimately he was forced out of business.[113]

All such oppositional activities were locally organized. An appeal for a nationwide consumers' and workers' boycott, which potentially could have been effective in their struggle, was of limited use because it required a high degree of national organization.[114] In general, it was the cutters, the best-organized craft within the clothing business, who used this weapon most effectively. In 1893, cutters employed by Alfred Benjamin organized a nationwide boycott of their employer's cloaks, a boycott which damaged the company's business and resulted in a lockout. Similarly, in the same year, a cutters' boycott, supported by other clothing workers who refused to work on garments cut by scabs, successfully persuaded buyers throughout the country to return their goods to the manufacturers. In response, the manufacturers sought to use the law to prevent the cutters from issuing boycott circulars, but the court refused to grant an injunction.[115] In 1901, the cutters again embarked on a boycott of goods from Cohen, Goldman, and Co. In circulars sent to the firm's out-of-town buyers, they described its sweating methods and threatened to inform all workers in their areas about the firm's "obnoxious products." As a result, the firm suffered serious losses.[116]

Unlike the cutters, unskilled workers who lacked national backing supplemented local economic sanctions and boycotts with social ostracism through public denunciations and symbolic parades that stigmatized labor's opponents. These public denunciations "against individuals who offended against certain community norms" were reminiscent of *charivari,* or rough music, described by E. P. Thompson, although they used noisy insults rather than the musical format.[117] These attacks were a form of social retribution that penalized offenders by ridicule. The public nature of this ostracism made it a powerful weapon. Scabs who "sold out their brothers" faced the threat of having their names branded in the labor press.[118] In 1904, a particularly dramatic example of strikebreakers' public humiliation occurred when a woman striker denounced her own brother and father as cowards in front of a crowd of tailors gathered near their headquarters.[119]

Another powerful tactic that required careful organizing was picketing, which was extensively used during the 1894 cloakmakers' strike and achieved favorable results. Although employers attempted to send work to outlying communities, strikers successfully picketed the striking shops and kept a close watch over the interborough ferries to prevent scabs, identifiable by their sewing machines, from reaching Manhattan. Brownsville and Brooklyn were under virtual siege. Those who wished to come to Manhattan needed a pass and were met by picketing groups who guarded the elevated stations. Those scabs who succeeded in reaching Manhattan to work for New York manufacturers had a "welcome they will never forget" when they went back to Brownsville to see their families on weekends. According to Rosenberg's account, they returned to their homes in police wagons, accompanied by a dozen policemen riding in front and back. Men, women, and children of Brownsville went out to "welcome" the scabs, carrying black candles, an old-world symbol alerting the community to the danger of epidemic or plague, as well as a symbol of social ostracism. They shouted in Hebrew, "Righteousness delivers from death." The scabs did not dare to leave their homes and needed police protection on Sunday, when they had to be re-escorted to Manhattan.[120]

Workers often initiated such campaigns to intimidate, single out, and isolate scabs. During the cloakmakers' strike of 1891, which began against the firms of Blumenthal and Co. and Benjamin and Caspary, the particularly effective "Committee No. 1" was organized by the strikers. The committee took upon itself the picketing of firms in outlying areas that accepted work from the Manhattan firms paralyzed by the strike.[121] The committee also terrorized a scab working for the firm of Benjamin and Caspary, who was followed by an "ugly and threatening group" wherever he went.[122] The effectiveness of these and other campaigns of social ostracism was dramatically illustrated by the tragic case of Joseph Katzman, a tailor of good union standing. In 1897, being the financial mainstay of his family, he felt he had to continue working despite a strike and pleas from his fellow workers to join the walkout. The striking tailors turned Katzman's life into "a burden" by jeering and calling "hard names" whenever he appeared in the street. Ultimately, he was forced to leave his family, possibly to spare them embarrassment, took a room in a hotel and committed suicide by jumping from a third-floor window.[123]

In 1902, meat strikers and protesters targeted synagogues as strategic arenas for public condemnation of butchers. Women played a central role in these actions, making public appearances in the synagogues to appeal to the male congregants to discourage their wives from buying meat, despite rabbinical objections to the violent tactics employed by women during the boycott.[124] During the 1894 cloakmakers' strike, workers followed two scabs into their synagogue, where they proceeded to denounce them to the congregation.[125] These and similar provocations brought about a police watch near synagogues during an 1896 strike.[126] In 1907, cloakmakers striking against Simon and Co. resorted to similar tactics during prayers at a synagogue their employer attended, informing the congregation of his "good deeds" and pleading with them to ostracize him. For a while, Simon stopped attending the synagogue for fear of his life, but subsequently he received police protection when attending the synagogue on the High Holidays.[127]

Class loyalties and divisions were also expressed in the synagogue. The case of the Dorf brothers shows how social conflict undermined family cohesiveness. During his first days as an immigrant, Max Dorf was assisted by his two brothers. Soon he progressed to becoming a cloak manufacturer and a man of standing in his community and synagogue where, with the support of his two brothers, he was elected vice president. However, in his shop he paid his brothers starvation wages for a sixty-hour work week. Max Dorf's brothers joined a strike against him. He vowed not to give them work again, complaining that they were socialists and were after a share of his wealth. One Saturday, when the whole family came to pray at their Broome Street synagogue, the two brothers and a cousin, also an employee of the company, staged a public walkout, making their protest clear to all those attending the services.[128] The walkout recalled a nineteenth-century form of protest when Jewish journeymen rebelled against better-off, established artisans by leaving their synagogues. Like their nineteenth-century counterparts, the employees of Max Dorf joined a friendlier congregation on Pitt Street. Having broken with their old synagogue, the two brothers continued to torment their brother by maintaining occasional noisy vigils outside his synagogue.[129]

Conclusion

The first wave of emigrants had left behind, in their homeland in Russia, a repressive political regime as well as their own traditional community elites; both of which denied them political participation. Coming to America opened up new opportunities for democratic participation within the new ethnic community and in the wider social sphere. In due course, immigrants transformed their way of life by entering the world of wage labor and mass consumption, adapting their political culture and language to contest a wider political terrain. Women were full participants in this process. In the context of new economic opportunities, Jewish women transformed the customary gender expectations, such as their contribution to the family economy, into personal empowerment.[1] As the old social arrangements dissolved and new arenas for popular participatory politics and agitation became available, the newcomers, men and women, found a new way to interpret their social and political circumstances in a manner consistent with the core concept of universal rights. This ideal derived from ties to their community, craft solidarity, and commonality of wage-earning experience. The solidarity and mutuality inherent in community membership was not a given or "fixed" characteristic marking Jewish ethnicity that was simply "transferred" from the home community. It evolved through the process of migration and settlement. The webs of formal and informal mutuality and support within the Jewish immigrant community inspired a new political perspective of universality and equality that found expression in struggles over rights in the workplace, the administration of the law, the use of public spaces, and the formulation of a new political vocabulary. Membership in the ethnic community, for the first generation of immigrants, overlapped with the solidarity inherent in the nature of the garment industry and its army of semiskilled and nonskilled workers. Despite some important differences, such as that between the cutters and other grades or workers in larger shops in contrast to those in tenements and backroom sweatshops, unskilled work in the needle trades was the main source of employment and therefore a unifying force. The particular political perspective of rights rooted in the mutualism of community and craft became a dynamic theme for the immigrants' definition of their own political culture and gave them opportunities for democratic participation in American political life. The close geographic space, the rise of democratic associations of mutual assistance, and the language of enslavement provided the workers with publicly available "cultural components" from which to devise strategies of mobilization for political action.[2] These components, in combination with publicly understood and shared political language, were the basis for industrial actions, neighborhood strikes, and consumer boycotts. Public contestations over the interpretation of concepts of fairness, justice, citizens' rights, and the relationship of individuals to their social context were issues proclaimed in these public enactments on the Lower East Side.

The working-class community was the driving force in the "communally intensive," adversarial eruptions such as picketing, crowd activity, labor, consumer and rent strikes, boycotts, social sanctions against scabs, mass funerals, and other displays of "public culture."[3] These practices used a language and a symbolic code that permeated all aspects of public and private life. It became an instrument to mobilize sympathizers in a broadly defined movement that upheld competing codes of social justice and condemned profiteering and individual gain at the expense of community welfare. Through these joint actions, the protagonists gained the power to challenge the authority of capital and to state their demands for an alternative social order. The social practices of the Jewish community were more than a means to enforce the norms of the community and reaffirm its cohesion; they served also as a transformative tool that enabled historical actors to struggle for control over such issues as definitions of community, its value system, and legitimacy of authority. The participants in demonstrations, riots, and protests transformed accepted meanings and created new ways to evaluate the relationship between work, market, and community.[4] In short, culture served as an agent of change by defining new political agendas. At the historical moment when the old social and political arrangements of the traditional community had disappeared and the new power structures had not yet taken root, this process endowed hitherto marginal groups with new power and authority.

The year 1905 is in some ways an arbitrary cut-off point for this study, although the date is significant in marking a revolutionary period in Russia that had an impact on the Jewish population and its politics. Observers and historians have also ascribed to this date an importance in the history of the Jewish community in the United States, asserting that those who arrived at this time were more politically conscious and articulate and therefore played an inspirational and instrumental role in the establishment of "modern" unions. While it is true that 1905 was a high point in the arrival of Jewish immigrants radicalized in the political struggles in Russia, this did not immediately lead to a breakthrough in the establishment of Jewish unions, nor did it signal a break with local struggles as practiced by the first generation of immigrants.[5] Jewish immigrants on the Lower East Side conti~~ to engage in industrial and political action in which strikes and communi~~ involvement went hand in hand for many years to come. Labor unrest remained a signal for community action. The fiercely fought bakers' strike in 1905 illustrates how an industrial action on the Lower East Side could bring out sympathizers in numbers larger than the actual number of striking workers.[6] Similarly, during the reefermakers' strike of 1907, nonstrikers and workers from other branches of the industry left their jobs to assist in picketing.[7] In the kosher meat boycott of 1917, which echoed the struggles of 1902, Jewish women initiated a "house-to-house campaign" against rising prices marked by protests, riots, and arrests on the Lower East Side and in other boroughs and cities. The meat riots soon became food riots directed against all profiteers who took advantage of the wartime shortages and inflation.[8] In 1917, women activists also petitioned the city's mayor and the White House for the distribution of $1 million worth of food stuffs, which prompted the *New York Times* to claim that the riot was the work of German agents.[9] These and similar "disorderly" practices remained the hallmarks of the Jewish community for years to come and are evidence that community actions retained their power, despite the arrival of more accepted political methods such as unions and political parties through the participation of post-1905 immigrants.

Nevertheless, with the advent of more solid union organization in the garment industry after 1909, the politics of the Jewish community moved into the more legitimated channels of orderly negotiations, membership dues, and binding arbitration procedures. Unions became the vehicles for regulating labor practices and provided an opportunity to participate in the bigger arena of power. After 1909, the new union organizations introduced a semblance of order into the needle trade industry, with the cooperation of the larger employers who also wanted to moderate the anarchy of cutthroat competition. The broad union objective was to obtain standardization of work in the clothing industry by regulating wage rates, hours, and conditions. Although short-lived "seasonal" unions and strikes continued as part of the political life of the Lower East Side throughout the period, the success of mass recruitment into the ILGWU after 1909 signaled a new era in the needle trades.

The ILGWU was a union based on broad industrial principles and ultimately became one of the first to reject the traditional notion of craft divisions.[10] With the mass uprisings of 1909 and 1910, at a time when the philosophy of the general strike based on industrial organization was gaining ground, it was, paradoxically, the traditionally close links between work and the community that irritated union leaders. The 1909 strike of dressmakers and waistmakers, which brought out other workers in related crafts and unemployed workers in support, illustrated the divide between the leadership

The committee recognized the rights of the unem-
phans," only when they threatened to scab.[11] The
rganizers in 1910 multiplied further when they faced
h not only workers and strikers but also their families,
the Lower East Side.[12] These features of community
d to frustrate union organizers, who hoped for orderly
and disciplineu ᵤ... ᵢ organization and proceedings.

The right to declare a strike was, in itself, an issue which had traditionally pitted union leadership against rank and file. Within the first four
months following the inception of the ILGWU, eighty-three strikes were
called, none of which were officially endorsed by the ILGWU. In 1905, hoping to prevent unofficial stoppages, the leadership attempted to centralize
union affairs by closely supervising the local's finances and by establishing
a procedure for declaring strikes. All strikes, for example, had to be approved by the individual trades within the ILGWU while strike benefits were
distributed solely to members in authorized strikes.[13] However, the "scrap-
ping" spirit of the rank and file persisted; between March 1911 and July 1913,
there were 304 shop strikes against firms belonging to the Protective Association whose members were bound by the Protocol.[14]

Union members continued to express deep dissatisfaction with the
goals defined by the famous Protocol of Peace in the years following 1910.
The Protocol, essentially a no-strike agreement, was signed by both sides of
industry to maintain industrial peace in the garment trades, on the basis of
compulsory arbitration. It was intended to guarantee job security to the
workers in return for giving up the closed shop. The Protocol obliged employers to observe the "preferential shop," whereby employers agreed to
hire union members if they were "equal in efficiency" to non-unionized
workers, thus opening the trade to non-union labor recruitment.[15] The Protocol used the power of the unions to stop unauthorized strikes and to represent members in the arbitration process in a nonpartisan capacity. The unbridgeable gap between the leadership, which was determined to keep
industrial peace, and the disaffected rank and file soon became apparent.
In 1912 the ILGWU actually sent in strikebreakers when workers refused to
return to work.[16] Some workers therefore regarded the Protocol as having
a bias toward employers and regarded themselves as "slaves of the Protocol."[17] Union leaders deplored the "immaturity" of rank-and-file members
who rejected industrial discipline, while members continued to resent compulsory arbitration.

Historians have emphasized the rise of the long-awaited Jewish unionism as a "forward-looking" and "modern" development in the history of the
Jewish labor movement. This interpretation obscures the fact that union organization was only one of the many collective institutions and practices developed by immigrants. Unions, whether "seasonal" or permanent, existed

side by side with voluntary, community-based self-help organizations, such as the landsmanshaftn, the Workmen's Circle, and the Socialist Party, which all coexisted with ad hoc, spontaneous, and seemingly anarchic community actions.[18] All of these multiple social practices "made sense" in seizing the available political opportunities and finding communal ways of appropriating political power.

The period between 1881 and 1905 in the history of the Jewish labor movement stamped a distinguishing, ideological identity on the Jewish community through its actions and language. The marked participation of Jews in the Socialist Party, for example, was an expression not only of the revolutionary experience imported from Russia but also of the legacy of the broad universalist, political vision forged in the public battles fought on the Lower East Side. In 1915, according to Charles Leinenweber, Jews represented the numerical "core" of the Socialist Party.[19] The party's popularity in Jewish neighborhoods was confirmed in November 1912, when Eugene V. Debs's campaign succeeded in drawing forty thousand marchers representing unions, clubs, and societies, while an additional fifteen thousand watched.[20] A familiar event, one that came to symbolize the communal solidarity of the Jewish immigrants with their Socialist candidates, took place in 1914, when Meyer London, a lawyer for garment unions, won the congressional election. An "impromptu demonstration" at 4:00 A.M., followed by a march in the streets, were among the celebrations marking that victory.[21] The Socialist Party's popularity on the Lower East Side grew further because of its opposition to World War I. During Morris Hillquit's mayoral campaign in 1917, the "whole East Side seemed to be on its feet" when thousands of men and women came to hear the candidate known for his uncompromising antiwar stand.[22]

These popular political displays, as well as the participation in organizations such as trade unions and the Socialist Party, reflected a specifically Jewish political language. Militant strikes, unions, violent boycotts, and political practices have been described as "a streak of madness, the purity of messianic yearning" or "an apocalyptic frenzy."[23] These hallmarks of Jewish politics also expressed a Jewish identity, evident in the early period of immigration, which survived long after the disappearance of the Jewish working class and its close-knit community of the Lower East Side.

NOTES

Introduction

1. Among historians who link the post-1905 immigrants to the establishment of politically "mature" unions are: Irving Howe, *World of Our Fathers: The Journey of the East European Jews to America and the Life They Found and Made* (New York: Harcourt Brace Jovanovich, 1976), p. 297; Melech Epstein, *Jewish Labor in U.S.A.* (New York: Trade Union Sponsoring Committee, 1950) vol. 1, p. 387; John Laslett, *Labor and the Left: A Study of Socialist and Radical Influences in the American Labor Movement, 1881–1924* (New York: Basic Books, 1970), pp. 98–109.

2. Moses Rischin, *The Promised City: New York's Jews, 1870–1914* (Cambridge, Mass.: Harvard University Press, 1962) is a pioneer study of the immigrants and their cultural, social, and economic life in New York. Among the important works focusing on labor and its organizational aspects are Epstein, *Jewish Labor in U.S.A.*; Louis Levine (Lorwin), *The Women's Garment Workers* (New York: B. W. Huebsch, 1924); Jacob M. Budish and George Soule, *The New Unionism in the Clothing Industry* (New York: Harcourt, Brace and Howe, 1920); Joel Seidman, *Needle Trades* (New York: Farrar and Rinehart, 1942); Melvyn Dubofsky, *When Workers Organize* (Amherst: University of Massachusetts Press, 1968). ILGWU was founded in 1900, but its organizational success dates to its first mass strike of 1909. ACW was formed in 1914 by men's clothing workers.

3. Howe, *World of Our Fathers*, p. 77.

4. Gerald Sorin commented on the "uprootedness" of Jewish immigrants in a study of the cultural background of 170 Jewish immigrant socialists. His findings suggest that a vast number of Jewish immigrants were rooted in the values of secularized Judaism, which made a central contribution in creating a viable new community of a uniquely radical character. Gerald Sorin, *The Prophetic Minority: American Jewish Immigrant Radicals, 1880–1920* (Bloomington: Indiana University Press, 1985).

5. Alice Kessler-Harris, "Organizing the Unorganizable: Three Jewish Women and Their Union," Milton Cantor and Bruce Laurie, eds., *Class, Sex, and the Woman Worker* (Westport, Conn.: Greenwood Press, 1977), pp. 144–65; Maxine Schwartz Seller, "The Uprising of the Twenty Thousand: Sex, Class and Ethnicity in the Shirtwaist Makers' Strike of 1909," in Dirk Hoerder, ed., *"Struggle a Hard Battle," Essays on Working-Class Immigrants* (DeKalb: Northern Illinois University Press, 1986), pp. 254–79; Susan A. Glenn, *Daughters of the Shtetl: Life and Labor in the Immigrant Genera-*

tion (Ithaca: Cornell University Press, 1990), chs. 3–6; Sydney Stahl Weinberg, *The World of Our Mothers: The Lives of Immigrant Women* (New York: Schocken Books, 1990), ch. 10; Kathie Friedman-Kasaba, *Memories of Migration: Gender, Ethnicity, and Work in the Lives of Jewish and Italian Women in New York, 1870–1924* (Albany: State University of New York Press, 1997). Also of interest, because of its incisive analysis of the roots of immigrant women's radicalism and their role in the secular public sphere, is Paula E. Hyman, *Gender and Assimilation in Modern Jewish History: The Role and Representation of Women* (Seattle: University of Washington Press, 1995).

6. The best example of immigrant wives' communal protest is documented in Paula E. Hyman's "Immigrant Women and Consumer Protest: The New York City Kosher Meat Boycott of 1902," *American Jewish History* 70 (1980): 91–105; also, Elizabeth Ewen, *Immigrant Women in the Land of Dollars: Life and Culture on the Lower East Side, 1890–1925* (New York: Monthly Review Press, 1985). For a discussion of Jewish women's definition of communal identity through informal neighborhood networks, see also Paula E. Hyman, "Gender and the Immigrant Experience in the United States," in Judith Baskin, ed., *Jewish Women in Historical Perspective* (Detroit: Wayne State University Press, 1991), pp. 222–42.

7. Expressions of community action and mutual support, the hallmark of many groups among the "new immigrants" entering industrial America, engendered hostility and suspicion on the part of organized labor and became the target of criticism by Americans in general. See, for example, Victor Greene, *The Slavic Community on Strike: Immigrant Labor in Pennsylvania Anthracite* (Notre Dame, Ind.: University of Notre Dame Press, 1968), pp. 141–44.

8. William Gamson, "Political Discourse and Collective Action," in Bert Klandermans, Hanspeter Kriesi, Sidney Tarrow, eds., *From Structure to Action: Comparing Movement Participation Across Cultures* (Greenwich, Conn.: JAI Press, 1988), p. 220.

9. Jonathan Sarna, tr., ed., *People Walk on Their Heads: Moses Weinberger's Jews and Judaism in New York* (New York: Holmes and Meier, 1982).

10. Edward P. Thompson, *The Making of the English Working Class* (New York: Random House, 1963).

11. Herbert G. Gutman, "Work, Culture, and Society in Industrializing America, 1815–1919," *American Historical Review* 78 (June 1973): 531–88.

12. The "continual adaptation" of people of diverse social and cultural backgrounds entering the American labor force was a defining feature for the formation of the American working class and for the development of American capitalism. Ibid., pp. 540–43. Also in Herbert G. Gutman, "Class Composition and the Development of the American Working Class, 1840–1890," in Herbert G. Gutman (Ira Berlin, ed.,) *Power and Culture: Essays on the American Working Class* (New York: Pantheon Books, 1987), p. 382.

13. Gutman, "Work, Culture, and Society," p. 561.

14. Ira Berlin, "Introduction: Herbert G. Gutman and the American Working Class," Gutman (Ira Berlin, ed.) *Power and Culture: Essays on the America Working Class*, p. 39.

15. Virginia Yans McLaughlin, *Family and Community: Italian Immigrants in Buffalo, 1880–1930* (Ithaca: Cornell University Press, 1977).

16. Mike Merrill's interview with Herbert Gutman in Henry Abelove, Betsy Blackmar, Peter Dimock, Jonathan Schneer, eds., *Visions of History* (New York: Pantheon Books, 1983), pp. 196–97. Labor historian Alan Dawley has suggested that the interaction between ethnic cultures and the conditions of immigrants' working life represents a process "in which both the cultures and the conditions were transformed." Alan Dawley, review of *Immigration and Industrialization: Ethnicity in an American Mill Town, 1870–1940*, by John Bodnar, *American Historical Review* 84 (February 1979): 268–69. Similarly, labor historian Leon Fink called for a greater emphasis on the transformative power of culture. Fink notes historians' interest in the influence of culture on labor's vitality in the nineteenth century and their neglect of the cultural element in empowering labor resistance in the twentieth century. He calls for a broader concept of culture, one which would not only "enshrine" the traditional, but also emphasize its dynamic quality. Leon Fink, "Looking Backward: Reflections on Workers' Culture and Certain Conceptual Dilemmas within Labor History," in J. Carroll Moody and Alice Kessler-Harris, eds., *American Labor History: The Problems of Synthesis* (DeKalb: Northern Illinois University Press, 1989), pp. 19–20.

17. For a discussion of the traditions of sociology of culture, see Ann Swidler, "Cultural Power and Social Movements," in Hank Johnston and Bert Klandermans, eds., *Social Movements and Culture* (Minneapolis: University of Minnesota Press, 1995), pp. 25–39.

18. Ann Swidler, "Culture in Action: Symbols and Strategies," *American Sociological Review* 51 (April 1986): 273. Swidler is skeptical of Max Weber's view that Calvinist values led to a distinct type of Protestant rational, capitalist, economic behavior. Ibid., p. 275. She maintains that Calvinist values could not provide the core inspiration for social behavior so long after the decline of its essential ideology. She also notes that Protestantism had "different political implications in different historical contexts." Ibid., p. 283.

19. Ibid., p. 280. Swidler's interpretation of culture differs from the view offered by Gerald Sorin. Sorin demonstrates how religious values were subsequently reinterpreted in a new secular context and became key elements in predisposing Jews to socialism and radicalism. Sorin, *The Prophetic Minority*, p. 3.

20. Swidler, "Culture in Action: Symbols and Strategies," p. 284.

21. Ibid. p. 280.

22. Margaret R. Somers, "What's Political or Cultural about Political Culture and the Public Sphere? Toward an Historical Sociology of Concept Formation," *Sociological Theory* 13:2 (July 1995): 133–34.

23. Ibid., pp. 129–30.

24. Ibid., p. 132.

25. Lynn Hunt, *Politics, Culture, and Class in the French Revolution* (Berkeley and Los Angeles: University of California Press, 1984).

26. Lynn Hunt, *The New Cultural History* (Berkeley and Los Angeles: University of California Press, 1989), p. 17.

27. Ann Swidler suggests, in fact, that culturally shaped collective actions and practices become strategies that have the ability also to "sustain alternative view of politics." Ann Swidler, "Inequality in American Culture: The Persistence of Voluntarism," *American Behavioral Scientist* 35 (March–June 1995): 619. In her study of African American social movements, Swidler shows that black radicalism arises from historically tried and tested channels of collective action that became the framework for organizing and mobilizing action. This form of organization created a different political perspective. The particular view shared by African Americans rejects the voluntaristic principle, which focuses on reforming the individual rather than solving social problems through established political frameworks. Unlike white Americans, who persistently uphold the view of America as a land of equality and opportunity despite a reality that testifies to the contrary, black Americans have a skeptical view of the American myth of individualism not just because of the experience of oppression, but also due to their collective pattern of action.

28. Kathleen Neils Conzen, David A. Gerber, Ewa Morawska, George E. Pozzetta, and Rudolph J.Vecoli, "The Invention of Ethnicity: a Perspective from the U.S.A.," *Journal of American Ethnic History* 12 (Fall 1992): 3–41.

29. Werner Sollors, ed., *The Invention of Ethnicity* (New York: Oxford University Press, 1989), p. xi.

30. Conzen et al., "The Invention of Ethnicity," p. 4.

31. Ibid., p. 5.

32. Kathleen Neils Conzen, "Mainstream and Side Channels: The Localization of Immigrant Cultures," *Journal of American Ethnic History* 11 (Fall 1991): 11.

33. Conzen et al., "The Invention of Ethnicity," pp. 5, 16, 32.

34. Pierre Birnbaum and Ira Katznelson, "Emancipation and the Liberal Offer," Pierre Birnbaum and Ira Katznelson, eds., *Paths of Emancipation* (Princeton, N.J.: Princeton University Press, 1995), p. 28. The article offers a constructive critique of the one-dimensional model of the traditional self-contained Jewish community as the only bulwark against the eradication of Jewish identity. The authors see emancipation and modernization as historical moments for reconstructing alternative Jewish community structures capable of evoking loyalty and a sense of belonging.

35. Ibid., pp. 18, 19.

36. Howe, *World of Our Fathers*, p. 205.

37. For a discussion of German national celebrations and public rituals, which were mostly "invented" by the middle class, see Kathleen Neils Conzen, "Ethnicity as Festive Culture: Nineteenth-Century German America on Parade," Sollors, ed., *The Invention of Ethnicity*. Although lacking regional identity or common religion, the emphasis of German immigrants on their common cultural heritage prevented conflict along class or religious lines.

38. Daniel Soyer, *Jewish Immigrant Associations and American Identity in New York, 1880–1939* (Cambridge, Mass.: Harvard University Press, 1997), pp. 3–9.

39. For a discussion of the relationship between local struggles and broader demands for citizenship rights in mid-nineteenth-century England, see Margaret Somers, "Citizenship and the Place of the Public Sphere: Law, Community, and Political Culture in the Transition to Democracy," *American Sociological Review* 58 (October 1993): 587–620.

40. Eli Lederhendler, *The Road to Modern Jewish Politics* (New York: Oxford University Press, 1989), pp. 9–10.

Chapter 1. Jewish Immigrants to the United States, 1881 to 1905

1. By 1914, out of a total Jewish population in czarist Russia of over five million, the number immigrating reached a million and a half. Samuel Joseph, *Jewish Immigrants to the United States from 1881 to 1910* (New York: Arno Press, 1969), p. 93. For data on Jewish immigration after 1910, see Simon Kuznets, "Immigration of Russian Jews to the United States: Background and Structure," *Perspectives in American History* 9 (1975): 39. Since Jewish immigrants did not constitute a separate category in the U.S. documentation of immigrants until 1899, both Joseph and Kuznets base their estimates for the years 1881–1899 on unofficial data from the reports of Jewish aid societies in the three main entry points of New York, Philadelphia, and Baltimore. For a discussion of the problems presented by the lack of official United States data for 1881–1899 and for other related issues, see Joseph, *Jewish Immigrants to the United States*, pp. 87–92, and Kuznets, "Immigration of Russian Jews," pp. 36, 37, 40, 41.

2. For a discussion of the causes of immigration from eastern and southern Europe in the late nineteenth century, see Thomas Archdeacon, *Becoming American: An Ethnic History* (New York: Free Press, 1983), ch. 5, and John Bodnar, *The Transplanted: A History of Immigrants in Urban America* (Bloomington: Indiana University Press, 1985), ch. 1.

3. Archdeacon, *Becoming American*, pp. 123–24.

4. Margaret R. Somers, "The Narrative Constitution of Identity: A Relational and Network Approach," *Theory and Society* 23 (1994): 624.

5. Kuznets, "Immigration of Russian Jews," p. 101, Table 11, p. 105. While pre-1899 statistical data about Jewish immigrants from Russia is scanty, nonstatistical sources, mainly autobiographical materials, indicate that neither the causes for immigration nor the composition of the immigrant group differed to any great extent from those of 1899–1914. For the purposes of this study, the data pertaining to the later period will provide the basis for insights into the period starting in 1881. For the analysis of the occupational structure of the immigrant group for the years 1899–1914, see Kuznets, "Immigration of Russian Jews," pp. 100–12. According to one source, the socioeconomic character of the immigrants who arrived in the pre-1900 period differed from the later arrivals. In the earlier period, there was a higher proportion of immigrants who had been previously engaged in petty trade and immigrants without defined occupations and who came from small shtetls, rather than towns or cities, and with little or no capital, most of whom came out of economic

necessity rather than choice. Elias Tcherikower, *The Early Jewish Labor Movement in the United States*, translated and revised by Aaron Antonovsky (New York: YIVO Institute for Jewish Research, 1961), pp. 71–72. The *Yudishes Tageblatt* remarked in a similar vein that the immigration of the late 1890s was made up of a "better class" of people than in the preceding years; *Yudishes Tageblatt*, 3 May 1892. Contrary to these two impressionistic views, however, the findings of Kuznets indicate that, like the earlier immigration, it was mainly economic necessity and dislocation that motivated the later group of immigrants to leave Russia. The relevant autobiographical material I use in this book consists of three unpublished collections located at the Jewish Institute for Social Research (YIVO). The largest body of material, Record Group 102, is the result of a 1942 YIVO contest on the theme, "Why I Left Europe and What I Have Accomplished in America." The collection contains approximately four hundred autobiographies, many added during subsequent years. The second collection, Record Group 113, part of the YIVO Oral History Project directed by M. Kligsberg in 1964–68, consists of forty-three transcribed interviews with labor leaders and activists. The third group, Aaron Antonovsky Editorial Records, consists of several questionnaires filled in by retired Jewish workers in Los Angeles, some of whom had worked in the garment industry in different parts of the country.

6. Kuznets, "Immigration of Russian Jews," pp. 109, 110, Table 12. The Pale of Settlement comprised the geographic areas where Russian Jews were allowed to settle. It included fifteen out of fifty western provinces of European Russia and ten provinces of Russian Poland. Barred from the countryside inside the Pale, Jews were restricted to incorporated cities and to villages. They constituted 58 percent of the urban population of Lithuania and White Russia but only 26 percent of the newly settled southern parts of the Pale. Approximately 4,900,000 Jews lived in the Pale in 1897, representing 11.5 percent of the local population and 94 percent of all Jews in czarist Russia. Ibid., pp. 69–72.

7. Ibid., pp. 105, 109.

8. Archdeacon, *Becoming American*, p. 133.

9. Ibid., p. 136.

10. Kuznets, "Immigration of Russian Jews," pp. 63, 73, 77, 110.

11. Jewish Colonization Association, *Recueil de materiaux sur la situation economique des Israelites de Russie*, 2 vols. (Paris: Alcan, 1906–1908), 2: Appendix Table 40, 1: 237.

12. Ibid., 1: 242, 382. The south and the Crimea profited from a demographic shift following new laws which opened these territories to the Jews. According to one source, the absence of established kahals, a more egalitarian draft system, and the availability of land attracted many inhabitants from the northwestern provinces in search of new opportunities. Michael Stanislawski, *Tsar Nicholas I and the Jews: The Transformation of Jewish Society in Russia 1825–1855* (Philadelphia: Jewish Publication Society of America, 1983), p. 165.

13. Glenn, *Daughters of the Shtetl*, pp. 13, 19. Second to employment in the needle trades came domestic service, representing 35 percent of all gainfully employed women. Ibid., p. 17.

14. Jewish Colonization Association, *Recueil de materiaux*, 1: 185, 289.

15. Ibid., 1: 394, Weinberg, *The World of Our Mothers*, p. 54.

16. In some towns of the Pale, there was one tailor for every twenty inhabitants. Jewish Colonization Association, *Recueil de materiaux*, 1: 308.

17. Within the Pale's borders, Jews constituted 11.5 percent of the Russian population. Of the total Jewish population of Russia, numbering over five million in the 1900s, only 4–6 percent met the standards required for domicile in the interior and the major cities. See Kuznets, "Immigration of Russian Jews," pp. 69, 71. The categories of those privileged to reside outside the Pale included master-craftsmen pursuing their trade. In practice, however, a variety of restrictions were applied by Russian guilds outside the Pale. The arbitrariness of local governments prevented artisans from taking advantage of the law. Ibid., p. 69. For a short summary of the czarist policies toward the Jews and legal developments, see Bernard Weinryb, "East European Jewry (Since the Partitions of Poland, 1772–1795)," in Louis Finkelstein, ed., *The Jews: Their History* (New York: Schocken Books, 1972). For demographic data, particularly on the ratio of the Jewish population to the non-Jewish Russian population within the Pale compared with the ratios outside the Pale for the 1860s and the 1870s, and the economic opportunities afforded to Jews living in Russia's interior, see Louis Greenberg, *The Jews in Russia: The Struggle for Emancipation* (New Haven: Yale University Press, 1945), vol. 1, p. 166.

18. The manufacture and distribution of vodka was often "farmed out" by the government to the nobility who, in turn, leased their rights to Jews. During the second half of the nineteenth century, however, this profitable trade was progressively removed from Jews by a succession of legal enactments. Stanislawski, *Tsar Nicholas I and the Jews*, pp. 171–74.

19. Quoted in Louis Greenberg, *The Jews in Russia*, vol. 1, p. 160.

20. Jewish Colonization Association, *Recueil de materiaux*, 2: 225, 227, Table 58. Baron noted an increase of 27 percent in the numbers of paupers between the years 1894 and 1898. Salo W. Baron, *The Russian Jew under the Tsars and the Soviets* (New York: Macmillan, 1964), pp. 128–29. According to Baron, in many communities as much as 50 percent of the population depended on charity during Passover. Ibid., p. 65.

21. Jewish Colonization Association, *Recueil de materiaux*, 2: 227.

22. Ezra Mendelsohn, *Class Struggle in the Pale: The Formative Years of the Jewish Workers' Movement in Czarist Russia* (Cambridge: Cambridge University Press, 1970), p. 14.

23. Jewish Colonization Association, *Receuil de materiaux*, 1: 266, 227.

24. Though difficult to gauge, the Russian government's policies may have contributed to the changes in the occupational structure of the Jewish population. Jewish russification, a broad governmental goal, was to be accomplished by granting legal and economic rewards to the productive elements in Jewish society. A statute issued in 1835, for example, allowed Jews possessing a craft to reside outside the Pale. Similarly, economically useful estates were granted special privileges in a series of

laws enacted in 1846 and developed further under the new reforms of Alexander II. Stanislawski, *Tsar Nicholas I and the Jews*, p. 49; Weinryb, "East European Jewry," pp. 363–65. This policy opened the interior provinces to merchants, graduates of universities, and artisans. However, the overwhelming majority of Jews, who lacked the means and were unable to challenge the administrative difficulties involved in the geographic move, remained confined to the crowded Pale, where they faced limited economic choices.

25. Jewish Colonization Association, *Recueil de materiaux,* 1: 260, 262. By the end of the century, Jewish workers, especially women, worked at home within the putting-out system. Glenn, *Daughters of the Shtetl,* p. 17.

26. David Cohen, "Baaley melacha be-Spola" [Artisans in the town of Spola], *He-Avar* 7 (1960): 170.

27. The price of a sewing machine was 60 rubles (roughly equivalent to $30). According to one testimony, after a down payment of ten rubles, the rest was paid in weekly one-ruble installments for two years. According to the same account, the tailors of Mogilev depended on loan sharks in order to acquire their machines. Isaac Levitats, *The Jewish Community in Russia, 1844–1917* (Jerusalem: Posner and Sons, 1981), p. 150. The interest on these loans was as high as 100 percent. Sara Rabinowitsch, *Die Organisationen des jüdischen Proletariats in Russland* (Karlsruhe: G. Braun, 1903), p. 61.

28. Avraham Solomon Melamed, *Hayim kemo she-hem* [Life as it is] (Constantinople: 1922), pp. 33, 119.

29. Jewish Colonization Association, *Recueil de materiaux,* 1: 247, 249, 276, 282, 283; 2: Appendix, Table 41.

30. Isaac Max Rubinow, *Economic Conditions of the Jews in Russia* (New York: Arno Press, 1975), a reprint of *Bulletin of the Bureau of Labor,* vol. 15, no. 72 (Washington, 1907), p. 524.

31. Jewish Colonization Association, *Recueil de materiaux,* 1: 249. Data for Minsk, Vilna, and Vitebsk for 1901 indicate the existence of larger shops employing ten to forty workers. Mendelsohn, *Class Struggle in the Pale,* p. 10.

32. Jewish Colonization Association, *Recueil de materiaux,* 1: 256, 257. For female apprenticeships, see Glenn, *Daughters of the Shtetl,* p. 27.

33. Jewish Colonization Association, *Recueil de materiaux,* 1: 256.

34. M. Alper, YIVO RG 102, no. 30, p. 9.

35. Cohen, "Baaley melacha be-Spola," p. 170.

36. Charles Nathan Reznikoff and Sarah Reznikoff, *Family Chronicle* (New York: Universe Books, 1971), p. 52.

37. Melamed, *Hayim kemo she-hem,* p. 8.

38. M. Alper, YIVO, RG 102, no. 30, p. 3. Though the forebear in the end had to marry one daughter to "a builder of wooden houses," her only consolation was that the groom was "a bit of a scholar and came from a good family." Ibid.

39. A. Berlow, YIVO, RG 102, no. 70, p. 4. Berlow immigrated to New York in 1895 at the age of fifteen.

40. Anon. YIVO, RG 102, no. 24, p. 22.

41. Cohen, "Baaley melacha be-Spola," p. 171. The custom of appropriating remnants of cloth—known in England as "cabbage"—was widespread among eighteenth-century English tailors and was considered by them as part of their remuneration. John Rule, *The Experience of Labour in Eighteenth-Century English Industry* (New York: St. Martin's Press, 1981), p. 126.

42. Melamed, *Hayim kemo she-hem*, p. 122. The stigma attached to the status of artisan and worker persisted into the twentieth century and became a target for the Bund's counterattacks. The Bund's agitators and organizers taught "that the worker is indispensable because he produces with his hands and blood all that we need. And that even God wasn't ashamed of being a tailor . . . and he himself sewed the first garment for Adam and Eve," remembered one immigrant. Ben Joseph, YIVO, RG 102, no. 81, p. 17.

43. Michael Stanislawski, "Russian Jewry, the Russian State, and the Dynamics of Jewish Emancipation," in Birnbaum and Katznelson, eds., *Paths of Emancipation*, p. 273.

44. Ibid.

45. Levitats, *The Jewish Community in Russia, 1772–1844*, pp. 128–29.

46. Lederhendler, *The Road to Modern Jewish Politics*, p. 47.

47. For a discussion of the relationship and the allocation of power between the czarist authorities and the kahal, see ibid., pp. 46–51.

48. Michael Stanislawski, *Psalms for the Tsars; A Minute Book of Psalms-Society in the Russian Army, 1864–1867* (New York: Yeshiva University Library, 1988), p. 23.

49. Melamed, *Hayim kemo she-hem*, p. 9.

50. Levitats, *The Jewish Community in Russia 1772–1844*, p. 63.

51. The folksong at the opening of the chapter is one expression of the memory of injustice. See also, Azriel Shochat, "Ha-hanhaga be-kehilot Rusya im bitul ha-kahal" [Leadership of the Jewish communities in Russia after the abolition of the kahal], *Zion* 42 (1977): 182–83.

52. Lederhendler, *The Road to Modern Jewish Politics*, pp. 13, 44; Stanislawski, *Tsar Nicholas I and the Jews*, p. 131.

53. Soyer, *Jewish Immigrant Associations*, ch. 1.

54. Y. Schatzky, "Amolike Yiddishe schneider fareinen un hevros" [Tailors associations and societies], *Fortschrit* 5 January, 1923, p. 10.

55. Bernard Weinryb, "Texts and Studies in the Communal History of Polish Jewry," *Proceedings of the American Academy for Jewish Research* 19: 101. According to Mark Wischnitzer, while Christian guilds had a say in the administration of towns, Jewish guilds were deprived of comparable influence. *A History of Jewish Crafts and Guilds* (New York: Jonathan David, 1965), p. 273.

56. Israel Halperin, "Hevrot baaley melacha yehudim be-Polin ve-Lita" [Jewish artisanal guilds in Poland and Lithuania], *Zion* 2 (October 1936): 76–84.

57. Ibid., p. 77.

58. Wischnitzer, *A History of Jewish Crafts and Guilds*, p. 244; Levitats, *Jewish Community in Russia, 1844–1917*, pp. 149, 150, 151. The masters' guilds and the *kahal*,

however, strove to suppress and frustrate these journeymen's attempts to establish their own places of worship. Ibid., p. 244; Halperin, "Hevrot baaley melacha yehudim," p. 84; Soyer, *Jewish Immigrant Associations,* ch. 1.

59. Rabinowitsch, *Die Organisationen des jüdischen Proletariats in Russland,* pp. 54, 57, 59. Similar associations of journeymen existed in Moghilev among cabinetmakers, printers, painters, and shoemakers, among others. In the case of the painters, however, the repeated secessions were of temporary nature; on each occasion, the journeymen rejoined their parent guild, bringing back their Torah scroll, which was then placed in the Ark of the masters' synagogue. Ibid., p. 74. These journeymen's associations survived into the twentieth century and became the base for the Bund's activities. Mendelsohn, *Class Struggle in the Pale,* p. 44.

60. Levitats, *The Jewish Community in Russia, 1772–1844,* p. 239. Levitats does not provide the date of the incident in Keidany. Stanislawski notes separatist tendencies on the part of Jewish artisans who, in one case, demanded representation on the town's council independently of the recognized Jewish authorities. Stanislawski, *Tsar Nicholas I and the Jews,* p. 131.

61. Rischin, *The Promised City,* p. 38.

62. Abraham Ain, "Swislocz: Portrait of a Shtetl," Irving Howe and Eliezer Greenberg, eds., *Voices from the Yiddish: Essays, Memoirs, Diaries* (Ann Arbor: University of Michigan Press, 1972), pp. 91–92.

63. According to Michael Stanislawski, the form of governance after the abolition of the kahal was not strictly defined. Stanislawski, "Russian Jewry," p. 268.

64. In reality, the Jewish communal leadership remained in power and was known at times to cooperate with the Russian authorities by indicating whom to draft. Shochat, "Ha-hanhaga be-kehilot Rusya," p. 194. Each community still had to meet set quotas of recruits. According to Shochat, Jews were also vulnerable to forced impressments, often by the local authorities and, at times, by Jewish agents who searched for residents who had left the community but were still subject to its laws. Ibid., pp. 163–82; See also Lederhendler, *The Road to Modern Jewish Politics,* pp. 52–57. Although theoretically the community lost its taxing power, in practice indirect taxes on candles and meat continued to finance community expenditures. Similarly, rabbinical judicial power, though illegal, except in civil and religious matters, remained in effect. Ibid., p. 211.

65. Azriel Shochat, *Mosad "ha-rabanut mi-taam" be-Rusya: parasha be-maavak ha-tarbut ben haredim le-ven maskilim* [The "crown rabbinate" in Russia: A chapter in the cultural struggle betweeen Orthodox Jews and maskilim] (Haifa: University of Haifa Press, 1975). The crown rabbis were nominated as administrators of Jewish population records and were expected to monitor and report to the Russian authorities all illegal activities in the community. A new phase began in the 1850s, when the Russian government hoped that crown rabbis, educated in progressive seminaries, would displace the traditional rabbis and thus exercise a secularizing influence on Jewish communities. These decrees were thwarted by internal opposition, as well as the inconsistency in czarist policies. Ibid., pp. i–xiii, 103.

66. Ibid., p. 107. Lederhendler, *The Road to Modern Jewish Politics,* p. 81.

67. Schohat, *Mosad "ha-rabanut mi-taam,"* p. 107.

68. In cases where the election of the crown rabbi was confined to the better-off members of the community, for example, in Kharkov, where only the merchants of the First Guild and the taxpayers could vote, opposing canditates had no chance of being appointed. Similarly, in Bobroysk, only property holders could vote. Ibid., p. 99.

69. Ibid., p. 181, footnote 140.

70. Traditionally, there were two types of charity organizations. One, under the kahal's jurisdiction, was financed by indirect taxes imposed on all members of the community. The other included all voluntary organizations, attached for most part to synagogues and supported by members' donations. With the general economic decline, however, the charities became increasingly dependent on an affluent few. Jewish Colonization Association, *Recueil de materiaux,* 2: 231.

71. Traditionally, a Jewish beggar could demand alms "as if it were his due" and often became abusive when refused. Quoted in Baron, *The Russian Jew under the Tsars and the Soviets,* p. 128.

72. *Knesset Israel* 1 (1886/7): 712.

73. *Ha-Carmel* 46 (1869): 359.

74. "A Letter From Elizavetgrad," *Ha-melitz,* 30 October 1886. A similar case, which illustrated the necessity to fend off not only the Russian government but also one's coreligionists, was described by Joseph Dyenson, an immigrant who came to the United States in 1892. Having reached draft age, he assumed his dead brother's name to avoid military service. The scheme failed because of Jewish informers, who demanded payment in exchange for not revealing his secret to the Russian authorities. J. Dyenson, YIVO, RG 102, no. 147, p. 29.

75. "A Letter from Elizavetgrad," *Ha-melitz,* 30 October 1886. Emigration to America coexisted with geographic mobility within the Russian Empire itself, especially in the regions of Russian Poland, where fewer restrictions allowed more freedom of movement. Although many Russian cities were closed to most Jews, larger cities within the Pale attracted many in search of better fortune. Thus Ekaterinoslav, profiting from its railway links, grew rapidly in the last quarter of the nineteenth century, attracting many Jews from rural areas. Similarly, Odessa attracted many Jews from the Ukraine and southern Russia. Like the response of New York's German Jews to the waves of immigrants, the better-off Jews of Odessa also warned hopeful immigrants to get rid of the notion that "in Odessa one can dig up gold in the streets with spades." *Yudishes Folksblatt,* 29 May 1885, p. 314.

76. B. M. Laikin, YIVO RG 102, no. 144, pp. 3, 11, 12.

77. Dr. S. J. Levy, YIVO RG 102, no. 32–32a, p. 7.

78. B. Reisman, YIVO, RG 102, no. 38–38a, pp. 2–3. Reisman refers to a Talmudic passage that asks, "Which is the righteous path of life a man should choose?" The correct answer reads: "The path which will enoble man's deeds."

79. Stanislawski, "Russian Jewry," pp. 274, 275.

80. Howe, *World of Our Fathers,* p. 11. The new concept of historical time inspired

the birth of modern Jewish mass movements of Zionism and Socialism. See also Rischin, *The Promised City*, ch. 3.

81. For a perceptive discussion of the Jewish intelligentsia and its links to the revolutionary movements of the day, see Steven Cassedy, *To the Other Shore: The Russian Jewish Intellectuals Who Came to America* (Princeton, N.J.: Princeton University Press, 1997), pp. 1–35.

82. Ibid., p. 51.

83. Their role as the intellectual vanguard of the immigrant community in New York will be discussed in chapter 6.

84. A. Berlow, YIVO, RG 102, no. 70, pp. 30, 23.

85. J. Esrick, YIVO, RG 102, no. 138, p. 1.

86. Ibid.

87. Anon., YIVO, RG 102, no. 24, pp. 10, 22.

88. P. Bernhardt, YIVO, RG 102, no. 62, p. 4.

89. Anon., YIVO, RG 102, no. 75, pp. 29, 30.

90. *Yudishes Folksblatt,* 12 February 1887.

91. S. Langer, YIVO, RG 102, no. 57, p. 3. The miraculous discoveries that America produced, which surpassed human imagination, further augmented its mythical character. Thus Edison's awesome invention, by which "turning a switch can light all of America" lent to America the aura of a magic place beyond imagination. M. Zeidman, YIVO, RG, no. 36, p. 6.

92. Ben Joseph, YIVO, RG 102, no. 81, p. 12.

93. B. Fenster, YIVO, RG 113, p. 1. Looking back on his life in America, the same immigrant concluded that, unlike the old country, in America, "we participated in things."

94. S. Ginsburg, YIVO, RG 102, no. 156, p. 7.

95. A. Gumner, YIVO, RG 102, no. 44, p. 102.

96. Anon., YIVO, RG 102, no. 24, p. 1.

97. E. M. Wagner, YIVO, RG 102, no. 45, p. 143.

98. Anon., YIVO, RG 102, no. 24, p. 22.

99. Jewish Colonization Association, *Recueil de materiaux,* 2: Table 63.

100. Hyman, *Gender and Assimilation,* pp. 54, 77–80.

101. Weinberg, *The World of Our Mothers,* pp. 12, 16.

102. Sydelle Kramer and Jenny Masur, eds., *Jewish Grandmothers* (Boston: Beacon Press, 1976), p. 18.

103. Glenn, *Daughters of the Shtetl,* pp. 43–49; quoted ibid., p. 45.

104. A. Berlow, YIVO, RG 102, no. 70, p. 18. Also women, like men, relied on friends and relatives in America to send tickets and to extend a helping hand upon arrival.

105. Kramer and Masur, eds., *Jewish Grandmothers,* pp. 1–16.

106. Ella Wolf, YIVO, RG 113, p. 3.

107. Sanford Ragins, "The Image of America in Two East European Hebrew Periodicals," *American Jewish Archives* 16–17 (November 1965): 144–45.

108. Although personal reports carried more weight than printed accounts, the latter still found an attentive reception in some segments of the population. One immigrant recalled that his decision to come to America was influenced largely by articles in *Ha-melitz*. Melamed, *Hayim kemo she-hem*, p. 225.

109. U.S. Congress, House, *A Report of the Commissioners of Immigration upon the Causes Which Incite Immigration to the U.S.*, 52nd Cong., 1st sess., 1892, p. 120. Also, U.S. Congress, Senate, *Immigration Commission Reports*, Senate Report 633, 61st Cong., 2nd sess., 1907, vol. I, p. 188.

110. Anon., YIVO, RG 102, no. 117, p. 12. Letters were also an effective means of disseminating information and reaching a large audience of neighbors and friends. Ibid.

111. The letters discussed below are part of a collection in Polish, edited by Witold Kula, Nina Assorodobraj-Kula, and Marcin Kula, *Listy Emigrantow z Brazilii i Stanow Zjednoczonych 1890–1891* [Letters of Polish emigrants from Brazil and the United States, 1890–1891] (Warsaw: 1973). The collection also contains some sixty letters sent by Jewish immigrants, mostly from the United States, to their relatives in the towns and villages of the Plock region. For the most part they contained receipts for ship tickets, train tickets, money, or instructions relating to the voyage to America, which were intercepted and withheld by the Russian authorities, who were determined to stop the flow of emigration.

112. Ibid., letters 273; 322; 266; 320.

113. "One has to work harder here than in Poland." Ibid., letter 282; letters 268, 273, 294, 295, 316, 320, 332.

114. Ibid , letter 295. While some letters warned the reader of the inability to maintain one's Jewishness and of the difficult life awaiting older immigrants, one son promised his father a good old age and a guarantee that in America one could be as religious "as at home." Ibid., letter 285. According to Kuznets, the number of returnees was highest for those aged forty-five and over and lowest for the younger group. Kuznets, "Immigration of Russian Jews," p. 99.

115. Ibid., letter 262, 282. In some letters, success stories served to illustrate the writer's optimism and aimed to inspire those reluctant to come. Letter 273, for example, informed the recipients of the letter at home of a cousin who learned tailoring and within one year saved one hundred dollars. See also letters 262, 284.

116. Ibid., letters 323; 261; 286. Also letters 313, 330.

117. Joseph, *Jewish Immigration to the United States from 1881 to 1910*, p. 93. The number of immigrants dropped to 25,161 in 1893, compared to 64,253 in 1892. Thereafter, their numbers decreased steadily, reaching the lowest number, 13,063, in 1897, and then increased to reach a new peak of 125,234 in 1906, after which they began to decrease again for several years.

118. *Yudishes Folksblatt*, 19 November 1881, p. 126. These refugees viewed the French Jewish philanthropic organization that was instrumental in enabling them to sail to America, as a living symbol of the Revolution's achievements and as a defender of its ideals.

Chapter 2. Conflicted Cultures

1. The role of kinship ties as a factor in the decision to emigrate is discussed in Bodnar, *The Transplanted,* pp. 57–71.

2. Robert Putnam has suggested a firm link between "contemporary civic norms and practices" and the regional social-economic traditions in Italy. Hierarchical "clientelism" of the south and the *mezzogiorno,* which was encouraged by such institutions as the Catholic Church, the large estates, and the mafia, failed to foster civic engagement and party mobilization, resulting in regional impoverishment and political quietude. In contrast, "horizontal" reciprocal voluntary and spontaneous associations based on "social trust," which had been characteristic of Northern Italy's history, constituted part of its rich civic democratic tradition. According to Putnam, the two patterns affected the long-term social and economic development of Italy's northern and southern regions. Robert Putnam, *Making Democracy Work: Civic Traditions in Modern Italy* (Princeton, N.J.: Princeton University Press, 1993).

3. Zoza Szajkowski, "How the Mass Immigration to America Began," *Jewish Social Studies* 4 (October 1942): 291–310.

4. The Alliance Israelite Universelle had been an active advocate for Jewish welfare throughout the world on numerous occasions. Its involvement in the Damascus affair of 1840, for example, was well known. As early as 1866, the Alliance hoped that Jewish emigration to the United States would alleviate the problem of Russian Jews. Ibid., pp. 295, 296. Sir Moses Montefiore, the representative of British Jewry, had gained similar fame, particularly through his activities on behalf of Russian Jews and his interest in the Jews of Palestine.

5. Quoted in an article denying the existence of the letter in *Yudishes Folksblatt,* 8 October 1881, p. 23; 15 October 1881, p. 35.

6. H. Schafier, Alliance agent in Brody to Central Committee of Alliance in Paris, 21 September 1881, YIVO, RG 406, docs. 324, 325.

7. See requests for passage money received by Brody committee, YIVO, RG 406, docs. 821–1031.

8. Minutes of Conference in Vienna, 2 August 1882, YIVO, RG 406, doc. 251.

9. M. A. Kursheedt, Secretary of Russian Emigrant Relief Fund of New York, to H. S. Goldschmidt of French Alliance in Paris, 21 October 1881, YIVO, RG 406, doc. 583.

10. Hebrew Emigrant Aid Society (HEAS) report, 21 July 1882, YIVO, RG 406, doc. 681. German-Jewish American relief circles hinted that money toward the upkeep of "undesirable immigrants" at European points of embarkation would be increased rather than allocated for their support in the United States. M. A. Kursheedt, to N. S. Joseph of Mansion House Committee, 9 June 1882, YIVO, RG 406, doc. 635.

11. H. Schafier to Central Committee of the Alliance in Paris, 21 September 1881, YIVO, RG 406, docs. 324, 325. Ibid., doc. 830.

12. "The Emigration of Russian Jews," an official letter of HEAS published in the London *Jewish Chronicle,* 27 January 1882.

13. M. A. Kursheedt, to S. H. Goldschmidt of the Alliance in Paris, 21 October, 1881, YIVO, RG 406, docs. 569–84. Settling the newcomers on land seemed to the European philanthropists a constructive solution. The example of the Mennonites' successful settlement in the United States further strengthened their convictions that agricultural settlements would guarantee the immigrants freedom of religion, while also providing them with a sound economic base. Printed circular of the Alliance, 24 March 1882, YIVO, RG 406, doc. 55.

14. M. A. Kursheedt to S. H. Goldschmidt, 21 October 1881, YIVO, RG 406, doc. 581; doc. 575; doc. 577; docs. 570–71.

15. Aleksander Harkavy, a member of the Am Olam group, tells of a Jewish society in Hamburg that purchased ship tickets for the entire group. Aleksander Harkavy, *Perakim me-hayay* [Chapters from my life] (New York: Hebrew Publishing Company, 1935), p. 39.

16. HEAS Report, 21 July, 1882, YIVO, RG 406, doc. 681.

17. M. A. Kursheedt to N. S. Joseph of the Mansion House Committee, 14 June 1882, YIVO, RG 406, docs. 637, 638. Also, William Seligman of New York to Zadoc Kahn, Chief Rabbi of Paris, 28 June 1882, YIVO, RG 406, doc. 647. It also appears that the Mansion House Committee used the tactic of dispatching refugees from England directly to Boston and other East Coast cities which would then promptly send the new arrivals to New York. M. A. Kursheedt to N. S. Joseph, 14 June 1882, YIVO, RG 406, doc. 637.

18. William Seligman to N. S. Isaacs, 20 June 1882, YIVO, RG 406, doc. 641; 20 June 1882, doc. 642.

19. According to one source, the Mansion House Committee refused to support the American organizations on the grounds that they were insensitive to the immigrants' dietary requirements or to their religious observances, that they forced the immigrants to eat nonkosher food and gave them employment which necessitated the abandonment of religious observance. Augustus A. Levey, Secretary of HEAS, 4 June 1882, YIVO, RG 406, docs. 689, 692.

20. F. Wertheimer of Vienna to Baron Edmond de Rothschild of Paris, 1882, n.d., YIVO, RG 406, doc. 389. Also Julian Goldsmid to Baron Edmond de Rothschild, 11 July 1882, YIVO, RG 406, doc. 387. N. S. Joseph, 11 July 1882, YIVO, RG 406, doc. 201.

21. N. S. Joseph to M. Veneziani, a personal delegate to Baron de Hirsch in Brody, June 27, 1882, YIVO, RG 406, doc. 644. Esther Panitz estimates the number of immigrants helped by charitable organizations as ten thousand. Esther Panitz, "The Polarity of Jewish Attitudes toward Immigration (1870–1891)," *American Jewish Historical Quarterly* 53 (December 1963): 113.

22. Minutes of the conference in Vienna, 2 August 1882, YIVO, RG 406, doc. 251.

23. Zoza Szajkowski, "How the Mass Immigration to America Began," p. 305.

24. Ibid.

25. Henri Strauss, a steamship agent in Antwerp to Senator Bischoffsheim in Brussels, 9 July 1881, YIVO, RG 406, doc. 548.

26. See chapter 1, note 111.

27. Kula et al., eds., *Listy emigrantow,* letters 274, 289; letters 316, 279, 277, 296; letters 316, 320.

28. Ibid., letters 286, 323, 261.

29. Henri Strauss, of the National Steamship Company, Antwerp, to Senator Bischoffsheim in Brussels, 9 July 1881, YIVO, RG 406, doc. 548. It should be noted that men served as an "avantgarde," and it is questionable whether the large proportion of women among Jewish immigrants indicates a pattern of family migration. Joseph, *Jewish Migration to the United States from 1881–1910,* pp. 127–32; Kuznets, "Immigration of Russian Jews," pp. 94–99. Letters and autobiographical evidence point to the tendency of unmarried women to emigrate; thus the significant presence of women does not necessarily imply they were wives. Equally doubtful is the assertion that the large number of children, defined in some sources as those under the age of fourteen and others as under the age of sixteen, is further proof of immigration as a family movement.

30. Kula et al., eds., *Listy Emigrantow,* letters 267, 287.

31. Rose Cohen, *Out of the Shadow,* (New York: Jerome S. Ozer, 1971) a reprint of George H. Doran, 1918, pp. 23, 27.

32. Statistics for the years 1908–1914 indicate that relatives financed the passage of more than 60 percent of all Jewish immigrants. Kuznets, "Immigration of Russian Jews," p. 113. Though there is a lack of comparable data for the earlier period, apparently this pattern was inseparable from the process of immigration since its beginnings. Kula et al., eds., *Listy Emigrantow,* letters 284, 287, 302, 306, 323, 326, 331; J. Dyenson, YIVO, RG 102, no. 147.

33. Kula et al., eds., *Listy Emigrantow,* letter 122.

34. The trend of parents sending daughters did not begin until the later years of mass migration. Glenn, *Daughters of the Shtetl,* pp. 48, 49.

35. Emma Goldman, *Living My Life* (New York: Alfred A. Knopf, 1934), p. 11; Alice Wexler, *Emma Goldman in America* (Boston: Beacon Press 1984), p. 7. Other women, Sarah Liss for example, paid for the passage of her mother in 1891 and sent detailed instructions, warning her about the dangers of Hamburg, the point of embarkation and the first metropolis for a majority of immigrants. Kula et al., eds., *Listy Emigrantow,* letter 297.

36. Samuel Cohen, *Transplanted* (New York: 1937), p. 71. Cohen tells of his brother who, in 1880 at age eighteen, decided to emigrate and purchased a ticket with the financial help of local relatives. However, before his departure, he became engaged to a young woman who had two tickets of her own, one for herself and one for her original fiancé, who had backed out of the engagement. Cohen himself came to America with his brother and sister-in-law by taking advantage of the available ticket.

37. S. Ginsburg, YIVO, RG 102, no. 156, pp. 8, 9. Ginsburg borrowed money in his village and, once in America, decided that 6 percent interest was a fair repayment rate because "I saw that one had to work hard to earn, much harder than I imag-

ined." He also advised his wife, who remained in Russia, that if the lender questioned the amount of interest, she should bring the case to a rabbi, who would weigh her case and have the final say in the matter.

38. H. Schafier, an agent of the Alliance in Brody, to Paris Alliance office, 21 September 1881, YIVO, RG 406, docs. 324, 325. Similar groups, from the Am Olam movement in Kiev, Vilna, and Minsk, were motivated to emigrate in order to establish agricultural communes. For further discussion of the group, see Nora Levin, *While Messiah Tarried: Jewish Socialist Movements, 1871–1917* (New York: Schocken Books, 1977), pp. 47–53. For the most part, Am Olam groups were told, upon arrival in the United States, that there was no land available, put in hostels for newcomers and left to their own devices. Aleksander Harkavy, a member of the Am Olam group, recounted his experiences in *Perakim me-hayay.* See also *YIVO Bletter,* vol. 19, p. 277. Only a few of the agricultural plans came to fruition, resulting in short-lived experiments in Louisiana, North Dakota, and Colorado. Howe, *World of Our Fathers,* p. 84; ibid., 32–34.

39. An immigrant who came in 1888 joined a group of about twenty people from his wife's hometown because "we wanted to go together." E. M. Wagner, YIVO, RG 102, no. 45, p. 143. Such groups were not unusual in cases when emigrants did not have an exit permit and had to be smuggled across the border from Russia to Germany or Austria.

40. *Yudishes Folksblatt,* 22 January 1887, pp. 55–57; 9 January 1885, pp. 19–23. Cohen, *Transplanted,* p. 93. With the continuous flow of immigrants to the German ports of Hamburg and Bremen, the German authorities tightened their control over the movements of transit passengers. Those arriving in Berlin were detained in special facilities until their departure to Hamburg or Bremen and were forbidden to enter the city. U.S., Congress, House, *Report of the Commissioners of Immigration upon the Causes which Incite Immigration to the United States,* 52nd Cong., 1st sess., 1892, p. 23.

41. A. Berlow, YIVO, RG 102, no. 70, pp. 37, 38; U.S. Congress, Senate, *Report of the Committee of the Senate upon the Relation between Labor and Capital,* 48th Cong., 1st sess., 1885, vol. 2, p. 1216. The crews of German ships, which carried the majority of Jewish immigrants, were reported to have maltreated their passengers more than crews of British ships. The German ships also lacked sanitary facilities and were slower than their British counterparts, which made the trip from Liverpool in ten days as opposed to the nineteen it took a German boat to reach New York from Hamburg. *Yudishes Folksblatt,* 9 January 1885, p. 21.

42. Anon., "Carpenter from Mohilev" YIVO, RG 102, no. 83, p. 39.

43. E. M. Wagner, YIVO, RG 102, no. 45, p. 150.

44. *Yudishes Folksblatt,* 5 February 1887, 14 October 1882; Howe, *World of Our Fathers,* pp. 42–50.

45. *Yudishes Folksblatt,* 5 February 1887, p. 87.

46. Anon., YIVO, RG 102, no. 24, p. 31.

47. Kula et al., eds., *Listy Emigrantow,* letters 324, 274; letters 302, 291.

48. Anon., YIVO, RG 102, no. 24, p. 12; Melamed, *Hayim kemo she-hem,* part 2, p. 239.

49. A. Balson, YIVO, RG 113, p. 8; M. Havelin, YIVO, RG 102, no. 21, pp. 20, 21. A weaver by profession, Havelin rejected job opportunities until he found friends from the army who helped him buy a grocery store.

50. J. Dyenson, YIVO, RG 102, no. 147, p. 41.

51. Quoted in Levin, *While Messiah Tarried,* p. 70.

52. Cohen, *Transplanted,* p. 103.

53. Ibid.

54. Ibid.

55. J. Dyenson, YIVO, RG 102, no. 147, p. 44; Cohen, *Transplanted,* p. 181.

56. S. Ginsburg tells of a Henry Street resident who charged newcomers a commission for finding their relatives and friends, holding them as hostages in his house until they paid him. S. Ginsburg, YIVO RG 102, no.156, p 11.

57. Anon., "Hamesaper" ("The Storyteller"), YIVO, RG 102, no. 75, p. 24.

58. Harkavy, *Perakim me-hayay,* p. 52; Howe, *World of Our Fathers,* p. 47.

59. HEAS to H. Makower of the Central German Committee for Russian Jewish Refugees in Berlin, 21 July 1882, YIVO, RG 406, doc. 681.

60. Ibid; *Yudishes Folksblatt,* 19 November 1881, p. 126. The same source informed its readers in Russia that the aid committee paid $1.50 to each newcomer.

61. Harkavy, *Perakim me-hayay,* p. 53.

62. J. Gershin, YIVO, RG 113, p. 35. Gershin was particularly proud of the education he had received in the Bund, where "students and college boys and girls would teach us writing." Ibid.

63. Although the New York charities discontinued their policy of dispersion in 1882, they continued to run an employment service in New York. The abandoned dispersion project was subsequently revived in 1904 with the establishment of the Industrial Removal Office, which was administered and financed by the same charities.

64. A. Levey, Secretary of HEAS to N.S. Joseph of Mansion House Committee of London, 14 July 1882, YIVO, RG 406, doc. 668. In contrast to the "old immigrants" whose vitality, resourcefulness, and energy were tested by the arduous journey to America, their contemporary counterparts, lacking money, trade, and skills and benefitting from the low ship fares, presented an altogether inferior and weaker race of newcomers, complained contemporary critics of the "new immigration." George Price, "The Russian Jews in America," reprinted in *Publications of the American Jewish Historical Society* 48 (September–December 1958): 28–62, 78–133. Himself a Jewish immigrant from Russia in 1882, Price was reflecting the prevailing views of the 1890s.

65. *Ha-magid,* 15 November 1882, p. 357. A Hebrew newspaper published in Lyck, Eastern Prussia, *Ha-magid* reported the Wards Island story through its special New York correspondent.

66. Ibid. Also *Ha-magid,* 25 October 1882, p. 335; 22 November 1882, p. 365; *American Hebrew,* 20 October 1882; *New York Tribune,* 15 October 1882, p. 7; *New York*

World, 15 October 1882, p. 1; 16 October 1882, p. 1. Also Leo Shpall, tr., "The Memoirs of Doctor George M. Price," *Publication of American Historical Society* 48 (December 1957): 105–109.

67. Edward Corsi, *In the Shadow of Liberty: The Chronicle of Ellis Island* (New York: Macmillan, 1935), p. 61.

68. *New York World,* 16 October 1882, p. 1; *Ha-magid,* 25 October 1882, p. 335.

69. William Seligman to Zadoc Kahan, Chief Rabbi of Paris, 28 June 1882, YIVO, RG 406, doc. 647.

70. *Yudishes Folksblatt,* 7 January 1882, p. 12; 19 November 1881, p. 127.

71. *American Israelite,* 17 March 1882, p. 298.

72. Emphasis in the original. Quoted in Harold Silver, "Some Attitudes of East European Jewish Immigrants toward Organized Charity in the U.S. in the Years 1890–1900," Unpublished Dissertation, Graduate School for Jewish Social Work, New York, 1934, in New York Public Library, Jewish Division, p. 104.

73. *American Israelite,* 9 December 1881, p. 190; 18 August 1882, p. 50; 20 January 1882, p. 238; 17 February 1882, p. 266.

74. M. A. Kursheedt, of the Russian Emigrant Relief Fund, to the Alliance in Paris, 31 October 1881, YIVO, RG 406, doc. 576.

75. YIVO, RG 406, docs. 726–32.

76. "Lament from America," *Yudishes Folksblatt,* 25 June 1882, p. 484. The scabbing incident as related in the newspaper concerned, most probably, the freight-handlers' strike of May–June 1882.

77. Quoted in Philip Foner, *History of the Labor Movement in the United States* (New York: International Publishers, 1955), vol. 2, p. 18.

78. "Lament from America," *Yudishes Folksblatt,* 13 August 1882, p. 485.

79. Harkavy, *Perakim me-hayay,* pp. 46, 47.

80. "A story of a 'green' watchmaker," *Yudishes Folksblatt,* 19 February 1887, p. 121.

81. Ibid.

82. "Lament from America," *Yudishes Folksblatt,* 13 August 1882, p. 486.

83. Zosa Szajkowski, "Deportation of Jewish Immigrants," *American Jewish Historical Quarterly* 67 (June 1978): 301.

84. Cohen, *Transplanted,* p. 105. "Eating by day" refers to the custom practiced by the wealthier members of the community of providing meals to poor religious students on certain assigned days. Cohen, who was orphaned at an early age, lived on charitable handouts from Jews in nearby villages. The need of immigrants to work hard was also reflected in many letters newcomers sent to their relatives in Europe. Kula et al., eds., *Listy Emigrantow,* letters 266, 320, 282.

85. Cohen, *Transplanted,* p. 116. After acquiring some experience, Cohen, in turn, brought his brother to work in the same factory.

86. Ibid., p. 132.

87. Harkavy, *Perakim me-hayay,* pp. 55, 59.

88. Ibid., p. 58.

89. Ibid.

90. "Lament from America," *Yudishes Folksblatt,* 13 August 1882, p. 486.

91. M. Touritz, YIVO, RG 102, no. 121, p. 4. Anon., YIVO, RG 102, no. 24, p. 4.

92. J. Dyenson, YIVO, RG 102, no. 147, p. 44; M. Turitz, YIVO, RG 102, no. 121, p. 5.

93. For testimonies from Lower East Side peddlers, offered at a hearing investigating Rabbi Jacob Joseph's funeral on July 30, 1902, see the minutes of the Committee to Investigate the Riot: 12 August 1902, YIVO, RG 117. J. Dyenson reported that his daily peddling profits on the Lower East Side averaged forty-eight cents. J. Dyenson, YIVO, RG 102, no. 147, p. 44; Cohen, in *Transplanted,* told of his peddling saga in the early 1880s in different parts of New England, pp. 137–41; Louis Glass, who as a child of thirteen was told by his father, immediately upon arrival in America, to peddle in the Perth Amboy area, reported an admittedly high income of 100 dollars a week. L. Glass, YIVO, RG 113, pp. 5, 44.

94. Reznikoff and Reznikoff, *Family Chronicle,* p. 175. For example, S. Ginsburg, who was forced to peddle because he could not find employment during the economic crisis of 1893, told of his longing for waged work after his stint in peddling. S. Ginsburg, YIVO, RG 102, no. 156, pp. 17, 18; L. Glass, YIVO, RG 113, p. 5.

95. Of 26,078 working persons surveyed, 2,440 were peddlers. Baron de Hirsch Fund Papers, Jewish Historical Society, box 16, file: Census 1890. By 1900, the number of peddlers doubled, reaching 4,215 while the number of wage earners more than quadrupled, reaching 113,048. *Jewish Encyclopedia,* 1905 ed., s.v. "United States." Moses Rischin arrived at the considerably higher number of 25,000 "peregrinating tradesmen" for 1900. The ranks of peddlers swelled according to levels of unemployment, especially during slack seasons, according to Rischin. *The Promised City,* p. 56.

96. Andrew Heinze, *Adapting to Abundance: Jewish Immigrants, Mass Consumption, and the Search for American Identity* (New York: Columbia University Press, 1990), p. 193.

97. Ibid., p. 196.

98. Ewen, *Immigrant Women in the Land of Dollars,* p. 168.

99. Melamed, *Hayim kemo she-hem,* part 2, p. 189.

100. M. Alper immigrated in 1888, after rejecting the prospect of becoming a *melamed* (a religious teacher), YIVO, RG 102, no. 30. Also, E. M. Wagner, a disenchanted melamed, came to America in 1888 hoping to find a favorable environment to learn a trade, YIVO, RG 102, no. 45.

101. Anon., "Carpenter from Mohilev," YIVO, RG 102, no. 83, pp. 40, 42. Similarly, Haskell, YIVO, RG 113, a weaver, who came in 1898, failed to find a job in his craft and was forced to become a skirt operator. A. Balson, another case in point, was a shoemaker in Russia but became a reefer maker upon arriving in the United States in 1906, YIVO, RG 113; B. Golbin, a chairmaker in the old country, began work in construction and eventually became a presser because the construction union in Chicago refused to accept Jews. Although he finally gained admittance to the union,

he worked both in construction and in garments, depending on the season. YIVO, Aaron Antonovsky Editorial Records.

102. New York Labor Department, Inspection Bureau, *Annual Report*, 1892, p. 10.

103. Ibid.

Chapter 3. Jewish Immigrants and the New York Clothing Industry

1. Margaret R. Somers, "Narrativity, Narrative Identity, and Social Action: Rethinking English Working-Class Formation," *Social Science History* 16 (Winter 1992): 608.

2. For a discussion of the "residual" perspective as a tool to explain the nature of collective action and the limitations of that approach, see Leon Fink, "Looking Backward: Reflections on Workers' Culture and Certain Conceptual Dilemmas within Labor History," Moody and Kessler-Harris, eds., *Perspectives on American Labor History: The Problems of Synthesis*, pp. 5–29.

3. Dawley, *Class and Community: The Industrial Revolution in Lynn*, pp. 80–83.

4. Kuznets, "Immigration of Russian Jews," p. 109. Ezra Mendelsohn noted the existence of a Jewish proletariat in a number of cities by the 1880s. In Bialystok, for example, Jewish workers were employed in textiles, mainly in small factories and shops, or at home. They also found employment in cigarette manufacture and in tanneries, both characterized by nonmechanized labor processes. Jewish employers seemed clearly to prefer Christian workers, who were considered more reliable and less rebellious. Mendelsohn, *Class Struggle in the Pale*, p. 18.

5. The newcomers' labor identity is further complicated by their categorization as "skilled." For a discussion of the degree and the transferability of their skills, see Kuznets, "Immigration of Russian Jews," pp. 109, 119.

6. For a full discussion of the "cultural" paradigm and the integration of gender into class analysis, see Leon Fink, "Culture's Last Stand? Gender and the Search for Synthesis in American Labor History," in Leon Fink, *In Search of the Working Class; Essays in American Labor History and Political Culture* (Urbana: University of Illinois Press, 1994).

7. Unlike other industries, the expansion of production did not fully transfer workers into the factory. Although family-based production gave way to shops utilizing hired labor, the home worker employing his family continued to exist, especially in vest and pants production. U.S. Congress, Senate, *Report on Conditions of Employment of Women and Child Wage-Earners in the United States*, S.Doc. 645, 61st Cong., 2nd sess., 1910, vol. 2, p. 492. The immigrants also tended to replace skilled women workers, especially in the manufacture of men's garments, assigning them the least skilled and the lowest paid work. Ibid., p. 495.

8. Quoted in Leon Fink, "American Labor History," Eric Foner, ed., *The New American History* (Philadelphia: Temple University Press, 1984), p. 241.

9. The census figures, with the exception those of 1890, do not distinguish between custom-made and ready-made clothes. However, it would be safe to assume

that the ready-made sector's impressive share of the total remained at least as large, if not greater, in later years. According to the census figures, the number of workers in the men's ready-made clothing sector in 1890 constituted approximately 85 percent of the total, while the value of ready-made men's clothes amounted to about 80 percent of the total. These figures surpassed the proportion of ready-made clothing for the nation as a whole, which had risen in 1890 to 60 percent of clothing produced that year. U.S. Congress, House, *Report of the Committee on Manufactures on the Sweating System,* 52nd Cong., 2nd sess., 1893, Introduction, p. iv.

10. U.S. Department of Labor, Bureau of Labor Statistics, *Regularity of Employment in the Women's Ready-to-Wear Garment Industries,* Bulletin 183, Miscellaneous Series No. 12 (Washington, D.C.: Government Printing Office, 1916), p. 22.

11. Ibid., p. 16.

12. *New York Times,* 18 August 1885, p. 4. This expansion continued at a similar pace. In 1890, cloak manufacture employed ten thosuand workers; in 1900 the number of workers reached twenty-four thousand, and by 1910, it amounted to fifty thousand. Levine, *The Women's Garment Workers,* pp. 168–69. According to the *Immigration Commission Report,* cloak and suit manufacturers of New York employed 68,466 workers in 1907, half of whom were women. U.S. Congress, Senate, *Immigration Commission Report,* S. Doc., 633, 61st Cong., 2nd sess., 1907, vol. 11, p. 387.

13. Levine, *The Women's Garment Workers,* p. 145; *Immigration Commission,* vol. 11, p. 387.

14. U.S. Congress, Senate, *Report of the Committee of the Senate upon the Relations between Labor and Capital,* 48th Cong., 1st sess., 1885, vol. 1, p. 414. The Committee was set up in 1882 and began its investigation in early 1883.

15. The House of Brook, for example, employed twenty-eight people on their premises and fifteen hundred outside tailors; in 1849, Lewish and Hanford, another leading manufacturer, employed seventy-two inside tailors and thirty-six hundred outside. Egal Feldman, *Fit for Men: A Study of New York's Clothing Trade* (Washington: Public Affairs Press, 1960), pp. 96, 98.

16. Quoted in David Montgomery, *The Fall of the House of Labor: The Workplace, the State and American Labor Activism, 1865–1925* (New York: Cambridge University Press, 1989), p. 117.

17. *Report of the Committee of the Senate upon the Relations between Labor and Capital,* vol. 1, p. 746.

18. Division of labor had already existed within the family as a unit of production, with finishing almost always being assigned to women. *U.S. Industrial Commission on the Relations and Conditions of Capital and Labor,* 56th Cong., 2nd sess., 1901–1902, vol. 15, p. 346.

19. Ibid., p. 345. Also, Mabel H. Willett, *The Employment of Women in the Clothing Industry* (New York: Columbia University Press, 1902), p. 41. According to Pope, the most economical shops employed two operators, a presser and one or two workers performing the less-skilled labor of sewing buttons, trimming, and finishing. Jesse E. Pope, *The Clothing Industry in New York* (Columbia: Missouri University Press, 1905),

p. 67. Various configurations were developed from the basic structure. One New York contractor employed six operators, four basters, two pressers, and one trimmer. U.S. Congress, House, Manufactures Committee, *Report on the Sweating System*, H.R. 2309, 52nd Cong., 2nd sess., 1893, p. 116.

20. *Industrial Commission*, vol. 15, p. 336; Willett, *Employment of Women in the Clothing Industry*, p. 36; Ronald Mendel, "Workers in Gilded Age New York and Brooklyn," (Ph.D. diss., City University of New York, 1989), p. 129. The exploitation of the workers through the task system contributed to their militancy, as will be shown in chapter 4.

21. *Report of the Committee of the Senate upon the Relations between Labor and Capital*, vol. 1, p. 417.

22. Willett, *Employment of Women in the Clothing Industry*, p. 37.

23. *Report on the Sweating System*, p. 234. According to John Commons, the demand for speed and the progressively longer day also resulted in the exclusion of women—mainly tailors' wives—from basting and finishing processes, which they had performed up to that time within the home production unit. *Industrial Commission*, vol. 15, p. 346.

24. Ibid., p. 366. *Report on the Condition of Women and Child Wage-Earners in the United States*, vol. 2, p. 425. See also Bernard Weinstein, *Di idishe yunyons in Amerika: Bleter geshikte un erinerungen* (New York: United Hebrew Trades, 1929), pp. 248, 277, 278, 281.

25. *U.S. Census of Manufactures*, 1900, "Special Reports on Selected Industries," p. 301. The system was also introduced in the coat industry, where the detailed division of labor was said to save 50 percent of previous labor costs. According to the report compiled for the first decade of the twentieth century, these savings resulted from the utilization of highly skilled labor together with cheap nonskilled labor employed in finishing, with both being employed in full-scale mass production. *Report on the Condition of Women and Child Wage-Earners in the United States*, vol. 2, p. 426.

26. *Report of the Committee of the Senate upon the Relations between Labor and Capital*, vol. 1, pp. 418, 420. Contracting also proliferated in the manufacture of shirts, overalls, pantaloons, and cheaper grade goods. Starting with the large-scale production of uniforms during the Civil War, large manufactures in Boston, Philadelphia, and New York contracted work to women in outlying rural areas. *Report on the Sweating System*, pp. 11, 13, 16. Feldman, *Fit for Men*, pp. 103, 104. *Industrial Commission*, vol. 7, p. 193.

27. New York State Department of Labor, Bureau of Inspection, *Annual Report*, 1892, p. 12. Another variation of the principle of contracting was the system of "inside contracting," whereby the contractor, though working on the premises of the manufacturer, did the hiring of "helpers" and was responsible for their wages. The system of contracting at all stages aimed at the further reduction of labor costs and became synonymous with sweating.

28. New York State Department of Labor, Bureau of Inspection, *Annual Report*, 1892, pp. 12, 66. *Immigration Commission*, vol. 11, p. 384. The degree to which con-

tracting could substitute for factory production depended on the type and quality of garments. In the cloak industry, for example, out of one hundred cloak firms in New York in 1892, only six made their garments in their own factories, while the rest had them made by contractors. New York State Department of Labor, Bureau of Inspection, *Annual Report,* 1892, p. 10. Similarly, the manufacture of pants, coats, vests, and overcoats was mostly contracted out. *Report on the Condition of Women and Child Wage-Earners in the United States,* vol. 2, pp. 421, 422. Cloak manufacture underwent a marked decrease of contracted work in the 1900s, with only one quarter of all cloaks and suits being produced by contractors. Levine, *The Women's Garment Workers,* p. 169. According to John Commons, the contractors were displaced by small independent manufacturers, who began acting as their own agents, selling finished goods directly to wholesalers and mail-order houses. *Industrial Commission,* vol. 15, p. 322.

29. Out of 241 establishments of ready-made garments in 1888, 234 were owned by Jews. *Jewish Encyclopedia,* 1905 ed., s.v. "United States." See also *Industrial Commission,* vol. 15, pp. 320, 321.

30. *Report on the Sweating System,* p. 7. A contractor often worked for more than one manufacturer who, in turn, used numerous contractors. For example, E. S. Benjamin, a partner in one of the largest New York cloak firms, testified that the firm employed as many as two hundred to three hundred contractors. Ibid., p. 23. According to Benjamin, forty contractors did half of the firm's total work; the rest, it appears, received only small assignments. Work distributed to contractors was divided according to the stage of production, as well as by different garment.

31. *Immigration Commission,* vol. 11, p. 385; *Report on the Sweating System,* Introduction, pp. vi, vii.

32. Many tailor-artisans were enticed to emigrate from their native country by the promise of high American wages, reportedly one-third higher than those in England. The promise that tailors were the best-paid tradesmen in America was confirmed by entrepreneurs, as well as by immigrants, who were keen to attract European labor. Feldman, *Fit for Men,* pp. 94, 95. In the 1850s, leading wholesalers in cloak and coat manufacturing employed large numbers of German and Irish tailors. In 1885, of the 12,609 tailors in New York, 12,109 were foreign born; of these, 6,709 were German and 4,171 were Irish. Ibid., p. 95. Similar ethnic composition could be found among owners of large tailoring establishments for custom-made garments; out of 403 tailors of that category, 159 were born in Germany, 81 in Ireland, and 23 in England. Ibid. Although the foreign-born represented the majority of garment workers, immigrants' children represented only 14.9 percent among all the tailoring occupations. *Industrial Commission,* vol. 15, p. 319.

33. Ibid.

34. Waltham, Massachusetts, American Jewish Historical Society Archives, Baron de Hirsch Fund Papers, Box 16, File: Census 1890.

35. New York State Labor Department, Bureau of Inspection, *Annual Report,* 1897, pp. 43, 45.

36. *Report on the Condition of Women and Child Wage-Earners in the United States,* vol.

2, p. 495. See also, Nancy L. Green, *Ready-to-Wear and Ready-to-Work: A Century of Industry and Immigrants* (Durham, N.C.: Duke University Press, 1997), pp. 161–68.

37. Ibid., p. 493, 422. Also Willett, *Employment of Women in the Clothing Industry*, p. 34.

38. Mendel, "Workers in Gilded Age New York and Brooklyn, 1886–1898," p. 339.

39. Pope, *The Clothing Industry in New York*, p. 58.

40. While in small shops employing less than twenty-five workers the ratio was four males to one female, in larger ones employing twenty-five to fifty workers the ratio was three men to one woman, and in shops and factories of fifty to one hundred it was less than two males to one female. Mendel,"Workers in Gilded Age New York and Brooklyn, 1886–1898," p. 339. On the whole, Jewish women did not seek employment in the industry after marriage. Glenn, *Daughters of the Shtetl*, pp. 67–73. See also, Roger Waldinger, "Another look at the International Ladies' Garment Workers' Union: Women, Industry Structure and Collective Action," Ruth Milkman, ed., *Women, Work and Protest: A Century of U.S. Women's Labor History* (London: Routledge, 1991) p. 86–109.

41. Quoted in Tcherikower, ed., *The Early Jewish Labor Movement in the United States*, p. 152.

42. New York Labor Department, Inspection Bureau, *Annual Report*, 1892, p. 10.

43. J. Guterman, YIVO, RG 113, p. 1; Haskell, YIVO, RG 113, p. 1.

44. Ella Wolf, YIVO, RG 113, p. 7; I. Schoenholtz, YIVO, RG 113, pp. 1, 2. Levine, *The Women's Garment Workers*, p. 418

45. Pauline Newman, YIVO, RG 113, p. 6; Ella Wolf, YIVO, RG 113, p. 4. Operators and apprentices generally had to provide their own sewing machine at a cost of $40 to $60 in the 1890s. In some cases, the employer would rent machines and deduct a fee from the workers' weekly wages. Operators used to carry their machines with them from job to job and also out of fear that their boss might confiscate or steal them. I. Schoenholtz, YIVO, RG 113, p. 12.

46. Anon., YIVO, RG 102, no. 24, p. 32.

47. S. Ginsburg, YIVO, RG 102, no. 156, p. 13; L. Glass, YIVO, RG 113, pp. 9, 10; Cohen, *Transplanted*, p. 114; J. Dyenson, YIVO, RG 102, no. 147, p. 52; S. Langer, YIVO, RG 102, p. 57. Langer learned to be a presser in exchange for sleeping in the shop and being a watchman.

48. *Arbeiter Zeitung*, 28 August 1891, pp. 1, 5.

49. Ibid., 28 August 1891, p. 1; 28 September 1891, p. 1; 29 May 1891, p. 5; Epstein, *Jewish Labor in U.S.A.*, vol. 1, p. 48.

50. Epstein, *Jewish Labor in U.S.A.*, vol. 1, pp. 48–49.

51. Anon., YIVO, RG 102, no. 24, pp. 30, 31; Cohen, *Transplanted*, p. 102; J. Gershin, YIVO, RG 113, p. 30.

52. S. Langer, YIVO, RG 102, n. 57, p. 21. Langer eventually received two dollars, after an appeal to the Industrial Removal Office, an arm of the UHC, which sued the boss. He was finally apprenticed as a presser in a shop where he worked as a watchman whose responsibility was to light a fire for the irons every morning.

53. Anon. YIVO, RG 102, no. 24, pp. 32, 33.

54. Lena Weinberger, born in 1888 in the Vilna district, came to the U.S. in 1905, YIVO, RG 102, p. 11; Glenn, *Daughters of the Shtetl*, pp. 126–27.

55. S. Langer, YIVO, RG 102, no. 57, p. 21; L. Glass, YIVO, RG 113, p. 9.

56. Melamed, *Hayim kemo she-hem*, p. 205.

57. S. Langer, YIVO, RG 102, no. 57, pp. 25, 26.

58. Cohen, *Out of the Shadow*, p. 112; B. Fenster, YIVO, RG 113, p. 13; A. Herschowitz, YIVO, RG 113, pp. 1, 2; P. Newman, YIVO, RG 113, p. 4; A. Berlow, YIVO, RG 102, no. 70, p. 48.

59. Glenn, *Daughters of the Shtetl*, pp. 102–03.

60. Cohen, *Out of the Shadow*, p. 274.

61. J. Werlin, YIVO, RG 102, no. 71–71c, p. 52. Also Ella Wolf, YIVO, RG 113, p. 5.

62. B. Fenster, YIVO, RG 113, pp. 9, 10; E. M. Wagner, YIVO, RG 102, no. 45, p. 173; L. Rosenman, YIVO, RG 102, no. 31, p. 17; A. Scherer, YIVO, RG 113, p. 7; *Yudishes Folksblatt*, 14 October 1892.

63. Newcomers often displaced more experienced workers. A newly trained cutter, earning only five dollars, replaced his predecessor who had earned twelve. L. Glass, YIVO, RG 113, p. 10. Also, S. J. Levy, YIVO, RG 102, no. 32–32a, p. 31; *Arbeiter Zeitung*, 29 May 1891, p. 5. Immigrant workers displaced more experienced workers in other industries as well. B. Reisman, YIVO, RG 102, no. 38–38a, p. 74; S. Ginsburg, YIVO, RG 102. no. 156, p. 24; A. Berlow, YIVO, RG 102, no. 70, p. 45; *Arbeiter Zeitung*, 5 January 1894, p. 3.

64. *Report of Committee of the Senate upon the Relations between Labor and Capital*, vol. 1, pp. 414, 749.

65. Ibid., pp. 749, 752.

66. Ibid., pp. 414, 417, 748.

67. *Report on Condition of Women and Child Wage-Earners in the United States*, vol. 9, p. 151.

68. *Report of the Committee of the Senate upon the Relations between Labor and Capital*, Samuel Gompers' testimony, vol. 1, p. 284. Women generally earned considerably less and often as little as half that of men's earnings. See New York State Bureau of Labor Statistics, *Annual Report*, 1897, pp. 446–51 for some comparison of men's and women's earnings, as reported by different garment workers unions. The average annual earnings for men in 1897 ranged from $415.30 to $580.78, while the average earnings for women for the same year ranged from $245.28 to $312.98. *Industrial Commission*, vol. 15, p. 338.

69. Mendel, "Workers in Gilded Age New York and Brooklyn 1886–1898," p. 134. According to Mendel, the wage gap persisted even when women entered the more skilled occupation, due mainly to men's greater experience and pace, as well as their willingness to work longer hours. Ibid.

70. Glenn, *Daughters of the Shtetl*, pp. 117–22.

71. Ibid.

72. In 1892, approximately two-thirds of all New York City clothing workers were employed in tenements. New York State Department of Labor, Bureau of Inspection, *Annual Report,* 1892, p. 66. Nonorganized and organized cloakmakers in 1885, for example, received weekly wages ranging from $8 to $12. New York State Bureau of Labor Statistics, *Annual Report,* 1885, p. 519. See also *Annual Report,* 1896, pp. 736–43 for similar comparisons of wages earned by the organized and the unorganized workers in different jobs in the industry. A machine operator's earnings at the turn of the century were as low as $11 per week and as high as $60 in the custom-made trade. *Industrial Commission,* vol. 15, pp. 335.

73. Ibid. In 1888, according to the New York State Bureau of Labor, some machine operators earned $6 per week, while others earned $13. The weekly wages of organized cutters ranged between $12 and $35. New York State Bureau of Labor Statistics, *Annual Report,* 1888, vol. 1, p. 483. For wage differences among women workers for the same year, see ibid., pp. 403, 501, 508, 515.

74. In women's garment manufacturing, the busy season began in mid-September, reaching its peak in mid-October. The slow period began in November and continued until February. Then the second busy season began, lasting well into May. The months between May and August constituted a second dull season. *Regularity of Employment in the Women's Ready-to-Wear Garment Industries,* p. 31. The definitions of busy and dull seasons differ and, according to another source, the period of May, June, and July was the busy season for manufacturing winter clothes, while during October, November, December, and January summer clothes were made. *Immigration Commission,* vol. 11, p. 388; *Industrial Commission,* vol. 15, p. 338.

75. New York State Bureau of Labor Statistics, *Annual Report,* 1890, pp. 279, 280, New York State Department of Labor, Bureau of Inspection, *Annual Report,* 1892, p. 26, *Immigration Commission,* vol. 11, p. 386. According to James Reynolds of University Settlement, some pantsmakers worked eighteen hours a day for $1.50. *New York Times,* 2 June 1897, p. 3.

76. *Industrial Commission,* vol. 15, p. xxviii; ibid., p. 368. For comparisons of wages for shorter periods of three to four years, see New York State Bureau of Labor Statistics, *Annual Report,* 1896, pp. 736–43 (for the years 1891–1895). For the years 1897–1899 see *Industrial Commission,* vol. 15, pp. 335–38.

77. *Industrial Commission,* vol. 7, p. 192, testimony taken in 1899. John Swinton also criticized the newcomers for their willingness to work long hours: "They cannot understand that every garment made after 6 o'clock, or after a ten-hour day's work, is only a weight to pull them down." *John Swinton's Paper,* 23 August 1885, p. 4; Jacob Riis quoted in Rischin, *The Promised City,* p. 182.

78. *Report of the Committee of the Senate upon the Relations between Labor and Capital,* vol. 1, pp. 413, 414. According to one witness, machine noise restricted work to daylight hours. Ibid.

79. Ibid., p. 414.

80. Ibid., p. 418.

81. New York State Bureau of Labor Statistics, *Annual Report,* 1890, pp. 542, 565.

82. New York State Department of Labor, Bureau of Inspection, *Annual Report,* 1892, p. 10.

83. Immigration Commission, vol. 11, pp. 380, 381. However, it appears that at some point after the ten-year period, increases in earnings slowed down considerably and became dependent on factors besides the length of stay in the U.S., such as education. Thus, Jewish immigrants, other than Russians, showed greater gains in earnings after the first ten years of residency, an advantage also shared by Northern Italians over their counterparts from Southern Italy.

84. J. Dyenson, YIVO, RG 102, no. 147, p. 59. The same immigrant later became a conductor on the Third Avenue El, but because of troubles with thugs and "the slavery of the job," he changed his occupation again, first becoming a collector for an insurance company and then a traveling salesman. Ibid., p. 61.

85. A. Gumner, YIVO, RG 102, no. 44, np; Cohen, *Transplanted,* pp. 217, 156.

86. Louis Borgenicht, *The Happiest Man* (New York: G. P. Putnam's Sons, 1942), p. 220; Reznikoff and Reznikoff, *Family Chronicle,* pp. 90–93.

87. Melamed, *Hayim kemo she-hem,* p. 205; L. Glass, YIVO, RG 113, p. 9.

88. Jeff Haydu, *Between Craft and Class: Skilled Workers and Factory Politics in the United States and Britain 1890–1922* (Berkeley and Los Angeles: University of California Press, 1988), p. 20.

Chapter 4. Making a Home and Earning a Living on the Lower East Side

1. Margaret Somers, "Citizenship and the Place of the Public Sphere: Law, Community, and Political Culture in the Transition to Democracy," *American Sociological Review* 58 (October 1993): 589.

2. Robert Anthony Orsi, *The Madonna of 115th Street: Faith and Community in Italian Harlem, 1880–1950* (New Haven: Yale University Press, 1985), pp. 35, 105.

3. Ella Wolf, YIVO, RG 113, pp. 7–8.

4. Chapters 5 and 6 will show how immigrant culture often conflicted with the city's police and the judicial system.

5. Conzen et al., "The Invention of Ethnicity: A Perspective from the U.S.A.," pp. 9, 12.

6. Rischin, *The Promised City,* p. 93. The figures for the 1890s and the 1900s are approximations. According to Rischin, 75 percent of the total New York Jewish population in 1892 lived on the Lower East Side. In 1890 that population reached 225,000. In 1903, only 50 percent of 580,000 New York Jews lived on the Lower East Side.

7. Quoted in Howe, *World of Our Fathers,* p. 69.

8. The proximity of the Lower East Side to the Houston Street and Grand Street ferries and, after 1903, to the Williamsburg Bridge facilitated the expansion of Jewish settlement into Brooklyn, which had already begun during the 1880s. Rischin, *The Promised City,* p. 92. See also Jeffrey S. Gurock, *When Harlem was Jewish, 1870–1930* (New York: Columbia University Press, 1979).

9. Ibid., p. 84; George Price, "The Russian Jew in America," trans. Leo Shpall, *Publication of American Jewish Historical Society* 48 (September 1958): 56. Nonpayment of rents plagued the poor of the Lower East Side; in the years 1891 to 1892, in two court districts on the East Side, 11,550 dispossession warrants were issued. Rischin, *The Promised City*, p. 84. Also, Walter Scott Andrew, "Law and Litigation," in Charles Bernheimer, ed., *The Russian Jew in the United States* (Philadelphia: John C. Winston, 1905), p. 342; Maurice Fishberg, "Health and Sanitation," ibid., p. 289; Price, "The Russian Jew in America," p. 54.

10. "Letters to Lithuania," *Ha-Ivry*, 2 July 1893.

11. Howe, *World of Our Fathers*, p. 173. Howe's statement is based on Herbert Gutman's analysis of the 1905 census. Wives predominantly stayed at home, according to these findings, with only 2 out of 118 households listed as employed housekeepers. Ibid., p. 142. It is possible that women's work has always been underestimated in census data. Glenn, *Daughters of the Shtetl*, pp. 72, 77.

12. Pearl Halpern, YIVO, RG 113, p. 1.

13. Rischin, *The Promised City*, p. 84; Price, "The Russian Jews in America," p. 56. The Baron de Hirsch Survey of 1890 found 10 cents a night to be the average fee paid by a lodger, or a monthly average of $3.12. According to one memoir, a payment of seventy-five cents per week entitled a boarder in the 1880s to morning coffee, as well as laundry services provided by the landlady. Cohen, *Transplanted*, p. 119. See also Glenn, *Daughters of the Shtetl*, pp. 67, 72, 73.

14. Glenn, *Daughters of the Shtetl*, pp. 73–76; Kessler-Harris, "Organizing the Unorganizable: Three Jewish Women and their Union," p. 145.

15. Salo W. Baron, *Steeled by Adversity. Essays and Addresses on American Jewish Life* (Philadelphia: Jewish Publication Society of America, 1971), p. 281. The presence of women among Jewish immigrants in some years was as high as among the Irish; in 1894, for example, it reached 51.3 percent. Ibid.

16. Ibid., p. 274; Baron de Hirsch Fund's survey found in 1890 that the number of children was much higher; out of a surveyed population of 111,690, children below the age of 14 comprised 44,690, or 40 percent of the total.

17. Kuznets, "Immigration of Russian Jews," pp. 95–97.

18. Maurice Fishberg, "Health and Sanitation," in C. Bernheimer, ed., *The Russian Jew in the United States*, p. 286. The Baron de Hirsch survey of 1890 found the average family consisted of 4.81 persons. George Price, "The Russian Jew in America," p. 56; Isaac Max Rubinow, "The Jewish Question in New York City 1902–1903," *Publication of American Jewish Historical Society* 39 (December 1959): 95.

19. Cohen, *Out of the Shadow*, pp. 112, 69–70.

20. Selma C. Berrol, "Education and Economic Mobility: The Jewish Experience in New York City 1880–1920," *American Jewish Historical Quarterly* 65 (March 1976): 259, 261.

21. Superintendent Emmanuel Marx, Acting General Agent of Baron de Hirsch Fund, Baron de Hirsch Fund Papers (henceforth referred to as BHF), 12 April 1904, Box 57, Educational Alliance. Inadequate educational facilities often failed to ac-

commodate the fast-growing child population of the Lower East Side; during the 1890s, as many as fifty thousand to sixty thousand children in the elementary grades were turned away because of lack of available school space. Berrol, "Education and Economic Mobility," p. 259.

22. Epstein, *Jewish Labor in U.S.A.*, vol. 1, pp. 89, 91; Isidore Kopeloff, *A mol in Amerike* [Once upon a time in America] (Warsaw: Ch. Brzoza, 1928), p. 289.

23. Borgenicht, *The Happiest Man*, p. 193; Cohen, *Transplanted*, p. 186; Kopeloff, *A mol in Amerike*, p. 426.

24. Ibid., p. 290.

25. Ibid., pp. 294–95.

26. Cahan, *The Education of Abraham Cahan*, p, 220.

27. *Yudishe Folkszeitung*, 6 February 1888, p. 2; 20 February 1888, p. 2; Weinstein, *Di idishe yunyons in Amerika*, pp. 243, 360.

28. *Arbeiter Zeitung*, 9 June 1893, p. 2.

29. The case of the reefermakers and other examples of landsmanshaftn supporting strikers contradict some opinions, which ascribe the failure to unionize to the popularity of landsmanshaftn. Rischin, *The Promised City*, p. 182. For a discussion of the strike, see Soyer, *Jewish Immigrant Associations*, pp. 130–31.

30. Rischin, *The Promised City*, p. 77; Cahan, *The Education of Abraham Cahan*, p. 300.

31. Rischin, *The Promised City*, p. 183. Ethnic animosities between, for example, "Litwacks" (Lithuanians) and Hungarians and differences between observant Jews and the nonreligious were considered to be a serious obstacle to working-class solidarity by the Socialist leadership. "Unity," *Yudishe Folkszeitung*, 6 February 1888, p. 2.

32. Sarna, ed., *People Walk on Their Heads*, p. 61. Rabbi Weinberger was a vociferous critic of New York Jewry in the 1880s.

33. Rischin, *The Promised City*, p. 146. A contemporary survey found that only 25 percent rested on the Sabbath and that 60 percent of stores were open. Charles Liebman, "Religion in American Jewish History," *Jewish Journal of Sociology* 9 (December 1967): 231.

34. Ezriel Pressman, YIVO, RG 102, no. 189, p. 114, quoted in Moses Kligsberg, "Jewish Immigrants in Business: A Sociological Study," *American Jewish Historical Quarterly* 56 (March 1967): 313.

35. Borgenicht, *The Happiest Man*, pp. 190, 191.

36. B. Rabinowitz, YIVO, RG 113, p. 2.

37. Cohen, *Transplanted*, p. 103.

38. Weinstein, *Di idishe yunyons in Amerika*, pp. 266, 269, 270.

39. For the most authoritative study of the landsmanshaftn see Soyer, *Jewish Immigrant Associations*. Also, Howe, *World of Our Fathers*, pp. 184, 187; Rontch, ed., *Di idishe landsmanshaften fun Nyu York* (New York: Yiddish Writers' Union, 1938), pp. 16, 17. In 1938, there were still half a million members in New York organizations and a quarter of a million more in the rest of the country, ibid. Also, Howe, *World of Our Fathers*, p. 189.

40. For a related discussion of the role of voluntary associations in the formation of the French working class, see Maurice Agulhon, "Working Class and Sociability in France Before 1848," in Pat Thane, Geoffrey Crossick and Roderick Floud, eds., *The Power of the Past: Essays for Eric Hobsbawm* (Cambridge: Cambridge University Press, 1984), pp. 37–66.

41. *Yudishe Folkszeitung,* 20 February 1888, p. 2.

42. Rischin, *The Promised City,* p. 182. See also Michael Weisser, *A Brotherhood of Memory: Jewish Landsmanshaftn in the New World* (New York: Basic Books, 1985), p. 83.

43. "Unity," *Yudishe Folkszeitung,* 13 February 1888, p. 2.

44. Epstein, *Jewish Labor in U.S.A.,* vol. 1, p. 123. Barsky was a fascinating character, an amateur actor with a vision of the theater's potential as a means of propaganda for labor causes, who never succeeded in gaining a trade union leader's position. Ibid., pp. 124, 173, 235.

45. Soyer, *Jewish Immigrant Associations,* p. 7.

46. Ibid., pp. 78–79. "Ladies' auxiliaries," which undertook social and charitable activities but which did not provide material benefits, became popular in later years. Ibid., pp. 79, 192. According to Daniel Soyer, the American landsmanshaftn added an element of democracy in bestowing honors to individuals. In contrast to traditional ways, where lesser members deferred to those distinguished by learning or wealth, in America, one's peers bestowed the honor. Ibid., pp. 59, 82, 109.

47. Ibid., pp. 59–60; Sarna, ed., *People Walk on Their Heads,* p. 45.

48. Soyer, *Jewish Immigrant Associations,* p. 129.

49. Ibid., pp. 128–37.

50. Abraham Cahan, *Bleter fun meyn leben* [Pages from my life] (New York: Forverts Association, 1926), vol. 3, pp. 421, 422. According to Cahan, member associations within the Arbeiter Ring came under close scrutiny; those voting for "capitalist and scab parties" were expelled. See also Soyer, *Jewish Immigrant Associations,* pp. 55–56, 66–70, 80.

51. Quoted in Zoza Szajkowski, "How Mass Immigration to America Began," *Jewish Social Studies* 4 (October 1942): 301.

52. Jacob Riis, *How the Other Half Lives: Studies among the Tenements* (New York: Charles Scribner's Sons, 1914), pp. 104–34.

53. George Price, "The Russian Jew in America," *Publication of the American Jewish Historical Society,* 48, no. 2 (December 1958): 106–07. Although himself an immigrant, Price advocated regulated immigration. Ibid., pp. 113, 122.

54. Quoted in Silver, "Some Attitudes of the East European Jewish Immigrants," p. 40.

55. Report of the President of the Baron de Hirsch Fund Trust, 1893, BHF, Box 35, File 3, Reel 1, Memorandum of Judge Isaacs, n.d.

56. M. Isaacs to Baron de Hirsch, 22 May 1890, BHF, Box 35, File 2; Arthur Reichow to Jacob Schiff, 8 December 1898, ibid., File 3, Reel 1; M. Isaacs to Baron de Hirsch, 22 May 1890, BHF, Box 35, File 2.

57. Arthur Reichow to Jacob Schiff, 8 December 1898, BHF, Box 35, File 3, Reel 1.

58. "Plan for Action by the Jewish Alliance of America in Regard to Russian Jewish Immigration, 1891," YIVO, RG 406, Doc. 2911; Arthur Reichow to Julius Goldman, 9 June 1897, BHF, Box 35, File 3, Reel 1. Also Arthur Reichow to Julius Goldman, 9 June 1897, ibid.

59. Report of Clifton Levey, Secretary of Hebrew Emigrant Aid Society, August–September 1890, BHF, Box 57, File: New York Educational Alliance.

60. Quoted in Silver, "Some Attitudes of the East European Jewish Immigrants," pp. 119.

61. Michael Heilprin to Oscar Straus, BHF, 18 January 1888, Box 35, File 2.

62. Untitled, undated, BHF, Box 36, File 5: Various histories of the Fund.

63. Henry Rice to Baron de Hirsch Fund, 15 August 1889, BHF, Box 35, File 2; Isidore Loeb to Judge Isaacs, 19 February 1890, ibid. A circular from the Central Committee of the Fund, New York, 1 December 1890, BHF, Box 35, File 2; also Julius Goldman to Jewish Colonial Association in Paris, 9 February 1897, BHF, Box 35, File 3, Reel 1.

64. Judge Isaacs to Baron de Hirsch, 11 November 1889, BHF, Box 35, File 2; Judge Isaacs to Baron de Hirsch, 22 May 1890, p. 46, ibid.

65. The Twenty-Eighth Annual Report of United Hebrew Relief Association of Chicago, 1886–1887.

66. Ibid.

67. Introductory Report submitted by Clifton Levey, August–September 1890, BHF, Box 57, File: Outside Correspondence, Educational Alliance.

68. B. Hoffman to the President of the Baron de Hirsch Fund, December 1891, BHF, Box 57, File: Outside Correspondence; Educational Alliance.

69. Clifton Levey to the Central Committee on Education, 19 August 1890, BHF, Box 57, New York Educational Alliance.

70. Ibid; Report of Louis Schnabel submitted to the Education Committee of the Baron de Hirsch Fund, 4 September 1890, BHF, Box 57, File: Outside Organizations' Correspondence, Educational Alliance.

71. Ibid.

72. Report of the Superintendent, 31 December 1891, BHF, Box 57, File: Outside Organizations' Correspondence; Educational Alliance.

73. Weekly Report (No. 5), 9 September 1890, BHF, Box 57, ibid. Clifton Levey to the General Committee on Education, 19 August 1890, ibid. Also, Clifton Levey to the Subcommittee on Education, August–September 1890, ibid. Louis Schnabel to Committee on Education, 1 October 1890, ibid.

74. Samuel Joseph, *History of the Baron de Hirsch Fund* (Philadelphia: Jewish Publication Society, 1935), p. 257.

75. Report of the Superintendent, 31 December 1891, BHF, Box 57, File: Outside Organizations' Correspondence; Educational Alliance.

76. Louis Schnabel to A. S. Solomon, 28 February 1895, ibid.

77. Circular from Central Committee of the Baron de Hirsch Fund, New York, 1

December 1890, BHF, Box 35, File: Materials re establishment of the Fund; M. Isaacs to Baron de Hirsch, 22 May 1890, p. 44, BHF, Box 35, File 2.

78. Rischin, *The Promised City*, p. 101.

79. Quoted in Silver, "Some Attitudes of Eastern European Immigrants," pp. 75, 162. For a history of Educational Alliance, see Adam Bellow, *The Educational Alliance: A Centennial Celebration* (New York: Educational Alliance, 1990).

80. Quoted in Silver, "Some Attitudes of Eastern European Immigrants," p. 24.

81. Levin, *While Messiah Tarried*, p. 145. The educational goals of Socialist leadership and labor press are discussed in chapter 6.

82. *New York Herald*, 28 May 1893, p. 37.

83. Julius Goldman to Baron de Hirsch, 6 October 1896, BHF, Box 35, File 3, Reel 1.

84. For examples of arrangements between charities and manufacturers, see Silver, "Some Attitudes of the East European Jewish Immigrants," pp. 153–55.

85. Quoted in Silver, "Some Attitudes of Eastern European Immigrants," p. 162.

86. Ibid., p. 148; ibid., p. 147.

87. George Price, "The Russian Jew in America," *Publication of American Jewish Historical Society* 48 (September 1958): 56–60.

88. *Jewish Daily Forward*, 21 November 1900, p. 1, quoted in Silver, "Some Attitudes of the East European Jewish Immigrants," pp. 66, 67.

89. Cohen, *Out of the Shadow*, p. 168; *Arbeiter Zeitung*, 28 August 1891, p. 5.

90. Borgenicht, *The Happiest Man*, p. 222. The same immigrant walked through Italian neighborhoods without fearing for his life.

91. Committee to Investigate Riot: August 12, 1902, YIVO RG 117, pp. 72, 76. For details of the clash between the Jewish mourners and the Irish employees of the factory, see Leonard Dinnerstein, "The Funeral of Jacob Joseph," in David Gerber, ed., *Anti-Semitism in American History* (Urbana: University of Illinois Press, 1986), pp. 275–301. Also, Howe, *World of Our Fathers*, pp. 123–24, 194–95; Arthur Aryeh Goren, "Sacred and Secular: The Place of Public Funerals in the Immigrant Life of American Jews," *Jewish History* 4 (1994): 268–305.

92. A. Held, YIVO, RG 113, p. 3.

93. Abraham Bisno, *Abraham Bisno, Union Pioneer* (Madison: University of Wisconsin Press, 1967), pp. 79, 80.

94. Kim Voss, *The Making of American Exceptionalism: The Knights of Labor and Class Formation in the Nineteenth Century* (Ithaca: Cornell University Press, 1993), p. 91.

95. Ibid., pp. 55–59, 135.

96. Ibid., pp. 243, 245. Voss maintains that the Knights declined after 1886 due to state power, manufacturers' associations, and the rapid proliferation of less-skilled locals which drained union resources. Ibid., pp. 236–37.

97. Epstein, *Jewish Labor in U.S.A.*, vol. 1, pp. 109, 110; Weinstein, *Di idishe yunyons in Amerika*, p. 90.

98. Bisno, *Abraham Bisno, Union Pioneer*, p. 73.

99. Ibid., pp. 72, 73. As one solution to the conflict between labor and capital, the Knights advocated the establishment of workers', producers' and distributors' co-operatives. Martin Shefter, "Trade Unions and Political Machines: The Organization and Disorganization of the American Working Class in the Late Nineteenth Century," Ira Katznelson and Aristide Zolberg, eds., *Working-Class Formation: Nineteenth-Century Patterns in Western Europe and the United States* (Princeton, N.J.: Princeton University Press, 1986), p. 224; quoted in Montgomery, *The Fall of the House of Labor*, p. 121.

100. Robert Weir, *Beyond Labor's Veil: The Culture of the Knights of Labor* (University Park: Pennsylvania State University Press, 1996), p. 14.

101. Rosenberg, *Di kloukmakher un zeyere yunyons*, p. 10, quoted in Epstein, *Jewish Labor in U.S.A.*, vol. 1, p. 114.

102. Rosenberg, *Di kloukmakher un zeyere yunyons*, pp. 10, 11. A similar initiation ceremony was reported by Samuel Gompers in 1873. Weir, *Beyond Labor's Veil*, pp. 33–34.

103. Ibid., pp. 72–73, 307–08.

104. *Arbeiter Zeitung*, 9 September 1892, p. 3, 8 September 1893, p. 2. The Knights' emphasis on the concept of "nobility of toil" transcended a narrow definition of labor and came to include manufacturers and shopkeepers who accepted the principle of "producing classes" and who were sympathetic to the plight of labor. Leon Fink, *Workingmen's Democracy: The Knights of Labor and American Politics* (Urbana: University of Illinois Press, 1983), pp. 8–9.

105. Shefter, "Trade Unions and Political Machines," p. 254. The Knights' national leadership favored arbitration and was against strikes. Weir, *Beyond Labor's Veil*, p. 84.

106. *Arbeiter Zeitung*, 5 February 1892, p. 3; 19 February 1892, p. 2; 22 April 1892, p. 3. Weinstein, *Di idishe yunyons in Amerika*, p. 169; Bernard H. Bloom, "Yiddish-Speaking Socialists in America: 1892–1905, *American Jewish Archives* 12 (April 1960): 40–52.

107. Montgomery, *The Fall of the House of Labor*, p. 120. The German and Irish suit and cloak cutters' union, however, openly sided with the manufacturers against the Jewish strikers. Ibid.

108. Cahan, *The Education of Abraham Cahan*, p. 265. The Central Labor Union, a New York umbrella labor organization, was founded in 1882 by the Irish Land League and later joined by German American Socialist unions and Socialist members of Knights of Labor. The organization played an important role in New York politics, especially in Henry George's mayoral campaign of 1886. Dorothée Schneider, *Trade Unions and Community: The German Working Class in New York City, 1870–1900* (Urbana: University of Illinois Press, 1994), pp. 120–21. Although CLU was not known for its organizational efforts among the unskilled immigrants, it took up a pardon campaign on behalf of Joseph Barondess in 1892. For Barondess' involvement in the "Jamaica affair," see Levine, *The Women's Garment Workers*, pp. 60–63.

109. Epstein, *Jewish Labor in U.S.A*, vol. 1, p. 78. It should be noted that in some ethnically diverse locals of the Knights of Labor in New Jersey, translators were se-

cured for meetings, and teachers were hired to teach English. Voss, *The Making of American Exceptionalism,* p. 162.

110. Weinstein, *Di idishe yunyons in Amerika,* p. 331.

111. Oscar Feuer, YIVO RG 113, p. 6.

112. Morris Schappes, "The Political Origins of the United Hebrew Trades," *Journal of Ethnic Studies* 5 (Spring 1977): 24.

113. Ibid., pp. 24, 25, 31.

114. Cahan, *Bleter fun meyn leben,* vol. 3, p. 64, describes the May Day parade of 1890.

115. *New York Sun,* 4 September 1894, p. 3.

116. Ibid.

117. Ibid., 5 September 1894, p. 1.

118. Quoted in Bloom, "Yiddish-Speaking Socialists in America: 1892–1905," p. 44.

119. Gutman, "Work, Culture, and Society in Industrializing America, 1815–1919," p. 543

120. In Voss's view, "new unionism," i.e., organization across skill and occupation, died with the decline of the Knights. Efforts to revive an all-inclusive labor movement were successful only in the 1930s, when a weakened AFL and a strong initiative on the part of the government brought the less skilled into the mainstream labor movement. Voss, *The Making of American Exceptionalism,* pp. 244–45.

121. Robert Asher, "Jewish Unions and the American Federation of Labor Power Structure, 1903–1935," *American Jewish Historical Quarterly* 65 (March 1976): 215–27.

Chapter 5. Themes of Collective Action

1. Martin Shefter has established that the many modes of collective organization challenged, to a greater or lesser extent, "those of acquisitive individualism that was preached by the upper and middle classes and the patterns of behavior that factory managers and public officials allied with those classes were seeking to impose upon workers." Shefter, "Trade Unions and Political Machines," p. 199.

2. *New York Tribune,* 29 March 1893, p. 1.

3. This view of the community's ability to reach beyond its traditional cultural trajectory contradicts Craig Calhoun's thesis. In his view, in the early days of the industrial revolution, communal ties were the social bond unifying workers for collective action. Community in its "dense familiarity" was crucial in working-class radicalism against capitalist exploitation. Craig Calhoun, *The Question of Class Struggle: Social Foundations of Popular Radicalism during the Industrial Revolution* (Chicago: University of Chicago Press, 1982), ch. 8, passim.

4. Sidney Tarrow, "Mentalities, Political Cultures, and Collective Action Frames: Constructing Meanings through Action," Aldon D. Morris and Carol McClurg Mueller, eds., *Frontiers in Social Movement Theory* (New Haven: Yale University Press, 1992), p. 189.

5. Melech Epstein, for example, traced the growing strength of Jewish labor

from "Early Failures" (chapter 7) to "Maturity" (chapter 19) and "The Taste of Victory" (chapter 20) in his *Jewish Labor in U.S.A.* Similarly, the successful organization of the International Ladies' Garment Workers' Union in 1900 marked, for historian Louis Levine, the end of the period of "darkness." See *The Women's Garment Workers*, Part II, "Darkness and Revolt," pp. 105–95.

6. *New York Times*, 24 July 1901, p. 2. An "epidemic" of strikes was also reported in 1896. Ibid., 30 July 1896, p. 3.

7. *Folkszeitung*, 20 February 1888, p. 2. Barsky was an advocate of an industrial union that would embrace all garment workers, from the humble and least-skilled buttonholemakers to custom tailors.

8. Julius Gershin, YIVO, RG 113, p. 42.

9. Rosenberg, *Di kloukmakher un zeyere yunyons*, pp. 80, 83.

10. *New York Tribune*, 24 July 1901, p. 2. Additional forms of community action will be discussed in the next chapter.

11. *New York Times*, 22 July 1901, p. 2.

12. *Arbeiter Zeitung*, 7 September 1894, p. 2.

13. *New York Sun*, 8 September 1894, p. 2, 5 September 1894, p. 1. Isidore Schoenholtz, who immigrated in 1906 and served on the General Executive Board of the ILGWU in the years 1924–1926, equated the sweating system with Jewish enslavement, and its foremen to *nogsim ve-shotrim* (taskmasters) of Egypt. YIVO, RG 113, p. 1; *John Swinton's Paper*, 23 August 1885, p. 4.

14. Rischin, ed., *Grandma Never Lived in America*, pp. 379–80.

15. Ibid.

16. The Sanhedrin was the supreme Jewish legislative council and religious court in the second century B.C. Weinstein reported another case where the secretary of the Jacket Makers' Union was a sexton of a synagogue on Pitt Street as well as a treasurer of "an old-fashioned lodge" (referring probably to a landsmanshaft of old immigrants). Weinstein, *Di idishe yunyons in Amerika*, pp. 266, 270. *Yudishes Tageblatt*, 22 February 1892, p. 1; *Yudishes Folksblatt*, 13 August 1882, pp. 483–85; *Arbeiter Zeitung*, 5 January 1894, p. 1.

17. *Yudishes Tageblatt*, 22 February 1892, p. 1; *Yudishes Folksblatt*, 13 August 1882, pp. 483–85; *Arbeiter Zeitung*, 5 January 1894, p. 1.

18. Ibid., 8 July 1892, p. 3; 15 July 1892, p. 5. The issue of affidavits was one cause of the Baltimore tailors' strike.

19. *New York Times*, 22 July 1901, p. 2; ibid., 23 July 1901, p. 3; *Arbeiter Zeitung*, 23 May 1897, p. 1.

20. *New York Sun*, 5 November 1894, p. 1. Manufacturers and their superintendents sometimes combed the East Side to persuade and pressure workers' wives to get their husbands back to work. On this and other occasions, employers and their emissaries were met with verbal and physical attacks. Ibid.

21. *New York Times*, 23 July 1901, p. 3. A strike by the Children's Jacket Makers' Union was one case when a walkout preceded specific worker demands. Ibid., 30 July 1896, p. 3.

22. Rosenberg, *Di kloukmakher un zeyere yunyons*, p. 12; *New York Tribune*, 25 July 1900, p. 14.

23. *New York Sun*, 6 September 1894, p. 1; *New York Times*, 21 February 1895, p. 2; *New York World*, 23 September 1894, p. 7; *New York Times*, 31 July 1901, p. 12; ibid., 3 July 1904, p. 16.

24. Theresa Serber Malkiel, *The Diary of a Shirtwaist Striker*, (Ithaca: Cornell University Press, 1990), pp. 104, 105.

25. Shefter, "Trade Unions and Political Machines," pp. 217, 218.

26. Some contemporary craft unions still adhered to apprenticeship rules as a means to control labor supply. For example, in 1892 a union of cloakmakers decided "not to take any learners until there is a demand for workers in the trade." *Arbeiter Zeitung*, 8 July 1892, p. 3. A year later, the cutters' union stipulated that there would be one learner-apprentice for every ten cutters. Ibid., 20 April 1893, p. 2.

27. Shefter "Trade Unions and Political Machines," p. 259.

28. B. Fenster, YIVO, RG 113, pp. 12, 13; S. Langer, YIVO, RG 102, no. 57, p. 26; A.Herschowitz, YIVO, RG 113, p. 3. *Arbeiter Zeitung*, 28 September 1894, p. 2, reported on a shirt shop on Monroe Street known for its strict discipline; P. Newman, YIVO, RG 113, p. 6.

29. S. Langer, YIVO, RG 102, no. 57, p. 26; E. M. Wagner, YIVO, RG 102, no. 45, p. 187, also B. Lilienblum, YIVO, RG 113, p. 37; J. Dubna, YIVO, RG 102, no. 147, p. 13; R. August YIVO, RG 102, no. 266, p. 1.

30. A. Gumner, YIVO, RG 102, no. 44, np; A. Balson, YIVO, RG 113, p. 30; J. Guterman, YIVO, RG 113, p. 3.

31. Z. Scher, "The Shop: The Everyday Life of the Worker," in *United Hebrew Trades: Fiftieth Anniversary, 1888–1938* (New York, 1938), pp. 211–12. Scher was an organizer for the United Hebrew Trades.

32. Quoted in Howe, *World of Our Fathers*, p. 290. Also, *Zukunft*, April 1892, p. 18. John Commons was expressing his widely shared view of Jewish workmen to the Industrial Commission in 1901.

33. Rosenberg, *Di kloukmakher un zeyere yunyons*, pp. 12–13.

34. *New York Tribune*, 20 July 1901, p. 2. John Swinton criticized the unions for disappearing quickly after winning gains in strikes. *John Swinton's Paper*, August 23, 1885, p. 4.

35. *New York Times*, 4 March 1897, p. 4, also 23 July 1901, p. 3; *New York Tribune*, 29 March 1893, p. 1. The *Tribune* promised its readers that, whatever its outcome, the strike "will be full of interest to the student of sociology."

36. *John Swinton's Paper*, 23 August 1885, p. 4. Also, John Swinton, *Striking for Life. A Momentous Question: The Respective Attitudes of Labor and Capital* (Philadelphia and Chicago: A. R. Keller, 1895), pp. 182–83.

37. *New York Times*, 17 May 1897, p. 10.

38. Abraham Rosenberg quoted in Louis Levine, *The Women's Garment Workers*, p. 178.

39. Rosenberg, *Di kloukmakher un zeyere yunyons*, p. 139. The incident probably oc-

curred in 1907. Although Bonwit workers were not on strike, they had begun nego-
tiating the new prices for the coming season; *Arbeiter Zeitung,* 2 June 1893, p. 2.

40. Rosenberg, *Di kloukmakher un zeyere yunyons,* p. 188; Levine, *The Women's Garment Workers,* p. 151. The strike's rhetoric proved highly successful in 1909. After
Clara Lemlich's fiery speech at the Cooper Union meeting, fifteen thousand joined
the sriking workers' ranks. Ibid., pp. 153, 154.

41. *Arbeiter Zeitung,* 20 May 1892, p. 3; ibid., 5 January 1894, p. 3; ibid., 6 March
1896, p. 3.

42. Ibid, 26 May 1893, p. 6.

43. Kessler-Harris, "Organizing the Unorganizable," in Cantor and Laurie, eds.,
Class, Sex and the Woman Worker, p. 154.

44. The incident probably occurred during the late 1880s. Quoted in Weinstein,
Di idishe yunyons in Amerika, pp. 258–59.

45. The preponderance of Jews among cloakmakers in that strike is confirmed
by the *World,* which reported the case of four tailors, the only English-speaking members of the Dress and Cloak Makers' Union, who "could not get any satisfaction from
the union, which transacted its business in Hebrew." *New York World,* 24 August 1885,
p. 2. According to Abraham Rosenberg, the chronicler of the cloakmakers' struggles, the strike began as a local walkout when a contractor slapped a worker, and it
spread eventually to many cloakmaking establishments. Rosenberg, *Di kloukmakher
un zeyere yunyons,* pp. 7, 8. It is difficult to determine whether Rosenberg's account
refers to the 1885 strike or to the one that took place the following year. See also
Levine, *The Women's Garment Workers,* pp. 37–39.

46. *New York Sun,* 23 August 1885, p. 9; *New York World,* 18 August 1885, p. 2; *New
York Times,* 20 August 1885, p. 8; Levine, *The Women's Garment Workers,* pp. 32–43.

47. The strike failed to achieve its aim, mainly because of the union's disinte-
gration. See Rosenberg, *Di kloukmakher un zeyere yunyons,* p. 149. The union could
have survived had it not been for the pressers' unrestrained behavior. In fact, both
the strike and union collapsed because of the ILGWU's reluctance to call other
workers out on sympathy strike

48. *New York Times,* 4 June 1901, p. 6.

49. Rose Schneiderman with Lucy Goldthwaite, *All for One* (New York: Paul S.
Eriksson, 1967), p. 51.

50. For a discussion of the Protocol, see Levine, *The Women's Garment Workers,* ch.
22; ibid., pp. 251, 252.

51. Malkiel, *The Diary of a Shirtwaist Striker,* p. 84.

52. Levine, *The Women's Garment Workers,* pp. 44–55.

53. *New York Sun,* 27 May 1890, p. 5, ibid., 15 June 1890, p. 1; Rosenberg, *Di kloukmakher un zeyere yunyons,* pp. 19, 20. According to Rosenberg, the strike began as a
walkout when a union worker employed by Goldschmidt and Platt was fired for insubordination, after playing a prank on one of the bosses. After the firm refused to
reinstate the fired worker, all workers were locked out. Ibid. The *New York Times* and
the *New York World* provided another version of the strike's causes, reporting that

the manufacturers locked out their cutters because of a successful national boycott against goods manufactured by Alfred Benjamin. Other firms, fearing a similar boycott, joined in the lockout. *New York Times,* 10 July 1890, p. 5; *New York World,* 12 July 1890, p. 3; ibid., 17 June 1890, p. 4.

54. *New York Sun,* 12 July 1890, p. 6, 16 July 1890, p. 1. Once the agreement was reached, the cutters were willing to readmit the scabs to their union for a high fee of $100. Ibid., 17 July 1890, p. 1; 22 July 1890, p. 5.

55. *New York World,* 17 July 1890, p. 5. According to the *World,* much to the manufacturers' surprise, only five hundred skilled operators could be found to fill the strikers' places. Ibid., 26 July 1890, p. 5; *New York Sun,* 17 July 1890, p. 1; *New York Times,* 19 July 1890, p. 3; *New York Sun,* 26 June 1890, p. 3.

56. *New York World,* 21 July 1890, p. 12; *New York Times,* 19 July 1890, p. 3.

57. *New York World,* 20 July 1890, p. 3.

58. *Arbeiter Zeitung,* 12 September 1890, p. 2. *New York World,* 23 July 1890, p. 8. In its effort to discredit Barondess, the *World* consistently spelled his name "Baron-Deess," thus attributing megalomania to this charismatic cloakmakers' leader. Also, *New York Times,* 25 July 1890, p. 8.

59. Edward King, *Joseph Zalmonah* (Boston: Lee and Shepard, 1894), p. 63.

60. Levine, *The Women's Garment Workers,* pp. 52, 54. *New York Sun,* 21 July 1890, p. 7, 24 July 1890, p. 5; *New York World,* 4 July 1890, p. 12; *New York Times,* 4 July 1890, p. 1.

61. The agreement stipulated that scabs were to be discharged and encouraged to join the union. However, in contrast to a previous draft rejected by the strikers, there would be no time limit for strikebreakers to be admitted to the union. Among other concessions, there were wage increases, a closed shop in the cloak industry, abolition of inside contracting, reinstatement of all those who had been dismissed, and employment only of those committed to union membership. *New York Sun,* 25 July 1890, p. 2; Swinton, *Striking for Life,* pp. 182–83.

62. *New York Times,* 23 July 1890, p. 2; *New York World,* 4 July 1890, p. 12, 17 July 1890, p. 5.

63. *New York World,* 24 July 1890, p. 8. However, Judge Duffy's eloquence was wasted, since his audience did not understand English. *New York Sun,* 24 July 1890, p. 5; ibid., 22 July 1890, p. 8. The tactics of the cutters will be analyzed in chapter 6.

64. *New York Sun,* 20 March 1891, p.1.

65. The closed shop again became an issue in the Meyer Jonasson strike of February 1892. *New York Times,* 20 February 1892, p. 9, 1 March 1892, p. 2. This strike witnessed the weakening of Barondess's leadership. His involvement in the "Jamaica affair" of the previous year, his imprisonment, and the ascendance of rival leaders and unions all contributed to the union's diminished power. Levine, *The Women's Garment Workers,* pp. 53–63; *New York Times,* 4 August 1901, p. 2.

66. Ibid., 26 November 1909, p. 5. The *New York Times* claimed that the women did not even know why they were striking and, in general, were very unfamiliar with unions. Ibid., 4 December 1909, p. 20.

67. For example, the Bureau of Labor reported that 75 percent of complaints submitted for arbitration between April 1911 and October 31—1,913 cases—were grievances relating to wages and "unjustifiable discharges." U.S. Bureau of Labor, *Bulletin* no. 14, 1914, p. 20, quoted in Levine, *The Women's Garment Workers,* p. 238.

68. Rebecca August, YIVO, RG 102, no. 266, p. 2.

69. *New York Times,* 28 December 1909, p. 8, 28 August 1910, p. 3. The preferential shop meant that although employers gave preference to union workers, they retained the right to hire non-union labor when the latter were more competent. "We want closed shop!" was the slogan the strikers carried on their banners. Ibid., 28 August 1910, pp. 1, 3. The injunction was issued because the demand for a closed shop allegedly constituted a conspiracy in restraint of trade.

70. Ibid., 7 September 1910, p. 20.

71. Quoted in Tcherikower, *The Early Jewish Labor Movemvent in the United States,* p. 304.

72. *Arbeiter Zeitung,* 14 March 1890; ibid., 21 September 1894, p. 2; J. Dubna, YIVO, RG 113, p. 14. The strike occurred while Dubna worked in the shop between 1908 and 1910.

73. A. Balson, YIVO, RG 113, p. 3; B. Rabinowitz, YIVO, RG 113, p. 2; J. Werlin, YIVO, RG 102, no. 71–71c, p. 66; *Arbeiter Zeitung,* 8 July 1892, p. 3; 19 August 1892, p. 3; 26 August 1892, p. 2. According to rules enforced in many shops, workers had to supply their own sewing machines (or pay for the use of machines provided by the employer) and pay for electricity where machines were power operated.

74. Ibid., 21 September 1894, p. 1.

75. *New York World,* 26 March 1886, p. 1; *New York Sun,* 19 March 1886, p. 3; *New York World,* 1 April 1886, p. 2.

76. *New York World,* 1 April 1886, p. 2.

77. Ibid.; *John Swinton's Paper,* 11 April 1886.

78. Rosenberg, *Di kloukmakher un zeyere yunyons,* pp. 7–8.

79. *New York Tribune,* 20 July 1901, p. 2, 21 July 1901, p. 2; *New York Times,* 21 July 1901, p. 1. Weinstein, *Di idishe yunyons in Amerika,* pp. 248, 249. Although the increase in wages was not an issue in the strike, the workers who insisted on union wages demanded they be based on piecework rather than week-work. *New York Times,* 23 July 1901, p. 2.

80. *New York Tribune,* 20 July 1901, p. 2; *Jewish Daily Forward,* 23 July 1901, p. 1.

81. *New York Times,* 22 July 1901, p. 2. Ibid., 23 July 1901, p. 3. In a similar attempt to make the manufacturers responsible for their contractors, in 1897 the Brotherhood of Tailors' Executive Committee threatened to call five hundred men from Fechheimer, Fischel, and Company out on strike unless the firm paid $75 owed by a contractor to his employees. Ibid., 8 September 1897, p. 3.

82. The task system was invariably hated, although workers' attitude toward piecework varied over time. In 1890, for example, shirtmakers demanded to be paid weekly, as did pantsmakers in 1894. In 1901, however, men's tailors wanted to abolish the task system but preferred piecework to a standardized weekly wage.

Arbeiter Zeitung, 14 March 1890; 21 September 1894, p. 2; *New York Times*, 23 July 1901, p. 3.

83. In 1886, the daily task consisted of 18 to 20 coats, requiring a workday of 16 to 18 hours, making it impossible to finish a daily task and resulting in reduced earnings. *New York World*, 21 May 1886, p. 3. According to another report, the daily task rate in 1886 was 10 to 16 coats, requiring a workday of 14 to 15 hours. The difference in garment quality might account for the wide range. See also Steven Fraser, "Combined and Uneven Development in the Men's Clothing Industry," *Business History Review* 57 (Winter 1983): 534–35.

84. The strikers set the lowest weekly wage at $16 for machine operators and $25 for "first-class," or highly skilled men. The wages demanded for basters, workers of lower skills, ranged from $14 to $22. *New York World*, 21 May 1886, p. 3; 25 May 1886, p. 2; 8 June 1886, p. 2. The two sides arrived at a compromise, agreeing that a failure to finish the daily task would not result in reduced pay. Ibid., 13 June 1886, p. 7.

85. *New York Sun*, 31 August 1894, p. 5; *New York World*, 4 September 1894, p. 8; ibid., 29 August 1894, p. 9; *New York Sun*, 31 August 1894, p. 5; ibid., 5 September 1894, p. 1; ibid., 31 August 1894, p. 5.

86. Ibid., 14 October 1894, p. 5; *Arbeiter Zeitung*, 28 September 1894, p. 1.

87. *New York Sun*, 15 October 1894, p. 3; 10 November 1894, p. 5.

88. Ibid., 15 October 1894, p. 3; 16 October 1894, p. 1; 17 September 1894, p. 6. Police Superintendent Byrnes met with manufacturers' representatives, offering them protection from strikers. Ibid., 17 October 1894, p. 7.

89. *New York Times*, 22 February 1895, p. 5; *New York Sun*, 17 September 1894, p. 6; ibid, 15 July 1895, p. 1; 29 July 1895, p. 1.

90. *New York Tribune*, 1 August 1895, p. 6; *New York Times*, 15 December 1895, p. 9.

91. For example, finishers, among the least skilled workers in the coat industry, had their wages reduced by 35 percent and were required to finish forty-eight coats, an increase of thirteen over the previous task of thrity-five coats. Ibid., 13 June 1896, p. 3; ibid., 2 June 1897, p. 3.

92. *Arbeiter Zeitung*, 5 October 1894, p. 2; 7 March 1897, p. 2.

93. For a discussion of industrial unionism in mining, steel, and garment industries, see David Gordon, Richard Edwards, and Michael Reich, *Segmented Work, Divided Workers* (New York: Cambridge University Press, 1992), pp. 157–62.

Chapter 6. The Politics of Morality

1. Quoted in Hyman, "Immigrant Women and Consumer Protest," p 97.

2. *Jewish Daily Forward*, 18 May 1904, p. 1.

3. Ibid., 7 December 1909, p. 5.

4. Edward P. Thompson, "The Moral Economy of the English Crowd in the Eighteenth Century," Edward P. Thompson, *Customs in Common* (London: Merlin Press, 1991), pp. 185–258.

5. My interpretation of the meat boycott follows the suggestions made by Margaret Somers concerning the food riots in seventeenth-century England. Rather than interpret them as expressions of a "prepolitical" population appealing to "paternalistic moral economy," she sees the riots as demands for legitimate citizenship rights. Margaret R. Somers, "Citizenship and the Place of the Public Sphere: Law, Community, and Political Culture in the Transition to Democracy," *American Sociological Review* 58 (October 1993): 609. Paula Hyman, in her study of the meat boycott, does not view women boycotters as engaged in a traditional protest but rather as sophisticated consumers who understood fully the workings of the market forces of supply and demand. Hyman, "Immigrant Women and Consumer Protest."

6. Editorial, *New York Times*, 24 May 1902, p. 8.

7. For an excellent selection of articles related to issues of gender and work, see Ava Baron, ed., *Work Engendered: Toward a New History of American Labor* (Ithaca: Cornell University Press, 1991). Especially relevant to issues of community-based activism and the shift to work-centered concerns that marginalized women's role is Elizabeth Faue's "Paths of Unionization: Community, Bureaucracy, and Gender in the Minneapolis Labor Movement of the 1930s" in the same collection.

8. Kessler-Harris, "Organizing the Unorganizable: Three Jewish Women and Their Union," p. 160.

9. Cassedy, *To the Other Shore*, p. xx. See discussion of that group in chapter 1.

10. Jonathan Frankel, *Prophecy and Politics: Socialism, Nationalism, and the Russian Jews, 1862–1917* (London: Cambridge University Press, 1981), p. 466; Cassedy, *To the Other Shore*, pp. 51–77.

11. Frankel, *Prophecy and Politics*, p. 483. Homestead (1892) and Coeur d'Alene, Idaho (1912), two landmark strikes that ended in defeat and underscored the growing power of corporations in state politics.

12. Bloom, "Yiddish-Speaking Socialists in America: 1892–1905," pp. 59–60.

13. Cassedy, *To the Other Shore*, p. 62.

14. Paul Buhle, ed., *Encyclopedia of the American Left* (New York: Garland, 1990), s.v. "Yiddish Left."

15. Howe, *World of Our Fathers*, p. 422; Paul Buhle, *From the Knights of Labor to the New World Order: Essays on Labor and Culture* (New York: Garland, 1997), p. 53. Paul Buhle's remark concerns the poet Morris Rosenfeld.

16. Cassedy, *To the Other Shore*, p. 78. Although the *Di Nyu Yorker Yudishe Folkszeitung* was the first paper identified with the labor movement, it closed down in 1889 after a three-year existence. Howe, *World of Our Fathers*, p. 111.

17. The *Forward* reached a circulation of over 200,000 in the years following World War I. Howe, *World of Our Fathers*, p. 545. The circulation of the 1890s *Tageblatt* clearly outstripped that of the budding socialist papers of the 1890s, reaching 100,000 readers in 1900. Ibid., p. 521; Rischin, *The Promised City*, p. 303.

18. "The Slave Dealers of Eighth Street," was the title of a three-column article by B. Feigenbaum in the *Arbeiter Zeitung* in September 1892. Quoted in Silver, "Some

Attitudes of the East European Jews," p. 136. Attack on charity's despotism was the focus of Morris Hilkowitz' article in 1891. Ibid.

19. Quoted in Cassedy, *To the Other Shore*, p. 113; ibid., pp. 100–103.

20. Rischin, *The Promised City*, pp. 152–54; Cassedy, *To the Other Shore*, p. 88; Rischin *The Promised City*, pp. 158, 162–63.

21. Quoted in Howe, *World of Our Fathers*, p. 418.

22. Ibid., p. 111.

23. Ibid., pp. 111–12.

24. Rischin, ed., *Grandma Never Lived in America*, p. 348.

25. *New York Times*, 22 July 1901, p. 2. For a discussion of oratorical styles, see chapter 5; *New York Sun*, 8 September 1894, p. 2; 5 September 1894, p. 1.

26. Howe, *World of Our Fathers*, pp. 112–13.

27. For a discussion of Jacob Gordin, see ibid., pp. 467–73.

28. Tcherikower, *The Early Jewish Labor Movement in the U.S.*, p. 303; Howe, *World of Our Fathers*, p. 243.

29. Hapgood Hutchins, *The Spirit of the Ghetto: Studies of the Jewish Quarter of New York* (New York: Funk and Wagnalls, 1965), p. 118.

30. Cassedy, *To the Other Shore*, p. 136; ibid., pp. 85, 135; Cahan, *The Education of Abraham Cahan*, p. 391; ibid., pp. 130–36.

31. King, *Joseph Zalmonah*, pp. 50, 217–19.

32. Benjamin Feigenbaum, a writer for the *Forward*, made his name as an inspirational and popular speaker. Howe, *World of Our Fathers*, pp. 242–43.

33. King, *Joseph Zalmonah*, p. 225.

34. E. Wagner, YIVO, RG 102, no. 45, p. 161.

35. *New York Times*, 4 August 1896, p. 9.

36. *New York Sun*, 19 August 1885, p. 3; 3 March 1891, p. 7. Also, *New York Times*, 19 August 1885, p. 5; 20 August 1885, p. 8; *New York Sun*, 6 September 1894, p. 1; *New York Times*, 4 August 1896, p. 9.

37. *New York Sun*, 30 March 1886, p. 1; 31 March 1886, p. 3; 1 April 1886, p. 1.

38. Schultz, the contractor, brought his case to court, where he was advised to lay the matter before the district attorney. Ibid., 3 March 1891, p. 7.

39. Ibid., 14 March 1891, p. 5; 16 March 1891, p. 8; Epstein, *Jewish Labor in U.S.A.*, vol. 1, p. 226.

40. *New York World*, 19 August 1885, p. 3; *New York Sun*, 19 August 1885, p. 3; *New York World*, 31 March 1886, p. 8; *New York Sun*, 31 March 1886, p. 3. In one case, to prevent sabotage, a contractor demanded his workers' watches as a guarantee that they would not tamper with the machines. *New York Sun*, 16 November 1894, p. 5.

41. *New York Sun*, 19 August 1885, p. 3; *New York World*, 4 July 1890, p. 12.

42. During the cloakmakers' strike of that year, Billet, an ex-worker turned contractor, who had provoked the ire of strikers during the preceding year and was in partnership with Greenbaum, another contractor notorious for hiring scabs, tried to escape effective persecution by moving their joint venture to Jamaica, Long Is-

land. However, that did not help. Despite barbed wire, guard dogs, and the distance from the Lower East Side, a number of striking cloakmakers traveled to Jamaica to take appropriate countermeasures. A melee ensued; it was alleged that the strikers used vitriol that was intended to damage the finished garments but instead unintentionally maimed Greenbaum's young daughter. *New York Times*, 10 March 1891, p. 12; *New York Sun*, 10 March 1891, p. 1; 11 March 1891, p. 1. According to Melech Epstein, a stove used by the pressers in Greenbaum's (in Epstein's version identified as Greenberg) shop overturned, and the little girl had her foot scorched. Epstein, *Jewish Labor in U.S.A.*, vol. I, pp. 226–27; Levine, *The Women's Garment Workers*, pp. 60–61.

43. *New York Sun*, 8 November 1894, p. 9; 9 November 1894, p. 9.

44. *New York World*, 12 November 1894, p. 9.

45. Ibid., 9 November 1894, p. 7.

46. *New York Sun*, 1 November 1894; *New York Times*, 8 August 1896; 11 August 1896, p. 3.

47. *New York Sun*, 3 April 1886, p. 1; 21 October 1894, p. 2; *New York Times*, 18 August 1910, p. 9.

48. Ibid., 26 August 1910, p. 16.

49. Ibid., 21 July 1905, p. 3.

50. *New York Sun*, 20 March 1891, p. 1; 10 March 1891, p. 1.

51. Ibid., 1 November 1894, p. 6; *New York World*, 1 November 1894, p. 6.

52. *New York Sun*, 25 October 1894, p. 5. Manufacturers traditionally threatened to open factories in Germany, which already had branches of some of New York's enterprises. *New York World*, 19 August 1885, p. 3.

53. The prices rose from 12 to 18 cents a pound. Hyman, "Immigrant Women and Consumer Protest," p. 93.

54. Paula Hyman concludes that the strike aimed to curtail demand through a neighborhood boycott, without fixing a target for a traditionally "just" or "fair" price.

55. *Yuddishes Tageblatt*, 15 May 1902, quoted in Hyman, "Immigrant Women and Consumer Protest," p. 99.

56. *New York Times*, 13 May 1902, p. 7; 16 May 1902, p. 6; 23 May 1902, p. 1.

57. *Brooklyn Eagle*, 18 May 1902, section 1, p. 6; 23 May 1902, p. 1.

58. *New York Times*, 16 May 1902, p. 6; 7 May 1902, p. 2; *Brooklyn Eagle*, 18 May 1902, section 1, p. 6.

59. *Jewish Daily Forward*, 15 May 1902, quoted in Hyman, "Immigrant Women and Consumer Protest," p. 100.

60. *New York Tribune*, 7 August 1905, p. 2. For a discussion of the strike see Paul Brenner, "The Formative Years of the Hebrew Bakers' Unions, 1881–1914," *YIVO Annual* 18 (1983): 39–120.

61. *New York Tribune* 11 August 1905, p. 8; *New York World*, 7 August 1905, p. 3; 9 August 1905, p. 3; *New York Times*, 8 August 1905, p. 4; 10 August 1905, p. 1. The bosses' association and the refusal of the union's International Executive Board to support a sympathy strike ultimately brought its defeat.

62. *New York Sun,* 17 November 1894, p. 8, 19 November 1894, p. 2. Contractors advocated a stiffer attitude and encouraged landlords to evict rebellious tenants. *New York Times,* 31 July 1895, p. 5.

63. *New York Tribune,* 6 July 1905, p. 4. One cause of rent increases was the frequent sale of property on the Lower East Side and other boroughs for speculative reasons. Another cause of rent rises may have been the new municipal laws, introduced in the 1900s, which defined more strictly mandatory repairs and the landlord's liabilities. Arlene K. Newman, "Ethnicity and Business Enterprise: A Study of Jewish Mutual Insurance Companies in New York" (Ph.D. diss., City University of New York, 1983), p. 6; *New York Tribune,* 6 July 1905, p. 4. Cohen, the landlord, became a prisoner in his own apartment, venturing out only under police protection. Ibid., 7 July 1905, p. 10; 12 July 1905, p. 10. However, the show of sympathy was marred by angry neighbors who tried to stop the noisy crowd by pouring buckets of water out their windows. For further discussion of the 1905 and 1907 rent strikes, see Jenna Weissman Joselit, "The Landlord as Czar: Pre–World War I Tenant Activity," Ronald Lawson, ed., *The Tenant Movement in New York City, 1904–1984* (New Brunswick, N.J.: Rutgers University Press, 1986), pp. 111–23.

64. *New York Times,* 28 December 1907, p. 2; *Jewish Daily Forward,* 31 December 1907, p. 1.

65. *New York Times,* 27 December 1907, p. 4; *Jewish Daily Forward,* 19 December 1907, p. 6, quoted in Arlene Newman, "Ethnicity and Business Enterprise," p. 68.

66. P. Newman, YIVO, RG 113, p. 8.

67. *Jewish Daily Forward,* 24 December 1907, p. 8; 24 December 1907, p. 8; 26 December 1907, p. 1. Although some landlords yielded to demands and lowered the rents, the strike continued to spread, affecting many tenements on the Lower East Side. Ibid., January 4, 1908, p. 1; 6 January 1908, p. 1. The strikers adopted the strategy of having some tenants stop payment, which was intended to bring about eviction. Those evicted were to be housed by their neighbors, thus remaining on the buildings' premises. Ibid., 24 December 1907, p. 8; 28 December 1907, p. 1; 31 December 1907, p. 1; 6 January 1908, p. 1.

68. *New York Sun,* 17 October 1894, p. 7; 9 November 1894, p. 9; *New York Times,* 4 August 1896, p. 9.

69. Quoted in Brenner, "The Formative Years of the Hebrew Bakers' Unions," p. 82.

70. The bias of the police was dramatically demonstrated when they failed to protect the mourners attending the funeral of Rabbi Jacob Joseph in 1902. The funeral, attended by an estimated cortege of 50,000 to 100,000 mourners, was set upon by Irish workmen as it passed R. Hoe's factory. A full-scale battle followed, and public anger at the police exploded for their failure to protect the Jewish mourners. Testimonies of witnesses gathered by a mayoral commission investigating the causes of the riot reflect popular resentment against the police. Minutes of Hearing by Commissioners Appointed by the Mayor of the City of New York to Investigate the Riot on July 30, 1902, YIVO, RG 117.

71. *New York Sun,* 6 March 1891, p. 5; 16 September 1894, p. 6; 16 October 1894, p. 1.

72. *Brooklyn Eagle,* 18 May 1902, section 1, p. 6; 23 May 1902, p. 1.

73. *New York Times,* 16 May 1902, p. 1; 17 May 1902, p. 2.

74. *New York Sun,* 19 August 1885, p. 3; *New York Times,* 3 August 1896, p. 5.

75. Ibid., 4 August 1896, p. 9; *New York Sun,* 24 July 1890, p. 5; *New York Times,* 6 August 1896, p. 3.

76. Ibid., 4 August 1909, p. 4.

77. Ibid., 24 July 1890, p. 5.

78. Ibid., 8 July 1910, p. 1.

79. Ibid., 28 August 1910, p. 1; 2 September 1910, p. 5; 28 July 1910, p. 4; 17 August 1910, p. 5; 18 August 1910, p. 9; 19 August 1910, p. 5.

80. Jewish socialists subscribed to the view that the state was an instrument of the ruling class. This view also contributed to their critique of the American labor movement, especially the Knights of Labor. Thus, the United Hebrew Trades, which was modeled closely on the United German Trades and under socialist leadership, ridiculed the Knights of Labor's nonpolitical character and its naive belief in the natural fraternity of all people, regardless of class. The *Arbeiter Zeitung,* the organ of the UHT, published an acerbic farewell article entitled "Adieu Powderly," on the occasion of Powderly's retirement as Grand Master, which not only ridiculed the ideas of an industrial army and of the establishment of cooperatives with the state's help but also criticized Powderly's unwillingness to support Uriah S. Stephens's efforts to win political power through the Workers' Party. *Arbeiter Zeitung,* 1 December 1893, p. 2. Similar criticism was voiced against the Central Labor Union, which, according to the Socialists, did not warrant confidence, since both Democratic and Republican politicians served as delegates and because it had strong ties to Tammany and traditional unionized workers. Weinstein, *Di idishe yunyons in Amerika,* p. 331.

81. For a summary of the strike, see Levine, *The Women's Garment Workers,* ch. 7.

82. *New York Times,* 7 July 1890, p. 4.

83. *New York Sun,* 7 July 1890, p. 1; *New York Times,* 7 July 1890, p. 7.

84. *New York World,* 10 July 1890, p. 1; 10 July 1890, p. 1; 11 July 1890, p. 2.

85. *New York Times,* 13 July 1890, p. 8.

86. *New York Sun,* 11 July 1890, p. 2.

87. Quoted in Levine, *The Women's Garment Workers,* pp. 50, 52.

88. *Brooklyn Eagle,* 22 April 1902, p. 1.

89. *Brooklyn Eagle,* 22 April 1902, p. 1.

90. *New York Times,* 16 May 1902, p. 6.

91. *New York Tribune,* 16 January 1906, p. 8; 7 March 1906, p. 1; 3 April 1906, p. 4.

92. *New York Tribune,* 7 August 1905, p. 2; 8 August 1905, p. 11.

93. *Arbeiter Zeitung,* 4 July 1890, p. 1; 24 April 1891, p. 3; 19 August 1892, p. 3; 23 December 1892, p. 2; 13 May 1892, p. 3; 14 September 1894, p. 1. Rosenberg, *Di kloukmakher un zeyere yunyons,* p. 79.

94. *Arbeiter Zeitung,* 25 March 1892, p. 2; 23 December 1892, p. 3; 15 July 1892, p. 3.

95. *New York Times,* 4 August 1895, p. 8. Similarly, in 1896, those who had work assisted the strikers by donating $175. Ibid., 30 August 1896, p. 8.

96. *New York Sun,* 4 April 1891, p. 2; 24 November 1894, p. 3; 26 November 1894, p. 6.

97. *New York Times,* 19 May 1902, p. 5. The leadership of the kosher bakers' strike of 1905 relied on the support of the international and on sympathy strikes of bakers' unions in New York. Neither had materialized. *New York Tribune,* 15 August 1905, p. 8; *New York World,* 15 August 1905, p. 3.

98. *New York Sun,* 18 December 1894, p. 3.

99. *New York Times,* 3 July 1904, p. 16.

100. Levine, *The Women's Garment Workers,* p. 50.

101. *Arbeiter Zeitung,* 8 September 1893, p. 2; 15 September 1893, p. 6.

102. Levine, *The Women's Garment Workers,* p. 81.

103. Rosenberg, *Di kloukmakher un zeyere yunyons,* p. 83.

104. *New York Sun,* 17 November 1894, p. 8; 22 November 1894, p. 5; *Arbeiter Zeitung,* 2 December 1894, p. 2.

105. *New York Tribune,* 6 January 1895, p. 9; *New York Sun,* 19 November 1894, p. 9; *New York Tribune,* 1 January 1895, p. 4.

106. *New York Tribune,* 2 January 1895, p. 7; 3 January 1895, p. 9; 4 January 1895, p. 4; 5 January 1895, p. 1.

107. *New York Times,* 3 January 1895, p. 14. Generally, the society's policy was no less hostile to strikers. It circumvented its rule "never to assist strikers so to enable them to maintain their contest, however justifiable the issue at stake may be," by extending assistance only after it declared the strike suspended.

108. *Arbeiter Zeitung,* 7 August 1898, p. 2; 31 March 1893, p. 6.

109. Ibid., 14 July 1893, p. 2; 21 July 1893, p. 3.

110. *New York Sun,* 29 March 1886, p. 1; 30 March 1886, p. 1.

111. *Arbeiter Zeitung,* 9 September 1892, p. 3; ibid., 20 March 1891, p. 2; 21 July 1893, p. 3.

112. *New York Sun,* 30 March 1886, p. 1.

113. *Jewish Daily Forward,* 18 May 1904, p. 1; 26 May 1904, p. 1.

114. One exception to the rule concerned suspendermakers, who sent letters informing Lobel and Coleman customers of the firm's vindictive treatment of its workers, who dared to voice dissatisfaction with their starvation wages. *Arbeiter Zeitung,* 13 April 1894, p. 3.

115. *New York Tribune,* 29 March 1893, p. 1; *New York Times,* 2 April 1893, p. 11; *Arbeiter Zeitung,* 31 March 1893, p. 2; 7 April 1893, p. 2; *New York Times,* 6 April 1893, p. 8.

116. Ibid., 7 September 1901, p. 16.

117. Edward P. Thompson, "Rough Music," in Thompson, *Customs in Common,* p. 467.

118. *Arbeiter Zeitung*, 31 March 1893, p. 6.

119. *New York Times*, 3 July 1904, p. 16.

120. Rosenberg, *Di kloukmakher un zeyere yunyons*, p. 81. Ibid.

121. Levine, *The Women's Garment Workers*, p. 60. The picketing committee was involved in the notorious Jamaica case that led to the arrest of Joseph Barondess. Ibid.

122. The desperate scab ultimately resorted to carrying a gun for self-protection. *New York Sun*, 20 March 1891, p. 1.

123. *New York Times*, 26 May 1897, p. 4.

124. *Jewish Daily Forward*, 18 May 1902, quoted in Hyman, "Immigrant Women and Consumer Protest," p. 94; *New York Times*, 19 May 1902, p. 5.

125. *New York Sun*, 11 October 1894, p. 8. An angry crowd of meat boycotters followed and attacked a meat wholesaler in Brooklyn who was going to his synagogue. *Brooklyn Eagle*, 24 May 1902, p. 1.

126. *New York Times*, 6 August 1896, p. 8.

127. Rosenberg, *Di kloukmakher un zeyere yunyons*, p. 167.

128. *New York Times*, 15 August 1897, p. 10.

129. *Arbeiter Zeitung*, 15 August 1897, p. 1.

Conclusion

1. Although institutions in the American host society reproduced inequalities, women nevertheless were no longer "appendages" of the male breadwinner, according to Friedman-Kasaba, *Memories of Migration*, p. 178.

2. See Introduction for discussion of "tool-kit" concept.

3. The use of images and symbols in public funerals by an array of political groups—secular radical, orthodox, and Zionist—for the purpose of mobilization of supporters and as tools to forge tradition, is discussed extensively and persuasively by Arthur Aryeh Goren, "Sacred and Secular: The Place of Public Funerals in the Immigrant Life of American Jews." Public funerals were accorded to prominent public figures representing social, political, and artistic worlds. Those of Rabbi Jacob Joseph (1902), the orthodox *Tageblatt*'s editor Kasriel Sarahson (1905), dramatist Jacob Gordin (1909), the victims of the Triangle shirtwaist fire of 1911, Shalom Aleichem (1916), Meyer London (1926), and Baruch Vladeck (1932) are some of the public funerals discussed by Goren. The subtle changes in the funeral ritual and the distinguishing marks of funerals for labor leaders reflect, among other factors, the emergence of the various constituencies and their political reach.

4. For observations concerned with the validity and the meaning of patterns of riots and public rituals, see Suzanne Desan, "Crowds, Community, and Ritual in the Work of E. P. Thompson and Natalie Davis," in Hunt, ed., *The New Cultural History*, pp. 60–68.

5. Charles Leinenweber, "The Class and Ethnic Bases of New York City Socialism, 1904–1915," *Labor History* 22 (Winter 1981): 51.

6. *New York World*, 9 August 1905, p. 1.

7. Levine, *The Women's Garment Workers,* p. 131.

8. For a discussion of the 1917 food riot, see Ewen, *Immigrant Women in the Land of Dollars,* pp. 176–83.

9. Ibid., pp. 178–79.

10. Although the ILGWU signaled the beginning of the organization of mostly unskilled workers along the principle of industrywide organization, tendencies to separate along skill and nationality persisted into the 1920s. Levine, *The Women's Garment Workers,* pp. 434–35, 459.

11. Rosenberg, *Di kloukmakher un zeyere yunyons,* pp. 203–13. The unemployed, however, met separately. Ibid., pp. 212–13.

12. Ibid., p. 213.

13. Rosenberg, *Di kloukmakher un zeyere yunyons,* pp. 113–14; Levine, *The Women's Garment Workers,* pp. 120–22.

14. Levine, *The Women's Garment Workers,* p. 241.

15. "Preferential union shop" was the invention of Louis D. Brandeis, the architect of the Protocol, who refused to accept workers' demands for "closed shop." Ibid., pp. 189–90.

16. Ibid., p. 252. In 1912, John Dyche, a newly appointed chief clerk of the union and a firm believer in the efficacy of the Protocol to build stable unions, promised the employers to discipline the membership and put an end to "wildcat" strikes. The strike occurred in 1912, when women finishers in the shop of J. C. Stratton protested against the foreman. The women finishers were soon joined by other workers, and all were told by the Joint Board to return to work within fifteen minutes. When workers refused, Dyche sent replacements. Ibid.

17. Ibid., p. 258.

18. Margaret Somers proposed this view in her study of class formation. In the case of the English working class, a rich array of political practices, such as machine breaking, existed side by side with "modern" political demands for universal suffrage. These practices were rooted in earlier "preindustrial" patterns of protest, which were "revised" and "adjusted" over the years, into the nineteenth century, as a result of the experience of capitalism and industrialization. Margaret Somers, "Narrativity, Narrative Identity, and Social Action: Rethinking English Working-Class Formation," *Social Science History* 16 (Winter 1992): 591–630.

19. Leinenweber, "The Class and Ethnic Bases of New York City Socialism, 1904–1915," pp. 37–51. See also Melvyn Dubofsky, "Success and Failure of Socialists in New York City, 1900–1918," *Labor History* 9 (Fall 1968): 361–375. For a historical discussion on the subject of the high numerical representation of Jews in the leadership and the rank and file of American radical movements, see Paul Buhle, "Themes in American Jewish Radicalism," in Paul Buhle and Dan Georgakas, eds., *The Immigrant Left* (Albany: State University of New York Press, 1996).

20. Charles Leinenweber, "Socialists in the Streets: The New York City Socialist Party in Working-Class Neighborhoods, 1908–1918," *Science and Society* 41 (Summer 1977): 159.

21. Howe, *World of Our Fathers,* pp. 314–17.

22. Morris Hillquit, *Loose Leaves from a Busy Life* (New York: Macmillan, 1934), p. 188, quoted in Leinenweber, "Socialists in the Streets: The New York City Socialist Party in Working-Class Neighborhoods, 1908–1918," p. 158.

23. Howe, quoted in Paul Buhle, "Themes in American Jewish Radicalism," p. 78.

INDEX